Light has a miraculous w̶ Bustard partook of this br̶ that showed up on her joy̶ into the world, and especially to those of us who encountered her on her shortened path of life. For those who did not get to meet her, I'm thankful for this collection of writings which serves as an introduction to Leslie and to her luminous work. Thanks be to God!

—LUCI SHAW
Author of *The O in Hope, Breath for the Bones: Art, Imagination and Spirit,* and *Reversed Entropy* (forthcoming from Paraclete Press)

This rich collection has so much to nurture and sustain the reader. It is a little trove of beauty and wisdom in the midst of ugly and confusing times. One might think a gathering of prose and poetry from someone who had to face severe illness and untimely death would be a difficult or depressing read, but these luminous little reflections show how Leslie lived ever more intensely, ever more keenly aware of beauty and blessing, as she learned to number and value her days.

But there is more on offer here than just attention to the beauties of life in this world, there is something deeper. We follow the author on her last journey deeper into Christ himself, into intimacy with the Love of God, and find, as we lift our eyes from the page, that we too feel closer to Jesus.

—MALCOLM GUITE
Poet, singer-songwriter, Anglican priest, academic, and author of *Lifting the Veil: Imagination and the Kingdom of God*

Tiny thoughts from an ordinary writer might not amount to much, but tiny thoughts from a poetic soul like Leslie Bustard are like small but brilliant diamonds: this book flashes with beauty and wisdom. This profound book is a collection, not of scraps, but gems. In these pages, is Light.

—CHRISTIE PURIFOY
Author of *Placemaker: Cultivating Places of Comfort, Beauty, and Peace* and founder of the Black Barn Online

I've known Leslie Bustard since she was a very young woman, but I knew her only in part, as I watched her dance in a crowd while I sang from stage. Now, through *Tiny Thoughts,* I can know her more fully in the expanse of her personhood—as a woman, wife, mother, creator, teacher, friend, poet, writer, Jesus-follower, and so much more. And despite the modesty of the title, there's nothing tiny about this book! It is grand. Not only in the richness and depth of its content, but in its universe-size gift to all of us. Well done, Leslie Bustard— well done. You overcame the world with beauty and your unwavering belief in the trustworthiness of Jesus. Now we have your field notes and an imaginative, faithful way forward.

—CHARLIE PEACOCK
Grammy Award-winning music producer and co-author with Andi Ashworth of *Why Everything That Doesn't Matter, Matters So Much*

With the gift of showing with words, Leslie is able to pull back the curtains of eternity and grant us a glimpse of the beauty of God's faithfulness through some of the most challenging of challenges. If you ever wonder, will God remain faithful? Leslie show us through her poems and prose in *Tiny Thoughts* that the answer is Yes! He was in her story and He is in yours.

—SARAH STONESTREET
Co-host of *The Strong Women Podcast*

It is hard not to use the word "inspiring" when thinking of Leslie, so animated was she by the breath of life, and so obviously borne along by the wind of the Spirit. That same Spirit flows through all these writings—displaying so well the charm, warmth, and infectious faith of their author. What a gift, and what a life!

—JEREMY BEGBIE
McDonald Agape Director and founder of Duke Initiatives in Theology and the Arts, and the author of *Resounding Truth: Christian Wisdom in the World of Music*

My friend Leslie Anne Bustard was an especially lovable person. This new, posthumously gathered collection of her essays and poems, both wholly relatable and awe-inspiring, is a gift. Many were written while she fought heroic, arduous battles with cancer, and her humility and grace throughout are miraculous. Through her words she continues to be a guiding light of tremendous magnitude and warmth, offering us a blueprint for striving to live a life filled with meaning and purpose.

—KAREN PERIS
Singer-songwriter for the innocence mission

TINY
THOUGHTS
THAT I'VE BEEN
THINKING

TINY
THOUGHTS
THAT I'VE BEEN
THINKING

SELECTED WRITINGS OF

LESLIE ANNE BUSTARD

EDITED BY
THÉA ROSENBURG

SQUARE HALO BOOKS

In Christian art, the square halo identified a living person presumed to be a saint. Square Halo Books is devoted to publishing works that present contextually sensitive biblical studies, and practical instruction consistent with the Doctrines of the Reformation. The goal of Square Halo Books is to provide materials useful for encouraging and equipping the saints.

COVER: *See You Soon, Leslie* ©Bruce Herman, 2023.
Oil and gold leaf on kaolin clay panel; 30" x 30"

©2024 Square Halo Books, Inc.
P.O. Box 18954
Baltimore, MD 21206
www.SquareHaloBooks.com

ISBN 978-1-941106-34-1
Library of Congress Control Number: 2023942518

Printed in the United States of America

This book is for my
beautiful daughters,
Carey, Maggie, and Ellie:
Enjoy life and love people
… and let them love you.
You girls are good
people to love.

contents

Grace & Peace
Leslie Bustard

I feel like I just got it—
I just got what it meant to
really rest in Jesus.
Rest in Jesus.
He really is trustworthy …

Lancaster General Hospital
Emergency Room | 03.28.23

Foreword

LESLIE ANNE BUSTARD loved to transform old photos, magazine clippings, quotes, and other beautiful ephemera into small collages ("scrapbook cards") that she filled with encouraging letters and sent to friends and family. This book is the last of those letters—one written during Leslie's final three years, into which she poured her love, wisdom, and prayers. Leslie believed that caring for others was a calling, and she pursued that calling with diligence and creativity, cultivating her gifts so that she could give them freely to others—to her husband, Ned, and daughters Carey, Maggie, and Elspeth; to her family and her church; to the students in her classrooms and the many, many people (myself included) who found a seat at her table. Hers was a warm and welcoming presence—effusive and bright-as-yellow.

But after she was diagnosed with both stage II breast cancer and stage IV melanoma, Leslie shifted, with a courageous sort of humility, from offering care to receiving it. And as she became less able to give time and energy to others, she began to offer more and more of what she could still give: herself.

Leslie's rubber stamp logo

During this time, she wrote poems and essays with startling abundance—more of them and more beautiful than seemed reasonable for a woman fighting two kinds of cancer. Though she had published a few pieces before her diagnosis, she spent her last three years publishing consistently in the writing communities that encouraged and supported her work, in addition to editing a book of essays and publishing a collection of her poems. The warmth and welcome of her writing drew others toward her, as though she'd thrown back the curtains in a dim room and readers couldn't help but turn toward the sunlight.

I met her the year before her diagnosis. While working as an editor for a magazine, I drew the lucky straw that allowed me to collaborate with her on a series of articles for publication. I say "lucky" playfully, because everything about our meeting felt artfully arranged by God: our correspondence quickly grew beyond the bounds of editorial comments and into the territory of true friendship. I had already given notice at the magazine (Leslie's articles were my last assignment), so when her husband, Ned, reached out to me about working with their publishing company, Square Halo Books, as an editor, the timing felt good and right. But then, just a few months later, Leslie was diagnosed with cancer (which felt—and still feels—horribly wrong).

Positioned as I was—across the country from Leslie, yet also somehow nearby as a friend, editor, and collaborator—I got to watch as Leslie's skill as a writer rooted and unfurled. In at least two of her essays, Leslie quotes Flannery O'Connor's prayer, "I do not know you God because I am in the way. Please help me to push myself aside." I could see Leslie doing exactly that—getting out of the way—which somehow allowed her to give of her true self more fully, in a way that pointed readers beyond her and toward Christ.

I have spent the last six months submerged in Leslie's writings—collecting, editing, and arranging them for this book—and let me tell you: her words only get deeper and more resonant with each reading. I have heard people call women like Amy Carmichael or Elisabeth Elliot their mentors, and I've wondered at that: how can you be mentored by someone you know only through their writing?

But I see it now: Leslie's words have that rare quality that shows readers not just how *she* lived, but how *we* might live, too. This quality shines especially fiercely through her words because she wrote them during a time when the Lord called her not simply to say what she believed but to live it out—one test result, one side effect, one sleepless night at a time. Rather than curling self-protectively around her sorrow, Leslie poured herself outward, into poems and essays and writings that illuminate for readers "the goodness of the Lord in the land of the living" (Ps. 27:13).

As she offered these words to us, the Lord multiplied her humble generosity and, through her, has given us something transformative and arrestingly beautiful—a book that witnesses to His goodness toward her, His beloved daughter, even in the midst of profound suffering and loss. We would have loved more time with her, and one day we will have it. But for now, we have this: a collection of her writings—a letter written with all of herself poured in.

—*Théa Rosenburg*

...

EDITOR'S NOTE

The title of this book comes from a conversation Ned and Leslie had while driving along the winding farm roads of Pennsylvania. "Do you know what tiny thoughts I've been thinking?" Leslie asked. Which of course Ned teased her for, in a way that guaranteed that the phrase "tiny thoughts" would become one of those jokes that make a marriage feel so lived-in and comfortable. As Leslie underwent treatment for cancer, these words served as an opening to many conversations between Ned and Leslie, and they suit this book beautifully, as it is an assortment of things from tiny poems to not-so-tiny essays. Part I of this book contains the best of Leslie's poems, prayers, essays, and recipes, all arranged like one of her beloved charcuterie boards—filled with sweet and savory things. Many of these pieces were published in other places first, while others were given as talks, gleaned from her correspondence, or previously included as chapters in other books. Though Leslie often acknowledged and explored her struggles with cancer in these writings, this portion of the book is not *about* cancer. These are the writings of a daughter of God learning to walk faithfully beside her Father during the ordinary days and the difficult ones.

Part II of this book is a selection of Leslie's CaringBridge entries, which she wrote faithfully throughout her time in what she called "cancer-land." Leslie was an ambassador for beautiful things, so these entries were much more than updates on her physical status: they were as full of the art, poetry, and music she loved as they were details about her health.

The entries included in this part are only a handful of the many notes Leslie wrote for her readers, and they've been carefully edited (and occasionally expanded using content from her blog) so they can serve as a cohesive, narrative arc for Leslie's final, incredibly fruitful, three years.[1] (In fact, those of you who like to know the chronology of things may prefer to read Part II first.)

In both parts of this book Leslie extends a kind of hospitality toward her readers that invites us not into her home but into her inner life and imagination. In doing so, she shows us what it can look like for one woman to surrender to her Father's care even when the answers He gives her differ vastly from the ones she'd hoped for.

PART I

. . .

Essays & Poems

RESTING IN THE REALITY OF MY NAME: THE GIFT OF NAMES AND IDENTITY

I kneel before the Father, from whom every family in heaven and on earth derives its name . . . And I pray that you, being rooted and established in love, may have power, together with all the Lord's holy people, to grasp how wide and long and high and deep is the love of Christ, and to know this love that surpasses knowledge.
—Ephesians 3:14–15, 17–19 NIV

One night thirty-five years ago, my friend Ned and I were in his car, driving back to campus from a concert and discussing, of all things, what we planned to name our children. I shared my desire to give my daughter my mom's maiden name, Carey, as well as my own middle name, Anne (which was also my mom's middle name). Ned was going to give his firstborn son his name— to be the Third. That night I didn't pick up on any particular foreshadowing; I didn't realize that I was seeing some subtle clue of what made Ned *Ned*. But two years later we were married, and in three, he was cuddling our first daughter: Carey Anne Bustard.

More names would follow, including those for Carey's two sisters, Margaret Ellen[2] and Elspeth Iona.[3] And many others would come from Ned's imagination. For example, he named his graphic design business World's End Images, and then our little homeschool Saint Clive's Academy, our home BookEnd,[4] the backyard swing set tower Minas Gûl,[5] and our book publishing company Square Halo Books. His penchant for naming added roots to our family culture.

I think this passion for naming began when Ned was a young boy. Before Marvel's movies became popular, Ned read their comic books voraciously. These stories inspired him to turn his siblings and friends into their own superhero team, The Revengers.[6] He gave everyone names (his was Knightlight), designed their costumes, and decided on their powers.

Decades later, Ned resurrected the team and created a new generation of superheroes. Starting with our girls and me, then adding in his nieces and nephews and the girls' friends, he created a diverse plethora of new Revengers . He delighted in naming each member and fitting the name and power to the person's personality, peculiarities, or talents. I was Peacemaker, and he was

Great Man. Carey was Power Princess (later Reverie), Maggie was Magpie, and Ellie was Iona. Some of the other members included Chocolatier, Will-o-wisp, Stryker, and Indestructiboy.

Over the years, I have enjoyed Ned's imagination in naming and come to appreciate how it is a reminder of the call that God gave to Adam (Gen. 2:18-20). Before God created the woman to be Adam's strong ally, God brought the animals to Adam to name. Later, Adam named the woman—after the serpent deceived her, and after Adam had eaten fruit from the

The Revengers
Ned Bustard

tree from which God explicitly told them not to eat. Because of their disobedience, they experienced deep shame for the first time—the desire to hide and cover up, and a quickness to blame-shift. God meted out consequences for their sin but He also offered grace—His promise of a future salvation born of a woman. After all of this, Adam named the woman Eve, meaning "the mother of all the living." This name was a gift—one that spoke to their initial reality of being made in the image of God, and of Adam's desire that she be reminded of God's promises, not of their failures. They had been created to spread life into the world. Naming Eve was an offering of hope when both Adam and Eve needed it.[7]

The act of naming in the ancient Hebrew culture was a creative act. In bestowing a name upon someone or something, God's people participated in the creation of its destiny and identity.[8]

. . .

Before I became Leslie Anne Bustard, wife of Edwin David Bustard, Jr., I was Leslie Anne Symons, daughter of Anne and Richard Symons.

The surname Symons comes from a long line of fishermen in Cornwall, England, while Bustard comes from a long line of farmers in Donegal, Ireland. Even though these names are easily mispronounced and are not as familiar as Jones or Smith, I like the earthiness of them.[9] They sound like the names of humble people—like Mary, Joseph, or Jesus.

"Leslie" was an odd name to me when I was a young schoolgirl—not very girly or common. It sounded to me like a boy's name. Historically, it has been used for both boys and girls, but I was given the masculine spelling and pronunciation. As a young child, I had a deep desire to be accepted and feel acceptable. My father once told me they planned to name me Jennifer or Leslie. Teenager-me would have preferred Jennifer; all the Jennifers I knew didn't seem to struggle with feeling comfortable in their own skin.

The awkward feelings I had towards my name mirrored my own awkwardness with myself, as well as my struggle with what it meant to truly love God and believe He truly loved me. But He who began a good work in young Leslie continued to be faithful as she grew up and added the names of Wife, Mother, Teacher, Friend, and Writer to her days.

Reflecting on the various chapters of my life, especially the times my inner-struggle affected life at home with Ned and our girls, I have learned to recognize His faithfulness as He revealed more of Himself and more of His heart towards me. I know now that during those times when I named myself Too Worldly, or Pharisee, or Failure, He was with me. He was the one helping me seek after Him to find grace upon grace and light and life in Christ Jesus. As the Holy Spirit did His work—through Scripture, worship, life events, wise counsel, and poetry— a rooting reality of the glorious freedom of being a child of God formed in me.

Ned's proclivity for naming who and what entered his life found its telos in me. Early on in our marriage he nicknamed me "Luvkup." He even created a cute little red heart guy, with arms out to give a hug, to go with it. Although "Luvkup" and the heart guy make me smile, one of Ned's other names for me, "Wife-of-my-Youth," is a reminder of something more soul-satisfying.

A few weeks before Ned and I were married, a dear friend of ours shared that Ned's love for me was an example to her of Christ's love and how He chose to set His love on His bride the Church.

For me, her sweet words have shown themselves to be true.

I have many stories from the past three decades of how Ned has lived out Paul's command to husbands to love their wives as Christ loves the Church (Eph. 5:25–33). However, during the past few years, as I have developed two types of cancer (stage IV melanoma and stage II breast cancer), I have learned in deeper ways what it means to be Ned's beloved. This has, in turn, reoriented my heart to better see how I am God's Beloved.

Ned has carried the burden of sorrow and suffering with me. And along with so many other things, he has made certain I take my meds each day and arrive on time to appointments. He knows something isn't right when all I want is sleep or Multigrain Cheerios. He has carried my burdens, physically and metaphorically, all those days-upon-days when my immunotherapy (a treatment that fights melanoma) caused my knees, feet, hands, and arms to swell and get stiff, making it impossible for me to care for myself. He got me out of bed, washed me and brushed my teeth, dressed me, and then made meals and did laundry—he kept us going while also juggling his own work. In the ways I needed, he was strong and caring.

During the second and third years of this fight with cancer, I experienced many changes to my body that made me feel undesirable. My clothes size went up; my cheeks grew rounder. And each time I tried to follow an exercise routine or eating plan, something physical or emotional thwarted my intentions. I wondered, how could Ned still want me as I gained so much weight from my medicines, had weird folds in my arms where dozens of lymph nodes had been removed, had a reduction in one of my breasts from a lumpectomy, and then went partially bald from radiation to fight a brain tumor?

Psychiatrist Dr. Curt Thompson observes everyone wants to be seen, soothed, safe, and secure.[10] How true for me now and over the course of my whole life, too.

From my teenage years into adulthood, although I tried to hide it from others and myself, I was conflicted over how I perceived myself and how I was perceived. I might not be model-beautiful, but was I attractive? Was I thoughtful enough? Loving enough? Theologically correct enough? Did I serve enough? These heart conflicts didn't rule me, but they did whisper loudly (despite Ned's love and encouragement). I wanted to embrace the truth that charm and beauty are shifting sands, while fearing the Lord is a firm foundation upon which to build one's life; as I imagine it is for others, this was a daily spiritual battle. And now, with all the changes to my body due to the consequences of cancer, can I find satisfaction in being praised as a woman who fears the Lord even when my body is a mess and my beauty really proved to be fleeting? (Prov. 31:30) Could I welcome Ned's gaze and his words, "You are altogether beautiful, my darling; there is no flaw in you" (Song 4:7 NIV), as a soothing balm and a place of security?

. . .

I am very grateful to be alive, and I do understand why all these changes in my body have occurred, and I have tried to be attentive to what God is offering to teach me. I have been learning to see myself as not just my physical body, though it is also true that, because of the incarnation of God the Son, I am my body and that is good. The gift is that these changes in my body have not stopped Ned from being effusive. He continues to celebrate my creativity while I have cancer, while also expressing that I am still who he wants. Consequently, I've been teaching myself to believe him when he names me Beautiful, Precious, and Desirable. Knowing he cherishes me more than I can imagine is a great freedom. This freedom leads me back to loving him, my family, and myself more deeply.

And along the way, as Ned was showing me his love, God was saying, "This is me, Leslie. Ned's love is a picture of my heart towards you. I want you to know: *you are my Beloved.*"

As I started to hear this, I imagined and ruminated on different people whom Jesus welcomed into His life. To the woman at the well, even though He knew everything about her, He offered life. To the woman caught in adultery, He said, "I don't condemn you." He revealed Himself to His friend Mary Magdalene as she wept at the tomb. Sometimes I pictured myself as the Prodigal Son, who upon returning home was enfolded in his father's arms.

Bible verses about God's love took on a timbre of reality that I had not heard before. Truly wonderful was I John 3:1: "See what great love the Father has lavished on us, that we should be called the children of God!" (NIV). And Isaiah 54:10: "'Though the mountains be shaken and the hills be removed, yet my unfailing love for you will not be . . .' says the LORD" (NIV).

Though I knew this truth theologically, I started to understand even more deeply that when God looks at me, He doesn't just see my sin and say, "But I love you anyway." He looks at me clothed in the righteousness of Christ and loves me as He loves His Son. There is no "but"— no qualifications—to His love, to His cherishing, or to His promise to complete the work He has begun in me. These promises have always been there, inviting me into the glorious freedom of being His.

Before I was given the name "Leslie" or the surname "Bustard," I was named from eternity past "Child of God." And through a myriad of ways I have learned to carry in my heart, be formed by, and live into each of these names.

The New Shining Barrier
Ned Bustard

Although I didn't like the name Leslie when I was younger, I grew up to gladly be one-half of "Ned and Leslie." Becoming Ned's beloved Wife-of-my-Youth is a treasure.

"Leslie" means "to the fortress"—a description I failed to appreciate for many years but that I now see is quite right. One of my favorite verses says, "The name of the Lord is a strong tower; the righteous run into it and are safe" (Prov. 18:10 NKJV). What a joy to begin to realize that I am one of those who runs to the fortress and is welcomed into its refuge. And from that place of refuge I am secure, ever growing and deeply knowing in my heart what before I only knew in my mind—that the Creator of all, from whom every family in heaven and earth is named, calls me: *Beloved.*

SONG OF SONGS 2:10

*My beloved spoke and said
to me, "Arise, my darling, my
beautiful one, come with me."*
—Song of Songs 2:10

I have learned to hear
God call me His Beloved
because your love for
me is the parable He
wrote to teach me to believe.

After Matisse #16
Ned Bustard

unhistoric acts

The growing good of the world is partly dependent
on unhistoric acts . . .
—George Eliot

Like many prayers that are said for the sick,
and thoughtful meals given after a baby is born.
Or when friends come to paint old walls
and fix broken steps.

As in listening ears and encouraging words.
Cards and flowers sent on hard days.
Trucks for moving furniture.

The grandmother who watches her daughter's
children, sharing her days with them.
And all those who mow their neighbors' lawns
and drive them to the pharmacy . . .

The goodness of the Lord in the land of the living.

BURNING BUSH

Spring's blooming forsythia,
with its yellow branches reaching
up and out,
is a burning bush
    commanding attention.

But what if this bush had been cut back
with pruning shears—shaped into a neat
square, its brightness restrained?

As if the one who revealed His glory
on the mountain could be tamed,
and His words trimmed down to be less
    wild and demanding.

Burning Bush
Ned Bustard

when i grow up

For we are his workmanship, created in Christ Jesus for good works, which God prepared beforehand, that we should walk in them. —Ephesians 2:10

"What are you going to be when you grow up?"

As a child this was an exciting question—especially if we had read colorful picture books about dancers or fire fighters or astronauts or circus tight-rope-walkers. The world looked ready for exploring and conquering.

But that exciting question boomeranged back on us our senior year in high school when well-meaning adults asked, "What will you study in college?" The world now seemed a little too large with too many options.

Once we were over the hurdle of choosing a college major, we started asking ourselves questions like "How am I going to support myself?" and "Is this what I really want to be doing?"

Then, as we got older and found ourselves in new social settings, we were asked, "What do you do?" Each time we tried to find a way to answer this in a sentence or two, inwardly grappling with how much to share about the things that take up our days (or that we wish took up our days).

These all seem like fine questions, fitting for each stage of life. Answering them seems to be the tough part, for underneath the questions and the answers are deeper questions and deeper ideas about identity, calling, and how we spend our days. The simplicity of Annie Dillard's "How we spend our days is, of course, how we spend our lives"[11] can be both freeing and burdensome.

After my husband Ned and I were married, our main goals were getting jobs—so we could pay the rent and utilities, pay off college loans, buy groceries, and maybe go to a concert every now and then. As young people working at our first jobs and thinking about the future, our vision of a successful life was what we had seen growing up: working our way towards buying a house and a car (or two), having children, serving in church, spending time with friends, and going on vacations. We assumed this was the path responsible Christians followed for a good life.

Concepts of *identity* and *calling* had not been part of any of the conversations we had had together or with our friends. But within the first couple months of marriage, Ned was wrestling with what it meant to be a Christian and an artist, while I was looking through Scripture to learn what it meant to be a woman and a wife.

Though we weren't using the words calling or identity, we were face-to-face with the honest question "What is our life for?"

Since then we have explored various thinkers' ideas of identity and calling. Fredrick Buechner's oft-quoted definition of calling—"The place God calls you is the place where your deep gladness and the world's deep hunger meet"[12]—is still a poetic mystery to me. I love how he put the words together, but I don't know how this idea actually works itself out. I have wondered, "What really is my deep gladness? And how could that possibly meet the world's deepest hunger?"

Of course I keep reading Buechner, even if I can't get my head around that quote. But I've found that a better starting point for me when working through the idea of identity and calling are the words of Saint Paul: "We are God's handiwork, created in Christ Jesus to do good works, which God prepared in advance for us to do" (Eph. 2:10 NIV). These words have reminded me of God's love, and they have encouraged me to keep seeking the good works God has for me to do. How amazing, I have thought, that He gives me something to do for Him that can be for the good of those around me—I get to be in on His New Creation plans as a child of God by being a wife, mother, daughter, friend, teacher, writer.

I have heard people say that being God's workmanship is akin to being God's poem, as the word *poema* in Greek is translated into *workmanship*. Whether this is an accurate translation or not, I am drawn to this picture of calling because I love words and poetry. What a real comfort to think that Jesus, the Word of God made flesh, is forming us to be part of His long epic poem.

To continue the analogy of poems, the mystery of discerning one's calling and then living into it can feel like what happens to Billy Collin's poem in "Introduction to Poetry": in the last stanza the poem has been tied to a chair with a rope and "beaten with a hose to find out what it all really means."[13]

All my questions about discerning God's call, about ability and inability, as well as comparisons to others and the work of improving have been torturous. I much prefer Collins's images of holding a poem "up to the light like a color slide" or water-skiing through life waving hello to the poet.

By our early thirties, through the books we read and talks we listened to, through late-into-the-night discussions with mentors, as well as through wrestling with each other and with God, we delved into the idea of calling and what our callings were. One friend's words greatly helped:

Calling does not refer to just one job or one task. It encompasses the whole shape of our life: the web of relationships and diversity of work that God gives to each Christian … Calling is the comprehensive picture of the unique path laid out for each of us, consisting of the particular things God has asked us—and sometimes no one else—to do.[14]

Paying attention to the community God had placed in our life—especially our family, church friends, and neighbors—and to the work that went with our passions offered us glimmers of clarity. We learned through hard life experiences that our callings didn't always match our day-in and day-out jobs.

One concept my husband and I ruminated on was the reality of living *coram Deo*—before the face of God. All of life, no matter how ordinary or unseen, could be lived as an act of worship to Him. This was revolutionary to me, as I assumed only "spiritual" activities such as evangelizing and having daily devotions were what really pleased God.

Reading Edith Schaeffer's book *The Hidden Art of Homemaking* was true north on my life compass. In each chapter, she elaborated on how "the fact that you are a Christian should show in some practical area of a growing creativity"[15] and how, because we are "created in the image of an Artist, we should look for expressions of artistry, and be sensitive to beauty, responsive to what has been created."[16] This book helped me enlarge the idea of living *coram Deo*. I was excited about how caregiving (caring for the people in my family and community) and writing (bringing beauty and goodness into the places God put me) could fill my days.

We understood that even if Ned worked hard as an artist and designer in his own business, he might not be what the world called successful, with name recognition and a big bank account. One mentor encouraged us with these words:

True artists … make the most of every opportunity. They do not wait for a national platform to really apply themselves. They give their best to God in their home, church, community, or university—being seen as faithful in the little things that they might be found ready and prepared for the bigger.[17]

How could we partner together well, using our gifts, creativity, and passions in our everyday lives and for others? How could I intertwine beauty and goodness in the ordinary parts of our days and offer it to my community? Along the way, as we figured out some of the answers to these questions, we grew in our callings—which included being husband and wife, parents, church members, and friends—and Ned grew in his craft as an artist and designer. I grew in my skills as a caregiver and a cultivator by expanding my baking abilities, gathering friends together for book groups, enfolding newcomers at church, and inviting my daughters to help me make meals for others. We deepened our commitment to the people and places God had given us.

This vision of the goodness of ordinary life was one God placed before me to keep my eyes fixed on Him and His ways. A crucial essay that helped me understand this was "A Stick Becomes a Staff of God," by Denis Haack:

> I dream of extraordinary things, of course, of things spectacular enough that the blessing of God is palpable and sure. Of doing great things for God not so much for the sake of fame, but to know for sure that what I do or accomplish is clearly significant in the eternal scheme of things . . .
>
> [Yet it is] pride that makes us go a-whoring after the spectacular and the extraordinary. Our primary calling as the children of God is to be faithful in the ordinary and the routine. The ordinary of everyday life that is before us moment by moment is not to be despised or considered insignificant or secondary. It is to be embraced and celebrated as the very sphere for which we were made and in which the grace of God is so spectacularly at work.[18]

The richness of this essay included seeing how Creation (although truly a wonder) was actually the beginning of ordinary living and working as God's people, as well as realizing how many of Christ's miracles (although amazing) made it possible for people to go back to their ordinary lives. His work was restoring people to what they were meant to be. And as we think about Moses with his ordinary wooden shepherding stick, we see how God took it and used it to do fantastic things, so that in the end, ordinary people could be set free to go live as His people—doing ordinary work.

I may have been called to do ordinary work with ordinary people in an ordinary place, but that didn't mean that it would be boring or meaningless. My ordinary life could make for a really good story. Our friend Charlie Peacock wrote, "My life and my art are going to tell a story whether I try to or not. They will tell a story that says: This is what a follower of Jesus is. This is what he is about."[19]

My imagination grabbed hold of this idea—that all of life, even my ordinary-days-on-Pine-Street life, could be an act of worship as well as a good story. I realized that this was what I wanted for my life and in our home. Small touches of beauty in our day would add goodness to the story, as well as enfolding others into our lives. I wanted to share huge doses of laughter, tears, conversations, and food with my people.

When my girls were growing up these small touches of beauty included fresh flowers arranged in the morning, Ella Fitzgerald during fall evenings, candles at dinnertime, piles of new library books every other week, sunflowers growing in the garden, and teatime and dress-up under the lilac trees. As they grew I added pancake breakfasts with poetry, picnics in the park, and Shakespeare plays with friends' children. I envisioned our life story to include loving and serving not just our family but also old and young church members, neighbors, and our daughters' friends.

But living it out wasn't always easy.

During my late thirties and early forties, I often fell into anxiety and the trap of comparing myself to others. I might feel confident, purposeful, and enthused about what I was doing, but under my skin I worried I was too idealistic, or that I was play-acting and would eventually be found out as a fraud. Even if others couldn't see it, I often felt trapped in insecurity and discouragement, wondering if what I did would matter.

Tulip
Hannah
Claire
Weston

As I look back over all the years of discerning and living out my specific callings, God has graciously been teaching me several things. Of most importance: *I am His beloved* (Song 6:3). Learning to fix my eyes on Jesus and resting in His steadfast faithfulness can be my source of daily confidence and strength. And even though I am His workmanship and He is completing his good work in me, the good works He has prepared for me are not just about my own personal fulfillment. Rather, my callings as a caregiver and a cultivator can be for the good of the people God has given me and in the places He has put me. It's really about His New Creation story lived out in ordinary time.

The Spirit and Scripture point me towards learning how to love God and others, as well as learning to die to my pride and vanity. I've come to learn that as I lean into the Holy Spirit for help and trust Him for the outcomes, the insecurities and anxieties that have turned me inward begin to take up less space in my heart.

It has been good to experience the deeper freedom of being God's child.

Now I am in my fifties. I am at the point my twenty-something self could barely imagine. The beginning of my fifth decade continued on like the previous one—caring for family and friends and finding ways to be creative and to offer beauty and goodness in my community, which included teaching seventh and eighth grade literature and writing and producing high school and children's theater. But this ordinary life took an abrupt left turn with my diagnosis of two different stages and types of cancer. But while life has changed, I realize my callings have not. All the things God had been working in me and doing through me have continued, although on a different scale and in different ways.

Over the course of my adult years, God has given me this gift to slowly unwrap, and as I pull back the layers of anticipation and discovery, He has shown me the splendor of quotidian days. And now He has given me this sweet surprise—the good work of writing, of putting what I see and love into essays and poetry. My observations of beauty in the ordinary now find their way out into the world through images, phrases, paragraphs, and stanzas. Jesus, the Living Word, continues to invite me to respond to His call of love through the work of caring for people and cultivating places, and, the wonder of it all, through the crafting of words into poetry.

These days I might ask a young friend, "What do you want to be when you get older?" But most likely I'll look them in the eye and ask them what book they are reading. Or after shaking the hand of a newcomer at church, I'll ask, "What takes up your days?" Or maybe I'll ask what they have been doing lately that makes them happy. And if I'm asked the same question, I might pause and figure out how much to say or not to say, but then might simply answer with a smile, "I love on my people and write poetry."

crash course

I take a piece of white paper
from the pile on the kitchen table,
and a lone red magic marker,
and fill its space with tall capital letters—
   I love you.

After a few attempts at creasing
and folding, I google *how
to make a paper airplane*—
though you showed our children this
maybe an hour ago.

Crash Course
Ned Bustard

I want to see my airplane glide
into your hand after one sweeping loop
in the air but imagine it will nose-dive
into an elbow and crash land at your feet.

Outside, taking a cue from one of our girls,
I hold the paper airplane above my head,
and pointing it, walk over to you
in the middle of our yard.

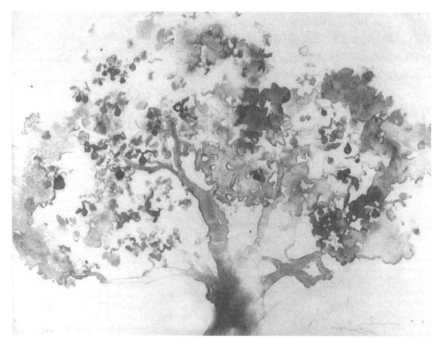

Shalom
Makoto Fujimura

LIVES SHAPED BY BEAUTY: THE GOODNESS OF ORIGINAL ART IN THE HOME

"If your house was burning down, which paintings should I try to save?"

Our friend Sophia had only been living with our family for a week when she half-jokingly shared this concern. Her question reminded me of the conversations my husband Ned and I periodically have together: if a catastrophe hit, what would we try to save?

Along with the memories we've made in our century-old city row home, the original artwork hanging on our walls have filled our rooms with precious and pleasant riches. This was not a question of hoarding and "storing up treasures on earth"; these paintings have become part of our family's story. We would try to save particular works of art from this hypothetical fire or flood in order to preserve something real to pass on to our children and, hopefully, their children.

During our conversation with Sophia, I was reminded of all the specific ways the Lord has abundantly fulfilled our desire for original artwork. In our first year of marriage, we started praying for well-made, beautiful artwork created by living Christian artists. We didn't know how we would pay for original artwork or how we would acquire any pieces; but we still asked. Now, nearly thirty years later, almost every wall in our home holds the gifts of beauty God has given to us, through many different ways, to steward and enjoy.

I want to add to the Beauty

In our early twenties, we collected cheap prints picked up during day trips to museums. Also on our walls were a few framed originals—a brass rubbing of a knight that Ned had made during a college mission trip and two watercolor paintings my aunt had commissioned depicting Ned and me on our honeymoon. These pieces planted a vision in us to add into our home a *solidness* that could only be found in original artwork and which mirrored what we were experiencing in our life together.

Author Jennifer Allen Craft affirms our vision in *Placemaking and the Arts*: "Our internal dispositions are externalized into our dwelling places, and in turn, our dwelling places influence and adjust our sense of self-identity."[20]

Years later, I started to see how our old prayer for original artwork was a way God had called us to be intentional—to "add to the beauty, to tell a better story,"[21] as the songwriter Sara Groves sings.

Paintings, sculpture, and handmade pottery or furnishings might be seen as unnecessary extravagance. However, as Craft posits, "The inclusion of the arts in all places of our lives may be one way in which to motivate our loves and cultivate a Christian sense of place and practice in the world. The arts might shape the places, and the sense of place, that shape us."[22] If our places do help shape us for love of God and His kingdom, then how we shape those places is necessary work in which to invest our creativity and resources.

Our hearts and imaginations are formed by the stories and images we experience each day. We can be tempted to become consumer-driven, fad followers. The world wears us down with constant messages of who to be and what to want. The environments in which we live our lives are not neutral.

When our children were younger, I was motivated to be purposeful and creative in how I shaped our spaces by filling them with artistic reminders that we belong to Jesus and are part of His kingdom story. "By wisdom a house is built and by understanding it is established; by knowledge the rooms are filled with precious and pleasant riches" (Prov. 24:3) hummed in my mind.

Recently, a friend recounted her own heart-shaping experience of bringing original artwork into her home. Each morning, as she drinks her coffee, she stands before *New Creation*, an ornate block print hanging in her Brooklyn apartment. After many months of attending to it each morning, she realized, "I get to breathe in the reminder that even though creation and our bodies are groaning, one day He will make all things new. We will join Him at His wedding banquet in our forever home!"

New Creation
Ned Bustard

BEAUTY FOR THE GLORY OF GOD

Although Home Goods can help us find a print that will match our sofa, original artwork serves a different, deeper purpose. As C.S. Lewis reminds us in *Experiment in Criticism*, "We sit down before a picture in order to have something done to us, not that we may do things with it."[23] Bringing original artwork into one's home is a transformative act. It helps us to be attentive to the longings and loves of our hearts. A painting will rarely draw out of us the same response each day; therefore, living with original artwork can help us look out into the world and see meaning and goodness. Along the way, these works of art can train our senses for glory, bear witness to our sorrows, and offer us moments of reflection.

For Ned's fortieth birthday, I asked family and friends to contribute money to his gift: *Shalom*, a lithograph on rice paper created by Makoto Fujimura in the wake of the 9/11 attacks. This piece originated from a picture of a quince tree Fujimura had sketched at The Cloisters in New York City. Speaking blessings and reminders to be rooted in God's ways, this image of a peaceful, strong tree, with soft light shining through the branches, hangs above our bed. When I slow down to attend to it with my eyes and heart, I get a glimpse of the flourishing peace God offers us.

Shaping beautiful spaces is one way we can image our Creator God who called forth His world and pronounced it good. God made the world filled with beauty—beauty seen in the heavens as the stars and planets shine, as well as the unseen beauty in the deep darkness of the seas.

God's design of the temple affirms that He is a God who creates His dwelling places to be filled with glory and beauty. Francis Schaeffer observed in his classic treatise *Art and the Bible* that God directed every detail of the temple's building and decorating plans. "The temple was to be filled with art work. 'And he [Solomon] garnished [covered] the house with precious stones for beauty.' (2 Chron. 3:6)... They had no utilitarian purpose. God simply wanted beauty in the temple."[24]

Why would we adorn our spaces with the beauty of original artwork? Just as we fill our home with the loveliness of fresh flowers, the delicious aroma of simmering chicken soup, or the warm glow of flickering candles, beauty helps us celebrate our good God. At the same time, we are reflecting His art-making character as we shape our spaces creatively.

Literary critic Alan Jacobs underscored this when he wrote, "Whether we would have it so or not, the things we make are reliable tokens of what we believe, because what we make declares our character in the same way that 'the heavens declare the glory of God, and the firmament showeth his handiwork' (Ps. 19:1 KJV).'"[25] How we decorate and fill our homes reflects what we believe.

CHICKENS, GOLDFINCH, AND GOOGLY EYES

Mary McCleary, a Texan artist, creates mixed media collages out of small found objects such as foil, beads, painted sticks, and small plastic toys. She explains, "I like the irony of using materials that are often trivial, foolish, and temporal to express ideas of what is significant, timeless, and transcendent."[26]

A creative partnership between Mary and Ned brought *The Goldfinch* into our home. This eye-catching image of a yellow bird perched inside thorny branches is three-dimensional; actual thorn branches, googly eyes, and blue paper triangles are a few of the pieces that make up this mosaic. Because goldfinches would live among thorns, it was adopted as a symbol for Christ. In many Renaissance paintings of the Madonna and Child, the infant Jesus holds a goldfinch, fore-shadowing that He will be crowned with thorns at His crucifixion. This piece hangs downstairs in our library and we see it every day; it both delights us with its intricate details and slows us down to remember Christ's sacrifice.

And this is what I have learned over the years: collecting original artwork has both added to the beauty of our home and has helped us tell a good story with our lives. Each piece of artwork is packed with seen and unseen stories. There are many ties that bind us together as a family, and the stories that are intertwined in the paintings that hang on our walls are some of those ties.

Goldfinch
Mary McCleary

Cream Legbar Hen, an intricate 12x12-inch linocut, hangs near our kitchen. Thousands of black and white lines make up the ferns and feathers, as well as the impressive figure of a hen. We have been friends with its creator Matthew Clark and his family for more than a decade. Ned and Matt have spent hours and hours together, collaborating and pulling prints. Several Christmases ago, Matt surprised us with this new print. Because the Clark family is dear to us, and because different pieces of Matt's art hang throughout our home, it was only natural that our daughter Maggie would deem it necessary to hang two of his pieces, both portraits of different roosters, in her own kitchen, alongside one of her dad's prints of Jesus and His disciples eating the Last Supper. She continues our tradition of adding beauty and kingdom reminders into her home, as well as celebrating the art makers in her life.

BEAUTY ON A BUDGET

There will be many seasons in life when we cannot afford to purchase original artwork for our homes. Beauty still tugs at our hearts; we can bring it into our lives in other ways. Visiting local art galleries or museums and finding what you love is one way to add beauty into life. Borrow art history books from the library. I have enjoyed and learned much by checking out children's library books about Giotto di Bondone, Mary Cassatt, and Paul Cézanne. Often a daughter or two sat beside me as I looked through the pages. Hanging postcards of favorite paintings on my fridge kept my beauty-yearning heart happy. I would rotate favorite post-

cards through the seasons. Weaving
art into one's life and home enriches
you and your loved ones; it plants the
seeds of loving true glory.

We are called to mirror God by
offering beauty to those around us—
welcoming others into our homes by
saying, "Look and see with me." As we
shape our spaces, we learn that they
shape us. As Proverbs 14:1 tells us, "A
wise woman builds her house, but
with her own hands the foolish one
tears hers down" (NIV). The stories
our lives tell within our own four
walls will reflect the God who saves
us and will be filled with joy, sorrow,
struggle, and peace. The beauty we
add into our places—including the treasures of paintings,
sculpture, or hand-crafted pieces—will intertwine with
our lives, training our senses for glory and grace.

Rhode Island Red
Matthew Clark

THE Tree Across THE STreeT

Let us stretch ourselves out towards him,
that when he comes he may fill us full.
—Augustine

The tree across the street,
the one I see framed in our front window,
was slowly losing its leaves,
until yesterday's wind came.
Now only a scattering of red and orange remain,
exposing a maze of branches

reaching out,
stretching up.

And then there is my heart,
how gradually I reveal it
to me to you

to God.

How my longings reach out
and then stretch
and stretch up,
waiting to be filled.

And in the spring,
the tree I see in our window shines
by afternoon sun,
rich with its pink flowers
and its green leaves.

Trees Along My Way

The trees in winter,
naked and exposed,

look as if they are a tangle of hands reaching up—
the limbs and branches taking hold of the sun for warmth
and grabbing at the blue sky for cover.

And as the sun goes down,
when sky holds indigo before it falls to black,
they are a silent silhouette of waiting.

We Missed the Snow Geese
Leslie Bustard

I Am the Bread
Ned Bustard

A WILDERNESS OF WAITING FILLED WITH LIFE

On Sunday, March 1, I stood in church for the first time in weeks. Our pastor encouraged us to lift our hands to receive life—to receive the benediction. In that moment, it was as if my two raised hands held in equal tension a deep gratefulness for the life God had given me and a desperate desire for even more. With tears in my eyes, I heard my pastor say, "May the grace of the Lord Jesus Christ and the love of God and the fellowship of the Holy Spirit be with you all." Enveloped in this blessing, I begged God for more strength and more hope, as well as more days and more years.

On December 27th a doctor told my husband and me that I had breast cancer. A week later, a biopsy confirmed it was stage I, triple-positive invasive carcinoma. I had started the new year trusting in the Lord's sovereignty and goodness. I could rest in Him—even as I looked ahead toward an unknown battle against cancer. In early January, the days got scarier when the doctors discovered I *also* had metastatic melanoma. The next two months were filled with tests and scans to learn if the cancer had spread to any other organs. My oncologist would,

as he said, "throw every test in the book" at me. On February 27—after one final
CT scan—my doctors were convinced that melanoma had spread to the top of
my intestine, moving me to stage IV cancer. Treatment plans were finally set in
place, including immunotherapy in the spring, breast surgery in the summer,
and then more immunotherapy. My first infusion of nivolumab and ipilimumab
would happen March 4, 2020.

. . .

*What does it look like to receive life from Jesus when He has called me to walk
through this valley?*
I know, as the Apostle John stresses through his Gospel, that if I look to Jesus
as the Son of God and believe in Him, I will have eternal life, and that He will
raise me up on the last day. What a great hope and comfort we have been given
in this—one I have held onto even as the veil of heaven seems a little thinner
now. But what does it look like to receive life from Jesus when He has called me
to walk through this valley of the shadow of death? What does it look like to see
the goodness of the Lord in the land of living now, as I wait on Him while still
desiring to make a life with my husband, family, and community?
*What does it look like to receive Jesus' life with open hands when the me in my
skin and spirit is struggling to keep from drowning in weariness and weakness?*
Friends have shared that my heart and my words have been an encourage-
ment to them as they read my CaringBridge updates, look at my Instagram posts,
or spend time talking and praying with me on my sofa. They have even said I
look more radiant than ever. How can that be? If it is true, that radiance can only
be because of Jesus in me.
It is Jesus in me, made real as He abundantly gives me courage to get through
one more doctor's appointment, scan, test, or day of waiting for results.
It is Jesus in me, His overflowing care made real to me through all the gifts
and cards that have arrived in doubles or triples each day, for weeks.
It is Jesus in me, His truths made real through the Bible verses that friends
have sent to me through texts, messages, and emails.
It is Jesus saying to me, in a myriad of ways that I cannot miss, "I go before you."

. . .

Malcolm Guite's sonnets in *After Prayer* have been lifting me these many
weeks. The first poem in this collection, "The Church's Banquet," arrested my
attention, and for days I could not let it go; each time I re-read it, a deep desire to
experience these truths pounded in my heart.

THE CHURCH'S BANQUET
Malcolm Guite

Not some strict modicum, exact allowance,
Precise prescription, rigid regimen,
But beauty and gratuitous abundance,
Capacious grace, beyond comparison.
Not just something hasty, always snatched alone;
Junkets of junk food, fueling our dis-ease,
Not little snacklets eaten on the run,
But peace and plenty, taken at our ease.
Not to be worked for, not another task,
But love that's lavished on us, full and free,
Course after course of hospitality,
And rich wine flowing from an unstopped flask.
He paid the price before we reached the inn,
And all he asks of us is to begin.[27]

As I continue through this valley of the shadow of death, the Lord has offered me a course-after-course banquet, in the presence of my enemies, with a cup of rich wine that flowed from an unstopped flask. During those many weeks of waiting, His generosity to me through family and friends was at times so much that I could only weep. Through these days, in a tangible way, Jesus showed me He truly is the Bread of Life.

My wilderness of waiting was not barren; it was full of His care.

. . .

Following the surgery to insert my port, I lost most of my appetite. The only food I cared about was white bread toast with butter and raspberry jam. I ate this combination for most meals, despite the wealth of dinners given to us by church members. One day, after seeing a friend's Facebook post about dreamy, homemade blueberry scones, I found myself wandering the aisles of Wegman's looking for something like them. When my friends learned that what I really wanted was bread or scones, they made a "Happy Snacks for Leslie" sign-up list as a way to care for me. After that, I started receiving bread in many different, yummy forms. One morning, while looking at all the bread on my kitchen table and trying to decide what would go into the freezer, I thought, "Jesus said, 'I am the Bread of Life'" (John 6:35). When I ate bread—whether a homemade wheat roll, a slice of artisan bread, a scone, or a sticky bun—I could taste and see that Jesus was good and was being good to me.

As I walked through this wilderness of waiting, He was tangibly showing me that He was giving me His life. My wilderness was not barren; it was full of His care.

This life from the Lord was not given to me because I prayed the right prayers or because I prayed enough. Most of the time, I simply recited the Lord's Prayer or confessed "I am weak; please help me." Although I know these short prayers are enough for God to move, I cannot shake the feeling that I was given this abundance because my family and friends have been interceding for me, day in and day out. Their prayers have been more than I could ask or imagine. Truly, I am the paralytic needing to be healed, and my friends have broken a hole in the roof to get me to Jesus.

. . .

On the morning of March 5, I stand at the stove, holding in both hands farm-fresh eggs. I feel their weight, and I enjoy their muted hues. I crack them open over the pan, and their bright yellow yolks form perfect circles. I scramble them lightly with freshly ground pepper, goat cheese, and cherry tomatoes; they taste just right. I haven't made a breakfast like this in weeks. In this moment—as I live with medication coursing through me and still don't know what lies ahead of me—I gratefully receive new life, sweet and ordinary. Held together by the grace of Jesus Christ, I see the goodness of the Lord in the land of the living.

I am one who has been given God's love—lavished on me, full and free.

DELICIOUS

Shafts of delicious sunlight struck down onto the forest floor ...
—C.S. Lewis

When the glow of morning
runs through our faded, yellow curtains.

Or when the car windows are rolled down,
and we are swallowed up
by the sun on open back roads
of farm country.

When I'm lying in green grass
face to the shining blue sky,
both eyes squinting through upheld fingers,
and bright rays warming my skin.

LONG

One cannot measure
an anxious heart—hope becomes
a long wait, stretching
into the watchful stillness
of the always now of God.

THE BIRD OUT MY WINDOW

as hawks rest upon air, and
the air sustains them . . .
—Denise Levertov

I keep returning in my mind
to a bird I saw yesterday.
She sat still on the topmost branch
of a nearby tree made leaf–empty
by a late autumn rain.
Of all places to perch,
this bird chose the thinnest,
loneliest twig.
With no other birds nearby,
she tightly held her own
against a white sky.
Her weight,
or a slight breeze,
caused the branch to sway.
With a tilt of her small head
and ruffle of feathers,
she looked side to side,
content,
so far away from solid ground.
I keep wondering:
is this what it's like to
be a sparrow in God's eyes . . .
peacefully perched up high,
confident that letting go
will not result in free fall?
I recall looking away for a moment
. . . then she was gone.[28]

GRANDMAMA'S LEGACY

When I married Ned, I inherited his grandmother's iron skillet and her recipe for Irish Soda Bread. Agnes Bustard's parents were "straight off the boat" from Ireland and carried with them the strong name of Strudwick. Agnes was married to Edwin Atlee Bustard, later called "Dr. B" by everyone who met him; where

he was lovable, she was a force to be reckoned with. A solid Bible teacher, evangelist, writer, and spiritual mentor, for years she also ran a month-long Summer Bible School event where children were taught theology, memorized entire chapters of the Bible, sang songs, learned about missionaries, and, of course, made crafts—just for the sticker prizes on their report cards (yes, they were given report cards because "this was Summer Bible *School* not *Vacation* Bible School"). She loved the Bible, she loved to teach the Bible, and she laughed a lot, but she was a tough cookie who did what she wanted. Although our wedding guests were not expected to wear hats, she wore one anyway and delighted in showing it off.

Agnes Strudwick Bustard

I always imagined that this recipe traveled with her parents straight across the Atlantic Ocean. But when I asked her about its history, she told me that she had learned this family favorite from a friend, who had cut the recipe out of a newspaper. I'm still grateful for it; it has made three generations of Bustards, our family included, very happy.

I must admit, I upped the sugar to sweeten it and swapped out the dark raisins for golden ones. I think my father-in-law approves.

Grandmama's Irish Soda Bread *(with my tweaks)*

INGREDIENTS

4 cups all-purpose flour
1 tsp. salt
1 tsp. baking soda
4 tsp. baking powder
¾ cup granulated sugar
8 oz. raisins (or more!)
2 cups buttermilk

Fifteen minutes before putting the soda bread in the oven, preheat oven to 400°. Grease and flour an iron skillet. (I think the iron skillet is key to this bread's success.)

In a large bowl, mix all ingredients well. Pour batter into the skillet. Bake for 15 minutes at 400°, then turn the oven down to 375° and bake for the rest of an hour. (This is what the original recipe says, but I usually bake it for 30–35 more minutes to keep it from getting too brown on the top and from drying out.)

Butter the whole thing while it is hot . Enjoy that first warm piece! The bread is still delicious cold, but that first slice is wonderful warm.

God Enjoys the Creation and Creates Eve

A Necessary Ally[29]

The phrase "Bloom Where You're Planted" has always grabbed my attention—so much so that white-distressed chalkboard frames embellished with this saying repeatedly found their way into my shopping cart. At one point, I even made this phrase the theme of a ladies' gathering I organized at my church.

For me, motherhood became another place to bloom as I used my creativity and strengths in new ways. When I had one child, the idea of blooming where God had planted me seemed attainable. But when two more children and homeschooling were added to my everyday life, I began to struggle with deep feelings of inadequacy. The daily work of feeding, clothing, and training little ones—while also teaching my oldest child phonics, handwriting, and math—never seemed to go the way I planned. I felt like I was wilting, not blooming. The classic hymn's lines, "Frail as summer's flower we flourish / Blows the wind and it is gone," described me in this season.[30]

But God planted a new truth in my heart: my blooming could look different than I had imagined. He had set me in a place and given me a purpose. And I was slowly coming to see how the first few chapters of Genesis could form a vision for my life.

A GOD-GIVEN RESPONSIBILITY

Genesis 1 illustrates how everything God created was overflowing with life. The lush Garden magnified the Creator's goodness—it was full of trees, flowers, and fruit, as well as animals, fish, and birds. God then shaped two persons and placed them there. This part of Creation—humanity—was made to image the Creator-King. Three times God stated that He would make humans—male and female—in His own image (Gen. 1:26, 27), and then He commanded them to "Be fruitful and multiply and fill the earth and subdue it and have dominion" (Gen. 1:28).

The man and woman God created—image-bearers equal in value and dignity—were to use their imaginations and abilities to take God's work and expand it into the world. This is called the *cultural mandate*. And just as Adam and Eve were given this work to do, so too, were their descendants. Together they were given the job of making, cultivating, and caretaking—and so are we.

This Creation Story truth helped me see that the place where I lived and the way I sought to cultivate it for my people were part of God's Kingdom Story. I grew to see that I could reflect the image of God through ordinary days of making meals, doing laundry, training children, planning celebrations, and establishing traditions in our home.

A GOD-GIVEN HELPER

My vision and imagination were then enlarged by studying Genesis 2. There I saw that God designed women to image Him in a distinct way. As Adam named the animals, he learned that it was not good to be alone. God said, "I will make a helper fit for him" (Gen. 2:18).

The phrase "helper fit for him" is a translation of the Hebrew *ezer kenegdo*. By the time Moses had written the Creation account, he had seen God act as a strong helper to the Israelites over and over. God was their strength, their rescuer, and their protector. When Moses wrote the account of the first woman being made, he used the word *ezer* to describe her, offering readers a vision of women as strong helpers.

God is not a junior assistant—the aid, strength, and support He gives His people is crucial. Therefore, I am not a junior assistant to my husband in the fulfillment of the cultural mandate in our home and community. "Necessary ally" is another helpful translation that can clarify the meaning of the word *ezer*.[31] God has made me a necessary ally, and He calls me to spend my days loving, serving, advocating for, and encouraging others where He has planted me.

GOD'S HELP FOR OUR NEED

God had gifted me for this work, but I was not a consistent necessary ally. Although I embraced this vision of being an *ezer,* the days were often long, the kids' noses dripped, the reading lessons stumbled along, and the work of training my kids in the faith and in obedience seemed fruitless. My imperfections screamed in my mind, and my inadequacies pierced my heart. One day a mentor said, "Leslie, you already pray for God *to help you;* ask Him to open your eyes to see how He *is helping you now."*

So I prayed.

When I was weary, I learned to pray, "I am poor and needy; come quickly to me, O God. You are my help and my deliverer" (Ps. 70:5 NIV).

When I realized I was striving in my own strength, I learned to pray "wait in hope for the LORD" because I needed Him to be "my help and shield" (Ps. 33:20 NIV).

When I worried over the future, I learned to pray "I lift up my eyes to the mountains—where does my help come from? My help comes from the LORD, the Maker of heaven and earth" (Ps. 121:1-2 NIV).

A new picture of blooming has replaced my first one. Jesus promises, "I am the vine; you are the branches. Whoever abides in me and I in him, he it is that bears much fruit, for apart from me you can do nothing" (John 15:5). I am a child of God through faith in Jesus; He has made me a new creation and promises to complete the work He began in me. It is only as His life gives me life that I am able to give my life for others as an *ezer.*

You and I are made in God's image. With God as our strong helper—and trusting Him for the fruit of our work—we can be strong helpers for others. We can strengthen, build, defend, encourage, and create culture in our homes and communities. It is through living as necessary allies—for the people God has given us in the places He has put us—that you and I can *truly* bloom where we're planted.

YELLOW
FOR KAREN PERIS

"Bright as yellow"—like
how the sun shines through leaf-filled
branches; its warm rays
are outstretched arms greeting you
and me with great shouts of joy.

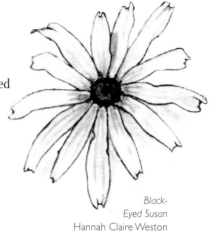

ACORN
FOR LUCI SHAW

*Black-
Eyed Susan*
Hannah Claire Weston

With smooth faces and
knubby caps, a few acorns
roll around in my palm, their
brown bodies a distraction—
in my pocket, a surprise.

INVITATION

As if pursuing blue skies,
then diving, skimming with swift
shadows rippling across
the lake's surface
was a call to *come*

and follow,
two black swallows arch
within my view—once, twice, and
back again.

LIGHT BEHIND THE LIGHT

For the past few weeks, my imagination has been filled with the paintings of a favorite artist. His unexpected use of colors—especially the vibrancy of his yellows, blues, and greens—is hard to forget, as are his bold brush strokes. Light shines out in most of his paintings—not just those set outdoors, but also those depicting the ordinary or rejected people he observed and captured on canvas. I have been drawn to this artist and his artwork because even though many in the church and the art world rejected him, he found the faith and fortitude to continue painting and to work out the vision that filled his heart. Wider acceptance and success came later; his paintings found their places in museums, galleries, and around the world, making him one of the greats in modern art history.

The reader might conclude that my narrative above describes the brilliant and tragic Vincent van Gogh. His use of color and light, as well as his lines, were bold. His subject matter included ordinary people. He was rejected during his lifetime, but later became one of the most beloved painters in the world.

However, this particular description is of the French painter Georges Rouault. Like Vincent van Gogh, who influenced him, Rouault was faithful to his vision of what, why, and how he wanted to paint. Although many, especially in the Catholic Church, rejected his work, he held onto his faith in Christ and his faith in his work. He found the courage to stick to the calling he believed God had given him.

. . .

Georges Rouault was born in 1871 in the basement of his family home during the Paris Insurrection. At fourteen, he was apprenticed to a stained-glass maker. He eventually contributed to the restoration of the windows of the Chartre Cathedral, one of the premier examples of Gothic architecture of medieval France. At the age of twenty, he started studying under the Symbolist Gustave Moreau, who later encouraged the young artist to find his own voice and path.

Another key element to his growth as a painter was an assignment he took, as a young man living in Paris, that involved sitting in on and recording what he saw in criminal court hearings. "His experience of the corruption of the French courts and the abject desperation that led most of the poor defendants to their crimes left him with little patience for outward displays of correctness and authority."[32] This experience planted the seeds for a vision that led him to create artwork that spotlighted the outsiders of society, such as prostitutes, and illustrated how Christ's grace and compassion was for them. Rouault was disgusted by the judges, by the rich, and by the church—those who did not care for others and believed they were above the law. In 1907 Rouault started painting prostitutes and clowns. The poet Andrew Suars wrote to Rouault about this, saying, "The beautiful style with which you have dressed them is a guarantee of their souls, and that their misery is worthy of salvation."[33]

Rouault continued painting and showed his work in public exhibitions, most notably the Salon d'Automne.. He also became part of the Fauvists movement led by his friend Henri Matisse. Vincent van Gogh's work, rich with color contrasts and emotion, influenced Rouault. As he continued painting in the early 1900s, Rouault became a major influence in the Expressionist movement. His works were shown internationally, especially in London and New York. Around 1917, his Christian faith and interest in the Catholic Church began to impact his art making, so much so that he is now considered the most passionate Christian artist of the twentieth century. In 1948, he exhibited his important *Miserere* series. He had started this in the late 1920s and continued working on it until he was ready to exhibit it. He died in Paris in 1958 at the age of 86.

To celebrate the 150th anniversary of Georges Rouault's birth, my husband hosted an exhibition of his work in the Square Halo Gallery . Although I had been aware of Rouault before, seeing this work in person inspired me to learn more. I found my interest in his artistic vision, and how his faith in Christ informed his work, grew the more I read about him. His courage and fortitude as an artist of faith—in an era when art and faith were isolated from each other, many doubted Christianity, and self-expression was all-important—encouraged me to keep researching Rouault and his artwork.

But what does it mean to be a courageous art maker and to practice fortitude in one's creative life?

The English word for courage comes from the French root word for heart, *coeur*. Stephen Roach, in his book *Naming the Animals,* writes, "Courage is to act from the heart. Courage is an inner strength realized with challenging circum-stances. It involves a willingness to risk failure, harm, or defeat."[34] He also says, "To act in courage takes confidence and trust that some necessary or desired good will come from our action."[35] Claude Monet and Pablo Picasso are examples of courageous artists. They each started their careers pursuing distinct visions of what and why they painted. In the beginning, their works were questioned and criticized; yet they kept on painting. Eventually they both found critical approval, praise, and popularity. Their courage paid off during their lifetimes.

In contrast, Vincent van Gogh and Georges Rouault were art makers who received little acclaim. But they kept to their visions, going against the popular movements of the day and refusing to bend to the critics' harsh words about their work. They didn't receive the glory in their lifetimes that they would receive after their deaths.

Georges Rouault was accused of being able to only "imagine the most atrocious avenging caricatures" and being "attracted exclusively by the ugly."[36] Art Historian William Dyrness said Rouault provoked "pious rage."[37] Even his favorite writer Leon Bloy told him to quit the direction his paintings were taking. Yet these detractors must not have paid close attention to what Rouault was doing with color, black lines, and subject matter. His colors were bright washes of vibrant reds, golden yellows and oranges, and antique-like blue-greens, with energetic and loose brushstrokes. His bold black lines, which created the forms in his paintings, were filled with these colors. Rouault used color combinations that art teachers often tell their students to avoid. Makoto Fujimura shared, "Bright yellow and sharp purple never should work well on painting, nor muted color mixed with black—in his hands these impossible colors speak deeply and resonate."[38]

The work he had done as a young stained-glass maker influenced his

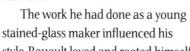

Christ and the Children
Georges Rouault

style. Rouault loved and rooted himself in this medieval tradition, and his black lines filled with color were meant to act as a type of icon—a way to allow the sacred and spiritual converse with the secular and material. Rouault said the eyes are "the doors of the spirit." As his paintings contained Jesus—with His disciples, with children, at His trial, and on the cross—Rouault desired to present the image of Christ as the true icon of the invisible. "His work had a meditative purpose in which the image is a medium for encounter between the visible and the invisible."[39] Those paying attention, even meditating, on Rouault's works understand the light that shines out of the darkness and the unseen reality that is behind the seen reality in his paintings.

The clowns, prostitutes, and kings were also subjects of his portraits—all equal in symbolizing brokenness. As an observer of humanity, he painted his people as "fit objects of grace, while more visibly born in and for suffering."[40] In a talk on his *Miserere* series, Sandra Bowden, artist and collector of Rouault's work, stated, "His work is not the easiest to appreciate because there is a darkness, a very realistic view of humanity, but there is always light in his work. But it is worth our effort to look deeply into the faces he portrays, to see how he portrays Christ being light in the middle of a world that has lost its way."[41]

...

Christ and the Woman Saint
Georges Rouault

As an artist rooted in medieval tradition and the Christian faith, Georges Rouault was a man of courage and fortitude. If courage means to act from the heart and to summon an inner strength to work through challenging circumstances, fortitude "is the virtue that enables us to conquer the fears that stand between us and the good to which God calls us . . . it reminds us of our calling to suffer and sacrifice, patiently, day after day."[42] Rouault exhibited courage and fortitude in several areas as he lived out the calling that he believed came from God.

Georges Rouault placed himself in a long line of a medieval tradition. An apprentice in stained-glass work, he loved the materials and the colors. As a painter, he used black lines and bold colors to mirror the stained-glass windows he created as a young man. As light shines through the colored glass in the windows, so did he backlight his color-filled paintings. As these medieval windows pointed the viewers to God, Rouault desired the same thing: "he wanted to portray Christ as the light in the middle of the a world that has lost its way."[43] Rouault remained steadfast in this artistic vision, even when self-expression had become the only reason for an artist to create. No longer valid and valued were the *medieval ideas of tradition* as the means to grow in creativity and *apprenticeship to a craft* as a means for artistic training—except in Rouault's vision for a life of painting. "In a sense . . . Rouault demonstrated that the highest form of self-expression is to be had through the embrace of a tradition that is both open to the future and to God."[44]

Another example of his courage and fortitude was his rejection of the fragmentation found in new and popular artistic movements of his time, such as that pursued by Pablo Picasso and Piet Mondrian. Where they painted in a way intended to make reality into two dimensional spaces (also called Super-Flatism), Georges sought to paint wholeness and grace and the reality behind reality. "He brought synthesis out of an age of fragmentation ... He was a little window that looked out into a vision of wholeness."[45] As his faith in Christ grew, he kept to this vision of grace and wholeness by painting both the suffering of Christ and of humanity and the light of salvation found in a crucified and risen Savior.

Finally, a central aspect of his courage and fortitude was his enduring faith in God. "He made no distinction between religious and secular; to him everything he painted or created flowed out of his deep faith in God.... He believed that his art flowed out of an interior life, so he maintained a solitary path, a lonely journey to depict the world as he saw it ... he relied more on his faith as a guide for making his art."[46] Painting was not about self-expression but about following the call God had given him.

Although his artwork and message was mostly misunderstood by the Catholic church, all his work was religious.

Appearance on the Road to Emmaus
Georges Rouault

As one rooted in a medievalist mindset, he wanted his artwork to help others know God more fully. In his book *The Soul of Desire*, Curt Thompson describes Rouault as "a painter who, as a Christian, worked out the grappling of his inner life through his art, pressed as it was between the world and the kingdom of heaven."[47]

With compassionate eyes turned toward the downtrodden and a belief in Christ on the cross, Rouault linked the sufferings of Christ to the sufferings of humanity. Georges Rouault portrayed Christ as the hope in the darkness and the light behind light that will never be extinguished.

After Rouault's
APPEARANCE ON THE ROAD
TO EMMAUS

[Rouault's] angle is "angelic"—halfway between heaven and earth.
—Makoto Fujimura

Things into which angels long to look:

Cleopas, learning that Jesus was no longer in the tomb,
walked with a friend to Emmaus from Jerusalem

and then listened to a stranger speak
surprising words concerning Christ.

That day was bright and sharp—
bursting into spring-life with its blues, and greens, and reds.

Each single blade of grass, each flower,
each step on the path
proclaimed a new promise to those burning hearts.

At a table spread with bread and wine,
his eyes would be opened,
and a stranger would be revealed.

AFTER ROUAULT'S
CHRIST AND THE WOMAN SAINT

I could be that woman kneeling before Christ.
As He leans in, His eyes look for mine.
I bend my head, unsure of His gaze.
His hand offers me a quiet invitation.
Yes, this could be me. It could be Rachel weeping
or Mary sitting at Christ's feet.
Or it could be my daughter, my mother, or
my neighbor. Here is Jesus saying, "Come
to me for rest, all you who are weary."
Woman, for you, too, He offers His hand.

AFTER ROUAULT'S
CHRIST AND THE CHILDREN

These little ones dance
around Jesus—the ones He
just blessed; laughing and
singing, they are unaware
that it is their faith we need.

THE GREAT GREEN PICNIC TABLE

I have had, through the years, a picture in my mind's eye of the perfect outdoor wooden table. I would decorate it with white table linens, tall candles in silver holders, vintage blue chintz plates, and shining silverware. Twinkling lights hang above this dream table and white peonies sit in just the correct spots along it, where they won't block anyone's view. This table would be at once classic and rustic—an inviting site for a gathering of twenty or so friends. My Tumblr page will attest to this vision, as I have posted many variations of this scene over the years.

The Green Picnic Table at BookEnd

My back patio, though, does not feature my dream outdoor table. It holds a generic green, heavy-duty plastic, one-piece picnic table. Let me repeat what I have owned for seventeen years: *a generic green, heavy-duty plastic, one-piece picnic table.*

One summer, seventeen years ago, Ned and I used a Costco membership to buy the same picnic table that our neighbors had just placed in their backyard. Our children were young, and we knew we needed something sturdy and in our price range. This particular table could sit lots of wiggly little bodies, take all the stickiness of melted Popsicles and outdoor crafts. It could also seat our family of five plus any friends we may invite to join us for a meal. An added bonus—it could double as a fort or hiding place. Although I really would have liked something lovely to look at, I went with what was practical.

Over the past several decades, acquiring the right table has been like the quest for the Holy Grail. Maybe I have desired the right table because my attention has so often been drawn to how tables, gathered-together people, and food are interwoven throughout Scripture—especially in those accounts of Jesus feasting or sharing meals with others.

One of the Gospel stories that never grows old for me is the record of Jesus walking on the road to Emmaus with Cleopas and another disciple. I love how this recollection of Easter Sunday continues on to a house and a table. It then culminates with the three of them sitting around that table breaking bread together. And it's in the breaking of the bread, while they are gathered together *at the table*, that Jesus reveals Himself to them as their resurrected Lord.

Gathering family and friends around a table—often my generic green, heavy-duty plastic, one-piece picnic table—has been one of the most heart-satisfying ways to show how much I want people to be known and to be loved. It has been a small way to image Jesus in my everyday life. As Andi Ashworth writes in *Real Love for Real Life*, "Christ has welcomed us into his presence and his kingdom, and we are to imitate him as we welcome others."[48]

Elaborating on the importance of gathering around a table, Andi says,

> Shared meals around a common table have many wonderful outcomes beyond simply nourishing the body. They create time for relational bonding through conversation, laughter, and listening to each other's stories. They provide a setting where the deeper needs of our souls— aesthetic enjoyment, comfort, feeling of belonging, and a sense of security that comes from being cared for—are tended to.[49]

Early this May, my green picnic table came out of winter storage for yet another summer. The original hardware lost somewhere in the basement, it is now held together by miscellaneous bolts. New this spring is the little puddle that collects in the middle of the table when it rains. Although I do "window-shop" each spring at Costco for a new table, I still haven't found something to replace it. I don't really want to spend the money, and, to my own surprise, I'm not quite ready to get rid of this table.

Around this table, we have celebrated June and July birthday parties, always with special friends and usually with some form of chocolate.

Around this table, friends have lingered late into the night, lit only by the light from the bulbs strung along the fence and the mismatched citronella candles placed between us.

Around this table, out-of-town guests have gathered for the Fourth of July and enjoyed grilled hamburgers and hotdogs, coleslaw, and potato salad. They have stayed long enough to run around the backyard, holding sparklers in their hands and blazing patterns in the darkness.

Around this table, teenagers have hung out, eating pizza and chips, drinking soda, and playing card games.

And around this table, church friends have gathered to eat dinner. Eight people can squeeze around it—three on each side and one on each end—with a picnic blanket on the grass nearby for young children, so they can eat and run around easily. For these gatherings, I'll use my colorful only-for-outdoor-eating plastic plates and serve a simple main dish—usually something that pairs well with locally grown corn-on-the-cob, hearty bread, and summer berry jam. For dessert, we'll have ripe red strawberries topped with homemade whipped cream and mini chocolate chips.

"A Liturgy for Feasting with Friends," from *Every Moment Holy*, applies even to this green table with the water-collecting dip in the middle:

Christ in Emmaus, from "The Small Passion"
Albrecht Dürer

But the joy of fellowship and the welcome
and comfort of friends new and old,
and the celebration of these blessings of
food and drink and conversation and laughter
are the true evidences of things eternal,
and are the first fruits of that great glad joy
that is to come and that will be unending.[50]

I still desire to fulfill my vision of the long wooden table, set with white linens and blue chintz and topped with perfect food and wine, lights and flowers—a gathering rich with feasting, talking, and laughing. Those photos I have collected on Tumblr are still playing around in my mind.

But the stories I have collected of family and friends around my great green, heavy-duty plastic, one-piece picnic table do make my heart glad. I have tasted, if only a little, of our New Creation future, as Isaiah declares "On this mountain, the Lord Almighty will prepare a feast of rich food for the people, a banquet of aged wine—the best of meats and the finest of wines" (Isa. 25:6 NIV). This is where my hope rests—the unending joy of being with all God's people around the table where Jesus welcomes us.

Tortellini Caesar Salad

If I am not grilling hamburgers or sausages for summer-time guests, I often serve this salad with corn-on-the-cob, thick bread, and jam. This salad is great for serving to a single family or to a large crowd, so with that in mind I haven't included specific amounts in the recipe. When you purchase your ingredients, you can buy what you need for the number of people you'll be feeding. One last note: if children are part of the gathering, and in case they are not salad fans, I offer enough tortellini and chicken so that they can have it as their main dish.

INGREDIENTS

Romaine lettuce
Cheese-filled tortellini
Sliced or shredded store-bought rotisserie chicken
Crispy bacon
Freshly shredded Parmesan cheese
Caesar salad dressing (I like Paul Newman's dressing)
Optional: A variety of salad vegetables (I like to add matchstick carrots,
    chopped yellow peppers, and halved cherry tomatoes)

Cook tortellini according to package directions. (Be careful not to over-cook!) Set aside to drain while you prepare the remaining ingredients.

Chop lettuce, cooked bacon, and vegetables (if using).

Combine everything in a large bowl and gently toss to distribute dressing. Top with one last flurry of grated Parmesan and serve.

KITE

A kite waltzes high
above the trees, its long line
tethered in my hand—
reminders to dance in the
wide space of God's gracious grip.

MERCY

A bird's bright song bursts the stillness
as I sit at the edge of the bed,
slowing into morning prayer. I hear

"Mer-CIE   Mer-CIE
Merce   Merce   Merce
Mer-CIE   Mer-CIE!"

Its song shapes my words:
"Your mercies are new every morning;
great is your faithfulness."

FOR HUGH RICHARD

You are here! We celebrated when
we heard you were
coming; we waited and imagined
and prayed. One day
you will chase butterflies with your sisters.
And you will know
the sun, the sky, and the green grass, and
the one who made you you.[51]

LOVE THINK SPEAK[52]

Far overhead from beyond the veil of blue sky . . . either
from the sky or from the Lion itself, . . . the deepest, wildest
voice they had ever heard was saying: "Narnia, Narnia,
Narnia, awake. Love. Think. Speak. Be walking trees.
Be talking beasts. Be divine waters." —C.S. Lewis

These three words—*love, think, speak*—
grabbed my attention the first year I guided
my seventh-grade literature class through *The
Magician's Nephew.* Aslan's call to his newly-ordained
talking animals to awaken and to love, think, and
speak was a call to image him to the rest of Narnia. This
reminded me of the awe-inspiring truth that humanity
is made in God's image; we love, think, and speak
because the Creator did so first.

Not only do these three commands of Aslan
remind us we are image-bearers of God to the
world, but they also show us that the words we use
and the various ways we use them are part of our
image-bearing work. The use and importance of

Hugging Girl (and *Kite,* previous)
from the cover of *Wild Things
and Castles in the Sky*
Leslie Bustard

words is woven throughout Scripture as we see God acting for and speaking to
His people, as well as commanding and teaching them (and us) how to speak
with love and wisdom.

As a parent, church member, teacher, aunt, and friend, I am called to the
imaginative and intentional work of shepherding, in large and small ways, the
hearts and minds of the children around me. And so are those who find them-
selves in communities with little ones, tweens, and teenagers. As we love, think,
and speak in our communities, we also need to bring into our children's lives
life-giving words, good stories, and meaningful conversations so that they, too,
can grow as image-bearers of God. Bible reading, worship, service, outdoor time,
movies and plays, stories, books, poetry, humor, artwork—these are seeds we
plant in our children's lives that can add to the treasure in their hearts. As Jesus
taught, "Out of the abundance of the heart his mouth speaks" (Luke 6:45).

In her book *Caring for Words in a Culture of Lies*, Marilyn McEntyre says,

> Words are entrusted to us as equipment for our life together, to help us
> survive, guide, and nourish one another. We need to take the metaphor
> of nourishment seriously in choosing what we "feed on" in our hearts,
> and in seeking to make our conversation with each other life-giving.[53]

The way our taste buds grow accustomed to the foods we eat and how those
foods affect the health of our body is an apt metaphor for how we decide which
words and ideas to offer our children. A child accustomed to sweet foods and
cheese-covered vegetables (I am very sympathetic to this) might struggle to
appreciate the variety of flavors and textures found in nutritional foods. A steady
diet of dumbed-down stories, illustrations, and conversations will not prepare
her for all the glorious ways words can be used in times of joy and delight and in
times of sorrow and suffering.

The stories we offer our children are important to their growth as people. As
James K.A. Smith says, "My feel for the world is oriented by a story I carry in my
bones."[54] These stories are experienced through a variety of written and visual
forms, including history, poetry, fiction, memoir, and songs. Children also learn
an orientation to the world through advertisements, social media platforms,
video games, TV shows, celebrity culture, and music videos. Smith elaborates,

> The imagination is acquired. It is learned. It is neither instinctual nor
> universal … Rather, the imagination is a form of habit, a learned, bodily
> disposition to the world. Embodiment is integral to imagination … This
> is why the arts are crucial to our collective imagination. Grabbing hold
> of us by the senses, artworks have a unique capacity to shape our
> attunement, our feel for the world.[55]

C.S. Lewis's words about stories solidified what I intuitively knew about
children and books when I became a mother. In his essay "On Stories" Lewis
states, "No book is really worth reading at the age of ten which is not equally
(and often far more) worth reading at the age of fifty."[56] This became my guide
for how to choose good books. I found, over time, that if I was reading a book out
loud and its illustrations or words were insipid or banal, I would get a knot in my
stomach. These books did not stay long in our home.

Lewis's belief that stories have formative power is intertwined throughout *The
Chronicles of Narnia*. *Prince Caspian*, the second book in the series as Lewis
wrote them, highlights the power of stories. The young Prince Caspian, whose
nurse and then his tutor told him stories of Old Narnia—full of talking animals,

high kings and queens, and Aslan—felt a strong connection with and loyalty to Narnia, so that later he longed to be crowned its rightful king. On the other hand, King Miraz—as well as previous Telmarine kings—perpetuated fear in his subjects by insisting that the stories of Old Narnia and Aslan were myths and that only evil came from across the waters and forests. His subjects lived in this fear and kept away from the seas and woods as much as they could.

"There was a boy named Eustace Clarence Scrubb, and he almost deserved it," begins *The Voyage of the Dawn Treader,* the book following *Prince Caspian.* It is a story that fleshes out Lewis's belief concerning the negative, formative power that the lack of good stories can have on a child's heart and mind.

From the very beginning of the book, we know that Eustace is truly an insufferable boy. His teachers and parents—whom he called by their first names—gave him facts and opinions, not stories or edifying conversations. "He liked books if they were books of information and had pictures of grain elevators or of fat foreign children doing exercises in model schools."[57] When Eustace entered into an adventure on the high seas, he had no imagination for its possibilities and lacked the largeness of heart necessary to welcome new people (or talking mice) into his life. He was full of disdain and self-righteousness—he needed a heart change.

Stories can train our imaginations and help us grow in empathy and sympathy, but stories can also help us understand how we fit into the kingdom of God, as well as prepare us for a life of being molded by the word of God. As Marilyn McEntyre writes,

> We derive our basic expectations from the narrative patterns we internalize...Stories provide the basic plotlines and in the infinite variations on those plots help us to negotiate the open middle ground between predictability and surprise.[58]

By reading an abundance of diverse stories—from *Beowulf* to *The Tempest* to *The Lord of the Rings* to *A Wrinkle in Time* to *Harry Potter*—children learn that although they may be a central character in a story, the story is not only about them; there is a bigger story outside themselves of which their story is part. Although Sam, in J.R.R. Tolkien's *The Lord of the Rings,* wishes for future storytellers to sing tales of his and Frodo's quest with the Ring, we know that he is one part of the epic fight for the life of Middle-earth. His part is vital, but he is not the only one to make brave sacrifices and face his enemies. When we get to the end of the story, we celebrate Sam, but we also celebrate the other heroic characters as we marvel at the story's victorious conclusion.

In the overarching story of God's kingdom and its chapters of creation, fall, redemption, and consummation, every individual is important. Every believer has a salvation and sanctification story that is part of eternity's new creation story. No one human, however, is the center or the hero of this ongoing plot. The Kingdom Story is about God drawing near to and dwelling with His people through the life, death, and resurrection of Jesus Christ. The Kingdom Story is about the Triune God. Reading stories that show protagonists as part of something bigger than themselves helps us see, even at a slant, that though we are important, the story is not only about us.

Reading widely and deeply can also bear fruit in how children enter into Scripture. Through stories, children encounter not just facts and ideas, but also poetic language, motif, foreshadowing, metaphor, and symbolism. God's word is divinely inspired truth that comes to us not only in historical accounts and commands, but also in poetry, prophecy, and parables. Understanding how a story works will help our children intuit how Scripture works as a large true story, full of connections, conflicts, and resolutions.

We are people who have words and stories deep down in our DNA. Our God created the world through His words, and He brought us into life and fellowship with Him through the Word-of-God-Made-Flesh. Jesus embodied to those around Him the life and light of God the Father. Through His words and stories, and then through His death and resurrection, our hearts, minds, and imaginations can be enlarged for the glory of God. As Paul writes, "For God, who said, 'Light shall shine out of darkness,' has shone in our hearts to give the light of the knowledge of the glory of God in the face of Jesus Christ" (2 Cor. 4:6). We can help our children be formed by Scripture as we help them enlarge their imaginations and minds through both reading Scripture and experiencing a multitude of well-told stories.[59]

Scripture is what can truly change hearts, minds, and souls, so knowing it should be a priority for us. Throughout Psalm 119, the psalmist declares the need for and the goodness of God's laws. All 176 verses focus on God's testimonies and instructions as the writer's life-blood. Verses 36 and 37 sum up this prayer:

Detail from
Little Pilgrim's Progress[60]
Joe Sutphin

Incline my heart to your testimonies,
 and not to selfish gain!
Turn my eyes from looking at worthless things;
 and give me life in your ways.

These young image-bearers of God will be formed by many, many things.
Therefore, we must provide the children in our lives with words, conversations,
and stories that will plant the seeds of abundance in their hearts and minds. As
Marilyn McEntyre affirms, "To accept the invitation of good stories is to enter into
deep and pleasurable reflection on very old philosophical questions: what can
we know and what must we do."[61] And with these seeds growing in their lives, our
children will have deeper roots to draw from in how they love, think, and speak.
 What a good work for all of us to participate in.

. . .

TRAVELING
TO LAITY LODGE

Flying above a
stretch of clouds,
I dream of beach
  and shoreline; I could
dive into all that blue, and
  float on my back for hours.

COMFORT

"Do not go gentle"
says the poet, but God says
"I will quiet you
with love"—Spirit, after I've
raged, settle deep your comfort.

Matthew 1:19–25

Today I often
imagine Joseph's courage
to give up his life
for Mary and also how
you follow in Joseph's ways.

Because you should know

My hands are busy with the ordinary,
as you walk into the day-filled kitchen.
"Will she stop and come to me?"
I imagine you are wondering.
Even so, your hands encircle me.

This table is strewn with blank paper,
waiting for its empty spaces to be filled.
"Will this be pleasing?"
I imagine you are wondering.
Even so, your hands work the lines and shades.

The keyboard has been silent through the night,
as you enter the third-floor office.
"Will they like it?"
I imagine you are wondering.
Even so, your hands are active with the designs.

Our girls stroll ahead of us, gesturing and laughing,
as we travel down the light-saturated street.
"Does the work of my hands matter?"
I know you wonder.
Even so, your hand slips right over mine;
yes, holding on fast and firm.

The Sower (After Millet)
Vincent van Gogh

van GOGH, AFTer MILLeT

The artwork of Vincent van Gogh continuously grabs my attention, pulling me in to look at both the "big picture" of his paintings as well as the details they contain. It is as if he has painted welcoming arms into the many layers and swirls of his paint; as we look at his work, we accept his invitation to see the world more deeply with him. Over the years, I have posted his paintings on Instagram and Facebook, often with the caption "A new-to-me van Gogh." If "likes" or "hearts" mean anything, these posts resonate with many folks—as well as with whatever tracks my likes, because after these posts I usually get more van Gogh sites to "follow."

Maybe it's because we, his viewers, are drawn to the story of this rejected, passionate, and vision-focused painter who mangled his ear. It's hard to forget his subject matter or the swirls and bursts of colors in his paintings—when I wander around a museum, I look for his sunflowers, or his trees, or his blue skies. Or perhaps we remember how he titled his pieces—it is hard to forget works with names like *Starry Night* or *The Potato Eaters*. His work is uniquely his own; it is difficult to confuse with that of other painters. Still, when I see a new-to-me piece and realize it is van Gogh's, I feel rather smart.

Along with delighting in his work, I have enjoyed learning about him. Reading the picture books *Camille and the Sunflowers* by Laurence Anholt (now titled *van Gogh and the Sunflowers*) and *Katie and the Starry Night* by James Mayhew to my daughters sparked my interest in van Gogh's story. So I began reading essays, listening to art historians, and even watching movies about his life (and then, of course, googling what was true and what was not). I went straight to the source and read excerpts of his letters to his brother Theo. I have been fascinated by his life, his vision, and his talent, but mostly with how his Christian faith intertwined in his life and his art making.

Recently, though, I realized I had missed an important painter who had been influential to van Gogh. One day, his painting *First Steps* showed up on my Instagram feed. This piece is very warm and homey. A father kneels down in his yard, with his hands stretched out toward his child and wife. The wife is walking behind their little one, as they make their way towards the arms of the father. The scene takes place in their garden, under the shade of a white flowering tree. Variations of green, white, and blue, as well as earth tones, fill the scene. There are splashes of sunshine. I particularly love the little child in light pink with her arms stretched out to her father.

This inviting painting is actually titled *First Steps, After Millet*. It was the "After Millet" that I noticed and wondered about. Jean-François Millet's *The Angelus* came to my mind, and so I looked up his *First Steps* and learned that he had started this piece with black chalk in 1858 and finished it with colored pastels around 1866.

Vincent van Gogh's *First Steps* is an oil on canvas that he painted in 1890. This piece is part of a collection of twenty-one paintings he did "after Millet" from 1889–1890.

The Sower
Jean-François Millet

Upon learning this, I began to search for more of these paintings and learned, to my chagrin, that several of my favorites are actually among those he did "after Millet."

Millet, a Realist painter, was an early influence in van Gogh's life as an artist. When Vincent was twenty-two years old and living in Paris, he saw an exhibition of Millet's drawings and was inspired. Six years later, when van Gogh was working on his figure drawing skills, he copied many of Millet's prints, calling the French man "Father Millet . . . counselor and mentor in everything for young artists," as Vincent wrote Theo in 1885.

Millet would continue to guide van Gogh, who was inspired not just by Millet as an artist but also by his life and vision. These proved important to van Gogh's growth.

Jean-François Millet lived from 1814–1875. Although he did achieve great financial success and was considered at the time one of the greats of early nineteenth-century painting, for much of his artistic life he was looked down upon by the French establishment for depicting peasants and farmers with respect. Millet showed the pride they took in their work and their land. This was considered inappropriate at the time. In Millet, van Gogh found an artist who mirrored his own deep respect and compassion for the ordinary farmer, the downtrodden peasant, and the work they did with their hands.

The Sower (After Millet)
Sandra Bowden

James Romaine writes about Millet and van Gogh:

A devout Christian, farmer's son, and artist committed to dignified representations of peasant life, labor, and piety, Millet inspired Vincent as a model of an artist motivated by faith. In 1883, Vincent wrote to his brother, "The longer I think about it the more I see that Millet believe in a something on High." Vincent paid Millet perhaps the highest compliment when he wrote to Bernard that, while Eugene Delacroix and Rembrandt van Rijn had succeeded in painting the image of Christ, "Millet has painted . . . Christ's doctrine." By this, he meant that Millet painted with, not only in his motifs but in his method, the values of faith, love, and humility that Vincent considered most Christlike.[62]

For three months in 1889–1890, van Gogh voluntarily became a patient at the asylum at Saint-Rémy. Here he took prints of Millet's work and translated them into his own paintings, using his techniques, colors, and ideas. He did twenty-one "copies."

Vincent wrote Theo about this work, explaining that these were more than just copies:

The Sower (After van Gogh, After Millet)
Ned Bustard

If someone plays Beethoven, he adds his own personal interpretation; in the music . . . it also counts and the composer doesn't have to be the only one to perform his compositions. Anyway. . . I put the black and white by or after Delacroix or Millet in front of me to use as a motif. And then I improvise in colour . . . seeking reminiscences of their paintings; but the memory, the vague consonance of colours while are at least correct in spirit, that is my interpretation.[63]

At some point, Theo declared that Vincent's "after Millet" paintings were some of the best work he had seen Vincent do and that he felt "big surprises still await us the day you set yourself to doing figure compositions."[64]

My favorite "after Millet" piece is *The Sower*—I loved this piece and the others that van Gogh did of a sower before I learned it was one of his "after Millet" works. However, I am also taken by how other artists I know have created their own "after" pieces of *The Sower*. My friend and artist Sandra Bowden has a large piece that is gold-leaf with Millet's *The Sower* etched in it. I must confess that for most of the years it has hung in our home, I thought it was "after van Gogh." My husband has done a linocut of *The Sower*—which, it turns out, is "after van Gogh, after Millet." I'm glad there is still much to learn in the world of art history and about what inspires other artists.

Millet's *The Sower* was also Vincent van Gogh's favorite piece. During my research, I learned that

> Although he never saw Millet's paintings of the subject, he possessed a print made after it. In 1881 Van Gogh drew a straight forward copy of the print, to practice his drawing. Seven years later, he took Millet's figure and included it in a painting of a Provençal wheatfield. In Van Gogh's version of *The Sower*, the peasant strides across a ploughed field, sowing next year's crop, pursued by ravenous birds. In the background lies a field of unharvested wheat, ripening beneath a symbolic setting sun.[65]

Hanging in our home is another linocut that Ned created: it depicts Jesus as the Sower, generously sowing seed; to the left, behind Him, is a black bird sitting on a large rock. Jesus is carrying a large cloth bag full of seeds. Under this linocut are the words of Malcolm's Guite sonnet, "The Good Ground" (I think Vincent van Gogh would have liked this):

THE GOOD GROUND
Malcolm Guite

I love your simple story of the sower,
With all its close attention to the soil,
Its movement from the knowledge to the knower,
Its take on the tenacity of toil.

I feel the fall of seed a sower scatters,
So equally available to all,
Your story takes me straight to all that matters,
Yet understands the reasons why I fall.

Oh deepen me where I am thin and shallow,
Uproot in me the thistle and the thorn,
Keep far from me that swiftly snatching shadow,
That seizes on your seed to mock and scorn.
  O break me open, Jesus, set me free,
Then find and keep your own good ground in me.[66]

What I enjoy in the work of Jean-François Millet, Vincent van Gogh, Sandra Bowden, Malcolm Guite, and my husband, Ned, is the pleasure of listening in on the continual conversation of artist with artist across the generations and cultures.

The Sower
Ned Bustard

With this thought in mind, I looked up another favorite artist, the Japanese print maker Sadao Watanabe, and found that he, too, had a sower.[67] I could see reflections of van Gogh (or Millet?) in his piece. Decidedly Japanese in its details, the work shows compassion and respect for the farmer and the story that Jesus told. This piece is another connection, another point, in the conversation that I hear and see art makers holding with other art makers, translating and expanding what they see and feel through their own choices of materials, colors, shapes, and design.

As Vincent van Gogh and Millet (who he conversed with) and other artists (who conversed with van Gogh and Millet) have paid attention and sought to see deeply, may we learn from them to do the same—to see with compassion, creativity, and care the people we are with and the places in which we find ourselves.

THAT SENSE OF HOPE
FOR SHAWN AND MAILE

How your bare feet feel on soft grass,
hard ground underneath;

Those sweet juices of an orange
filling your mouth;

That tenor note halfway through *Lux Æterna*
which always makes your heart yearn;

But also heavy morning mist
before the sun opens up the curve in the road.

Hope is now the long wait,
holding onto the one unseen who yet sees.

The kitchen at BookEnd

Houses of Cedar and the Home of God

The making of a space into a home—whether a three-room walk-up apartment or a three-story row home—is the work that has kept my hands busy and my imagination active for many, many years. Even when I was young, creating cute, cozy spaces motivated me; I loved decorating my dollhouse with new chairs or dishes, and I would rearrange my bedroom every few months, hoping to find the right direction of warm lamplight falling onto my bed. Wandering through the home furnishing section of the local department store Strawbridge & Clothier as a teenager eventually evolved into taking a spin or two around Ikea's multiple rooms with my husband and daughters while we looked for bedspreads, throw pillows, and other house accessories. I have sought to make each space I have found myself living in into a place that was not just for sleeping and eating, but for fostering life and love and good memories.

I am not alone in wishing and working for a "home sweet home" dream come true. Through the past few decades, decorators such as Martha Stewart and Joanna Gaines have been popular guides for choosing wall colors and tableware;

magazines like *House Beautiful* and *Architectural Digest* publish swoon-worthy goals, and reality television shows such as *Fixer to Fabulous* model for us how to accomplish home renovations. Proponents of minimalism or English Country Shabby have Instagram and Tumblr accounts to inspire us. And Barnes & Noble stocks many colorful home decorating books on their shelves.[68]

When we look at how people live around the world, we see that topography, climate, and resources, as well as cultural traditions, influence how living spaces have been created. Homes in Korea look different than homes in Kansas. But the hope for a "home sweet home" echoes throughout the world.

The drive for a place and a home, no matter how large or small, is intrinsic to being human. We are wired to make a place where we can protect and care for our people and ourselves. And because we are made in the image of a place-making God, we can cultivate homes that make life and flourishing possible. We can create spaces of beauty and goodness for others to live in.

Yet because humanity is sinful and broken, we can also make places that are characterized by power, or that are places for accumulating more possessions and showcasing wealth. Places where people live have also been places of trauma and abuse.

How do we, people following Jesus and seeking to be formed by Scripture, think about and pursue building and keeping our houses? Can Scripture influence not just how we live together but also how we create our places so they reflect the ways of God and not just the self-centered ways of the world?

God hasn't told us—as people living in the modern age—how to order or arrange our furniture, meal schedules, cleaning practices, or decorations. As Paul writes in the letter to the Ephesians, God has told us how to live together in unity as His people. But since God works in the physical-ness of our lives, then maybe how we think about our homes, how we live in them, and how we arrange them can mirror who we are as His people. We get these clues from Scripture. As Eugene Peterson said, "The Bible, all of it, is livable; it is the text for living our lives. It reveals a God-created, God-ordered, God-blessed world in which we find ourselves at home and whole."[69]

Encouraged by Eugene Peterson's words about Scripture—"Christians don't simply learn or study or use Scripture; we assimilate it, take it into our lives in such a way that it gets metabolized into acts of love"[70]—I sought to have my vision for homemaking and house-building be formed by Scripture. Several passages in particular animated my imagination. I am especially drawn to the beauty of Psalm 5:7:

But I, through the abundance of your steadfast love,
will enter your house.

The words *abundance, steadfast love,* and *enter your house* are rich with promises
of God's love and desire for us to be with Him. Entering God's house is about coming
to His tabernacle (and then later His temple). God is rich with unfailing kindness
and mercy; that He welcomes me to His place and presence is beyond imagining
but eternally true because of Jesus' life, death, and resurrection.

I love dreaming about what it would be like to quietly come into the tabernacle,
knowing that I have been invited by God to enter. His house is offered to me and to
others as a place of life and refuge. This welcome of God enlarges my heart to do the
same for others.

By wisdom a house is built,
    and by understanding it is established;
By knowledge the rooms are filled
    with all precious and pleasant riches.
(Proverbs 24:3-4)

This verse teaches me that it matters who I am in my heart and in my mind as
I seek to build my house—it matters if I am growing in wisdom and understand-
ing. And how do I know what wisdom is? How do I know what understanding
looks like? I keep my eyes on Jesus and on God's word. And fixing my eyes on
these things teaches me to practice using my words well, as well as my time and
my hands. I pay attention to what I'm striving after and how that influences my
emotions, and I think about how I create space for others; I want people to feel
welcomed and seen. Am I decorating to show off to others or to offer beauty? As
I take care of my home, whether through everyday chores or upkeep, or through
adding loveliness to our walls, I try to submit my ways to God's ways.

The next part of the verse—"by knowledge the rooms are filled with all
precious and pleasant riches"—reminds me of how God gave knowledge and
wisdom to all the Israelites involved with building the tabernacle and also
how the tabernacle was decorated with gold furniture and embroidered linen
curtains. These words encourage me to try to cultivate in my home the goodness
of human relationships, but also the goodness of lovely things and furnishings.
I'm reminded that these things in my home are not treasures to hoard on earth
but are, like the furnishings seen in the tabernacle, ways to create spaces of
peace and beauty.

My husband and I have been collecting original artwork since the early years of our marriage; we desire excellent work created by Christians, as well as work that highlights Scripture. By doing this, we have affirmed the importance of artists, craftsmanship, and storytelling. The works hanging on our walls are some of the precious riches we need to remind us that we are God's people.

Art from BookEnd

Exodus 25:8-9 says, "They are to make a sanctuary for me so that I may dwell among them. You must make it according to all that I show you—the pattern of the tabernacle as well as the pattern of all its furnishings" (CSB). Exodus 25–30 is full of specific instructions of the size and the materials used to make the tabernacle. These instructions include all the precious metals and jewels, the good wood, and the lovely materials for curtains that were to be found as part of God's dwelling place. God gave these specific instructions to the Israelites and even gave the Holy Spirit to certain men to be the artists. God gave these plans to the Israelites through Moses, and they were to follow His words. And God's glory would come down to dwell with them. The Hebrews would see what it meant to be set apart as His people.

Reading this section of Exodus leads us to Exodus 36–40, where we can imagine the actual making of the tabernacle, its furnishings, and the priests' clothing. For God's house to be built correctly and for worship to be established according to God's instructions, the builders had to submit to God's ways and words. They walked in wisdom as they built God's house and filled it with precious and pleasant riches. In this, they are our teachers.

The wisest of women builds her house,
but folly with her own hands tears it down.
(Proverbs 14:1)

And we who establish our own houses can follow in the footsteps of those who obeyed God's words and directions while building the tabernacle. I'm intrigued by how Proverbs 14:1 correlates with Jesus' words in Matthew 7:24–27. Jesus used the images of building one's house on rock or sand as a way to help

His listeners understand the consequences of heeding or not heeding the word of Christ. If one listens and follows His words, it is like building a house on a rock, which keeps the house from being destroyed. The outcome for a foolish person who does not follow Jesus' words is destruction (Matt. 7:24–27).

The words of Scripture—the words of Christ—form us from the inside out. We hear these words and we want them to form our hearts, our minds, and our motives. And then this formation comes out in our action and our words. But sometimes we just hear the words, and they don't form how we live day to day. And we become the woman who tears down her home because our words and actions don't bring life to those we are living with or caring for.

Our houses are the physical place where we live. They include the rooms where we sit together and talk and laugh and cry, where we share food and drink, and where we sleep and dream. In our homes, we pray and we celebrate. We discover our callings and creative abilities. Here, as we practice our creativity and interests, we start to learn what it means to follow the cultural mandate found in Genesis 1. But also, in our houses we care for others who come through our doors. Following in God's ways, we make room for people who need enfolding—church members, neighbors, hurting friends, and newcomers to our communities. In our homes we obey God's commands to love God and to love our neighbor.

The word "house" means a place to live in, but it also refers to the generations of a family—the people who come before us and after us. God not only built His house, the tabernacle and then the temple, but He built a house for Himself, made up of His people. Saint Paul reminds us,

> So then you are no longer foreigners and strangers, but fellow citizens with the saints, and members of God's household, built on the foundation of the apostles and prophets, with Christ Jesus Himself as the cornerstone. The whole building, being put together by Him, grows into a holy sanctuary in the Lord. You also are being built together for God's dwelling in the Spirit. (Ephesians 2:19–22 HCSB)

We are called, as part of God's household, to pray and work towards establishing our house—the people who come after us—to know and serve God, who invites us all into the abundance of His house. Although we do know that the final fruit of our work is in God's hands and purposes, we still seek to walk in God's wisdom as we love and care for our people. God has given us places and people to enfold and care for. As we try to build our house, we are following Jesus' directive to go and make disciples.

From God's first words in Genesis, as He spoke the world into form and planted a lush home in which He could dwell with His creation, to His specific instructions for how He wanted the Hebrews to build the tabernacle so His glory could dwell them, to Jesus coming to Earth to live with His people and thus beginning the building of a new house of worshippers, we finally will arrive to God's New Creation, where we will dwell together with God in Zion for eternity. As Jesus promised,

> In my Father's house are many rooms. If it were not so would I have told you that I going there to prepare a place for you? And if I go and prepare a place for you, I will come back and welcome you into my presence, so that you also may be where I am.
> (John 14:2–4 BSB)

May we be encouraged in our homemaking and house-building as we fix our eyes on the words of God, the ways of Jesus, the work of the Spirit, and the hope of the Home we have in Eternity.

BENEDICTION

We are filled with the good things of your house . . .
—Psalm 65:4

Morning sunshine filling the kitchen windows,
and a yellow knitted throw on my lap,

books lining our shelves,
and laughter around the table,

words in my head that I scribble on lined paper,
songs we sing together Sunday mornings,
water on a baby's head,

and every week,
Bread and Wine placed in my hand:
"the Body and Blood, given for you—
    take and eat."

ode to summer in my backyard

How much land does a man need?
—Leo Tolstoy

Enough space for a monarch to flutter
around the butterfly bush in the backyard
and then flit away, only to return—
as if it had forgotten more sweet nectar could be found.
And enough lawn for white clover
to scatter around the grass, and for a few
bumblebees to shimmy and hum
over pink-tinged florets.

A little bit more land for shadows of
trees and their branches to come and go,
sway and disappear throughout the day.
There needs to be space for a raspberry bush and
a patch of black-eyed Susans
(that will fall over by mid-August); also,
some soil to grow basil for fresh pasta sauce and
rosemary for roasted potatoes.
To make iced tea and lemonade—
an ever-expanding tangle of mint.

And for the wooden table and chairs
my daughters gifted me last spring,
a stone patio. Here we will share early evenings
of harvest-fresh meals and happy laughter.
I'll place flowerpots with bright
red geraniums and pink peonies close by.
Ants will scurry about, as
fireflies float up and away to the stars.

MYSTERIES OF THE WORLD PART I

I

On hot summer nights,
after chasing a sprinkle of fireflies,
I would stretch out on my bed—
sheets pushed to the edge—
and wait for a breeze to make
its way through my screens.
It seemed all the mysteries of the world
floated on the trill of katydids.

II

On bright summer days,
I would squint at a pile of clouds,
squeeze honeysuckle juice into my mouth,
watch a red ladybug travel the palm of my hand—
these were secrets of the universe.
The rattling wheels of roller skating,
sounds of a neighbor boy playing his piano,
an empty carcass of a cicada hanging on our porch door—
these wonders hung in the air, as
I cartwheeled through the yard before dinner.

MYSTERIES OF THE WORLD PART II

I remember little-girl-me
walking up and down
my neighborhood street,
searching the summer sky.
I believed God and Jesus,
Adam and Eve and winged angels
sat behind all those piles of clouds.
Glory peeked through crevices,
as they watched the world go by.

Heading west on Delta,
flying above earth,
resting my forehead
against a window,
I scan peaks and canyons
and oceans of sunlit white,
waiting to see what is there.

MYSTERIES OF THE WORLD PART III

On this blue-sky summer day,
as clouds spill over,
I peek through the wooden slats
of my garden door
and take a long, slow look
at this little patch of world.

Two house finches feast
at their feeder; several house sparrows
(or maybe Carolina wrens)
line up on a wire overhead, watching.

A huge hosta plant
with tall lavender flowers
hosts a hunting bumblebee.

Pumpkin plants
have overrun the back garden bed,
and butterfly bush branches are a tangle
of white.

Flowering mint, purple coneflowers,
and near-blooming black-eyed Susans
lean toward the sun to
play their seasonal parts.

Two ghost-like cabbage moths flirt
and race around

just like they did last summer.

summer salad solution

Recently I have been enjoying Joanna Gaines's cooking show *Magnolia Table*. Her personality and self-deprecating humor make me laugh and like her, but her words in the show's opening sequence are what made me a fan: at the beginning of each episode, she says, "Nothing about the way I cook is fancy or complicated, but over the years the kitchen has become such an important space for me" and "If your kitchen is not messy you are not having fun."[71] I find it very affirming to hear someone voice the way I have approached cooking for my family and friends—using tried and true recipes, rather than crafting complicated foods, and having fun during the process. (Also, how could I not want to watch an episode dedicated to all things biscuits?)

Regina Martin

Enfolding people into our lives around a dinner table and home-cooked food was easy in my twenties, but as we added raising children, and then homeschooling, and then producing plays and teaching full-time in a brick-and-mortar school, I realized that I needed to simplify my call to and love of caring for people in our home if I was to keep enfolding people. I know and love many cooks who have more developed skills in the kitchen or whose homes are more suitable for formal gatherings than mine is, and I'm grateful for the times they have hosted me. But to keep myself going, I try to keep my vision for culinary hospitality simple.

Many years ago, I decided I wanted to enjoy the planning and prepping involved in hosting friends and new acquaintances. I wanted to avoid feeling stressed by it or frustrated at the process. These meals needed to be about giving my guests an enjoyable and encouraging time together—not about me and the impressive things I could do in the kitchen.

To reach this goal, I needed to create simple but delicious go-to menus. In the spring and summer, I decided on big salads (or grilled hamburgers with all the toppings and sides); in the fall and winter, soup and salad or something pasta-y.

To round out the menus, I serve these dishes alongside fresh bread, fruit, and brownies. By simplifying these menus, I found I could take more time delighting in setting a welcoming table or picnic.

Now my life has really slowed down during this time of dealing with cancer. Some meds make my muscles and joints cranky, and some meds make me tired and unmotivated. But when I have the headspace and time, I still desire to bring people into my home. I am looking forward to having friends and new acquaintances sitting around my picnic table in the backyard this summer. My go-to meal, the one that feels very doable for me right now, is The Shrimp Shack Salad, with fresh bread and strawberries and mint. (Chocolate in some form will also be part of the menu, of course.)

The Shrimp Shack Salad[72]

INGREDIENTS

An assortment of salad veggies *(my favorites are matchstick carrots, shredded purple cabbage, chopped red peppers and cucumbers, halved cherry tomatoes, and thinly sliced radishes; sometimes I add a diced apple or two)*
A variety of fresh salad greens
1 cup dry quinoa *(multi-colored looks very pretty in the salad)*
Frozen shrimp *(small, medium, or large works fine)*
2 garlic cloves, minced
Ground ginger
Dehydrated minced onion
Salt and pepper
Homemade dressing *(recipe below)* or favorite store-bought vinaigrette

Place the frozen shrimp in a pot of warm water to defrost. Once shrimp are unfrozen, peel and devein the shrimp (if needed).

Prepare the quinoa according to package directions. Sometimes I cook the quinoa in vegetable broth (equal to the amount of water in the instructions) to add more flavor to the quinoa.

Heat a large frying pan or cast-iron pan (between medium-high and medium heat). Drizzle some olive oil, then add minced garlic and a couple dashes of ginger and minced onion (or more if you like). Stir around while the olive oil heats and then add the shrimp. Add salt and pepper to taste. Stir occasionally till shrimp are cooked through.

Place shrimp in a bowl to allow the cooked shrimp to cool down. (If I am using large or extra-large shrimp, I cut them in half.) When the quinoa is done, place this in another bowl to cool.

In a large salad bowl, combine the greens and the chopped salad veggies.

For simplicity's sake, instead of plating people's food, have everyone assemble their own salad. Allow your guests to put their salad on their plate and then add the shrimp and quinoa on top. Finish with salad dressing.

Salad Dressing

INGREDIENTS

2 parts olive oil to one part vinegar*
I dollop or tbsp. of honey mustard
I swoosh or tbsp. of honey or maple syrup
Salt and pepper to taste

Add ingredients into a glass salad dressing dispenser or canning jar (with a lid) and shake until thoroughly mixed.

*I enjoy honey-ginger vinegar as the vinegar in this dressing. It is very cool and refreshing. However, I also like using balsamic vinegar, apple cider vinegar, or red wine vinegar. If I am using the honey-ginger vinegar, I only use the olive oil; this dressing doesn't need the extras added into it. When using other vinegars, I add the honey mustard, honey/maple syrup, and salt and pepper.

The Living Room at BookEnd

Awakening to God's Gift of Light

When we moved into our century-old city row house, I was relieved to learn that our house faced east and west—the morning sun fills the kitchen windows, and later in the day, when the curtains are open, direct sunshine comes through the windows and falls over our old soft pine floors. Pevensie, our sweet black dog, can be found napping where the light has pooled. At night, when the house is dark and I cannot sleep, my gaze often lands on the irregular shapes of light across the bedroom ceiling. Depending on how tightly the curtains are closed, the lines of light originating from the street-lamps outside may be shortened or stretched thin.

The beauty and warmth of light has been a constant draw for me.

Many painters have felt the same as I do. Most of Rembrandt's paintings are a study of shafts of light coming from a source outside the painting and illuminating his subjects, leaving the rest of the scene in shadow and darkness. Claude Monet, so intent on the play of light, would paint the same subject, be it a haystack or cathedral, over and over again, capturing how the movement of light changed the object he was depicting with paint. He said, "Light is the most important person in the picture."

Scripture is witness to the mysterious relationship between light and life. In the beginning, as the Spirit hovered over the waters, the world was without form and void—chaos. But God said, "Let there be light" and creation took its first step towards order and life. We immediately learn that this light was good. God continued to speak to bring forth abundant life: vegetation, birds, animals, and humans. He also ordered different forms of lights to rule specific spheres—the sun for day and the moon for night (Gen. 1:14).

The Apostle John, rooted deeply in the words of Moses and the creation story, stated in the opening of his Gospel that all things were made through Jesus, the Word-of-God-Made-Flesh. He continued to reveal the Word as God, in whom was life, the light of all. This light gave life, and this light shines in the darkness, never to be overcome. Death and darkness cannot extinguish the true Life and the true Light (John 1:1–14).

Light and life are woven throughout Scripture. These word pictures are given as a beacon of hope in a world darkened by sin and sorrow, war and displacement. After a long dark night of the soul, one needs to be awakened by the light of the Morning Sun. Solomon wrote, "The path of the righteous is like the light of dawn, which shines brighter and brighter till full day" (Prov. 4:18). What comfort to know that God's chosen, the righteous, have a sure direction out of the darkness of sorrow and suffering brought on by our brokenness and the brokenness of this world.

Jesus—the prophesied light shining in the darkness—proclaimed, "I am the light of the world" (John 8:12). As a sign to this reality, He healed a man of blindness, allowing the everyday light into the man's eyes so that he could fully live life. The Kingdom of God was brought near to this newly-sighted man—no longer would the death-hold of darkness rule his days. This was a physical sign of the spiritual reality of Jesus being the true light. As Paul would later write to the church in Colossae, "He has delivered us from the domain of darkness and transferred us to the kingdom of his beloved Son" (Col. 1:13).

At Creation the light of the sun was placed to rule the day, while the light of the moon was to rule the night. In between morning and night, men and women could work as God called them to. When the New Heaven and the New Earth are established at the second-coming of Jesus, New Jerusalem—the everlasting city of God's people—will not need the sun or moon, because "the glory of God gives it light, and its lamp is the Lamb" (Rev. 21:23). We have a forever-more promise of being fully awake and alive in eternal light.

Many times when I see sunlight falling through branches of a tree, making the green leaves glow, or when I watch the sun on the horizon, spreading out hues of orange and pink, I feel at once a little more alive and a little more sad—an ache to be united to this beauty. I feel delight tinged with regret. C.S. Lewis affirmed this very human desire: "We want something else which can hardly be put into words—to be united with the beauty we see, to pass into it, to receive it into ourselves, to bathe in it, to become part of it."[73]

I feel Lewis's ideas keenly when

I see a multitude of stars winking in a black sky,
and the glow of the afternoon playing
with the whispery ends of tall, dry grass,
and sunlight shimmering and sparkling on a lake.[74]

Saint Jack
Ned Bustard

It is a transcendence of heaven into my everyday life that causes this longing ache; I want the eternal realty of light to invade my feet-on-the-ground reality.

Although this longing will not abate easily, practicing the presence of God and purposefully bringing light into my everyday life reminds me that hoping in the eternal is not a waste. It is placing a reading lamp beside a cozy chair, inviting someone to be at peace with a book or a nap. Or setting a dinner table with favorite foods and lit candles, then hearing my family laugh together around it. Or gathering friends around a fire pit in the backyard. Or paying attention to the morning light that seeps through my closed curtains, helping me to welcome in the day.

Because I need to remember that Jesus, the light of the world, has rooted my family and me in His kingdom story, reminders hang throughout our home in the form of paintings, photographs, and prints. Many of them illustrate the stories of Scripture. Two well-loved pieces which bookend our living room shed light on the mystery of a faith that holds together God's holiness and goodness, His light and His life in our lives.

On the front wall of our living room is a Marc Chagall lithograph depicting the face of an angel.[75] All the lines—thick and thin—are bold and organic. With a tilt of her head, her eyes looking down, her face exhibits both awe and serenity. A bright, gentle yellow washes over her.

Except for the swoosh of wings behind her head, she bears little resemblance to the angels in Isaiah's vision of God in the temple. Isaiah described these angels as having three pairs of wings, each pair covering different parts of their bodies. They called out to one another, "Holy, holy, holy is the LORD of Hosts; the whole earth is full of his glory" (Isa. 6:3). I imagine that, since they are continuously before the throne of God, their faces glow the way my angel's does.

Sacrament #2
Craig Hawkins

Across the room, a Craig Hawkins print of bread and wine hangs by the large archway that connects our living room to the library. The perspective of this piece is from above; we are able to see the circular rim of the cup with the wine filling in the space, as well as the specks of grain in the bread. The bread and the cup look contemporary and ordinary—not at all like the unleavened bread and cup of wine I think of at Jesus' Passover when He instituted the Lord's Supper. The dark gray lines that form the torn halves of bread with the small cup nestled between them are delicate compared to the bold movement which makes up Chagall's angel.

The glow of the angel reminds me of God's holiness, while the simple elements of the Eucharist point to God's goodness. Even though only the angel seems to be in the light, both pieces of art symbolize how light is connected to our lives. Paul wrote to the church in Corinth, "For God, who said, 'Let light shine out of darkness,' has shone in our hearts to give the Light of the knowledge of the glory of God in the face of Jesus Christ" (2 Cor. 4:6).

Jesus—this light that shines in the darkness—gives us His life, His death, His resurrection, His ascension, and even His holiness. And with these gifts, we awaken out of the shadows of sin and death into His marvelous light and His life.

A window view at regency park

But the path of the righteous is like the light of dawn,
which shines brighter and brighter until full day.
—Proverbs 4:18

As light streams underneath a closed door,
then once welcomed in, radiates wide—
whisking away every shadow—
today's dawn spread brighter
and brighter across the horizon—
bearing witness to the Word overcoming darkness.

carlingford lough prayer

That part of Rostrevor which overlooks Carlingford Lough is my idea of Narnia.
—C.S. Lewis in a letter to Warnie, his brother

The tide was low that early evening we
meandered along the beach of Carlingford Lough.

Cockle shells and limpet shells sat among
a scattered still life of seaweed and slate pebbles.

I picked up a bleached shell, its high arch so smooth
my thumb moved easily to worrying the inside.

Placing it rib-side down in my palm,
it looked ready to catch the last of the sun's rays—

just like my hands in prayer,
upturned.

RATHFRILAND MORNING

And some time make the time to drive out west . . .
In September or October, when the wind
And the light are working off each other . . .
—Seamus Heaney

Or one morning make time to brave moody skies.
Call the collie to your side as you walk
to the pond—you will find the farmers' lane
is quiet with Holly Blue butterflies
above the hedgerow and occasional
warblings of a wren. Honeysuckle
will be blooming bright among hawthorn and
ripe blackberries. Land, like clouds,
will spread far beyond. Stand still at a pasture gate
and wait for cows to meander near.
Their soft eyes will look up from eating, and
one by one they'll gather to you, jostling
to be closer. At the end of the lane,
two swans glide away from tall grass,
small cygnets following slowly behind,
as if distracted by all that shines.

THE CONCEPT OF COZY

My husband, Ned, teases me that my life is simply a series of ruts, but I like to think that my life is composed of seasonal rhythms and liturgies. The traditions in our home that mark the transition from September to October have barely changed these past few decades: Phil Keaggy's *Beyond Nature* playing in the morning; Lauridsen's *Lux Æterna* filling the air throughout the day; something big-band jazzy, such as Ella Fitzgerald's *Johnny Mercer's Songbook*, accompanying dinner preparations; pumpkins and gourds decorating window sills; trips to Cherry Hill Orchards for apples, apple cider, and cider donuts; and a variety of local apples cooking down to applesauce in the crockpot on Saturday afternoons. And soup—lots of soup. There are pots of soup ready for family on weeknights and more pots for friends on weekends.

Ned has also pointed out—and not disparagingly—that the highest good in the Bustard household is the concept of "cozy." As the weather changes to chilly, candles flicker when the sun goes down, lightweight throw blankets lay curled up on the couch, and soup simmers on the back burner of the stove. I make chicken vegetable soup on Sundays in preparation for Mondays, and taco soup for Wednesday when I am mid-week weary and need to make a simple meal. Cheesy wild rice soup is a household favorite, one that usually gets made when I don't have a shopping list on hand, because I can easily remember the ingredients while roaming the aisles at the grocery store Friday afternoons after work.[76]

On many cold-weather weekend nights we open our home to old friends or new, small gatherings or large. And this culture of welcome and cozy are the highest good in how I plan our meals and time together.

Many years ago, I decided that instead of being frustrated by how our long, narrow city row house dictated the size and shape of our gatherings, I would lean into it and use those boundaries to find my own hostessing groove. Because we had turned the dining room area into a library, which is separated from the living room by a tall, wide archway, I learned I could host up to twenty folks scattered around these two connected rooms for large "plates-on-your-lap" gatherings. Our kitchen table is just the right size to seat six people for a more intimate meal. Over the years, both arrangements have worked well. At one point I declared to Ned that I would, from now on, make soup for our winter gatherings, and then I invested in extra white soup bowls and sandwich plates and lots of spoons.

Cozy and welcoming are my gifts to our guests, while stress-free and enjoyable prep time is my gift to me. I love preparing my home for people. It makes me happy to create a space that says "I am glad you are here; make yourself at home." Pots of delicious-smelling soup, plus hearty bread, homemade applesauce, and Ghirardelli's double chocolate brownies cover the kitchen counters, ready and waiting to be enjoyed. Sprinkle in some good music, candles, and my dog, Pevensie, begging to be petted, and you have the ingredients for a perfect, cozy evening with friends.

The following are two of my favorite soup recipes. One is quite easy but always a crowd-pleaser. The other takes a little more time, but it is very satisfying on a cold night.

Swirling Leaves
Leslie Bustard

Taco Soup[77]

INGREDIENTS

1 lb. ground beef
1 16-oz. can refried beans
1 16-oz. frozen sweet corn
1 46-oz. container of tomato or vegetable juice
1 pkg. taco seasoning *(I try to find low sodium, all natural blends)*
TOPPINGS: Tortilla chips, shredded Mexican blend (or sharp cheddar) cheese, chopped avocado, diced onions, peppers, and tomato

In a soup pot, brown the ground beef and then follow the taco seasoning package directions. Once the taco meat is finished, add the tomato juice and heat through. Add refried beans and keep stirring till the refried beans have "melted" into the soup. Add corn and cook until the soup is heated through. At this point, you may stir in the cheese till melted, or use the cheese as a topping. Set the table with soup toppings so each person can add their own toppings.

Sweet Potato and Andouille Soup[78]

INGREDIENTS

¼ lb. Andouille turkey sausage, diced
4 tbsp. unsalted butter, divided
1 ¼ cups onions, finely chopped
1 tsp. dried thyme
1 ½ lbs. sweet potatoes, peeled and cut into ½" cubes
7 cups chicken broth
¼ cup brown sugar
¼ cup heavy cream
Salt to taste
Pepper to taste
Nutmeg or cinnamon to taste

In a large soup kettle, cook turkey sausage in 2 tbsp. of butter over moderate heat for 5 minutes. Add onions. Cook until onions are soft.

Add thyme and sweet potatoes. Cook while stirring for 5 minutes.

Stir in broth and brown sugar. Simmer, partially covered, over moderately low heat for 45 minutes, or until sweet potatoes are tender.

In a blender or food processor, purée soup in batches, transferring it when puréed into a good-sized saucepan. (I have also used an emulsion blender—but I always make a mess!) Stir in cream and remaining 2 tbsp. butter. Add salt and pepper to taste.

Garnish with a dash of nutmeg or cinnamon just before serving.

samaras I

Like whirligigs flying fast from children's hands,
our maple tree's seedpods fill the early autumn air.

They land without fanfare,
making a mosaic of the backyard.

During summer days, they stuck to my bare feet
and my puppy's tail
and found their way into the house,
under the kitchen table, in between floorboards,
up to the bedrooms—

reminding me of seeds the Good Sower scattered
generously over His land.

Today,
I was startled by a sapling in my neighbor's garden,
a shoot not weeded this spring,
    standing straight
    growing towards the sun
    bearing the beauty of new leaves.

samaras II

Whirling maple seedpods,
spinning a race to the ground,
are a picture of living in the moment.
They land green and flat,
as if they know their life
will be spent growing or dying.

samaras III

Clusters of Japanese maple seedpods
hang loosely on my neighbor's tree.
Each pod's skin tinged pink—
hinting at new life.

Beach Day

A large storm off the southern coast is
churning water, and pushing it up the beach,
straight for our towels and chairs.
After a few times pulling up and moving back,
we finally skirt the day's surprising high tide.

And isn't this our life?
We have staked our place,
only to see, out on the horizon,
the path of trouble leads to us.

SALVATION THROUGH THE STORM

"Do the next thing" repeats over and over in my mind.

Decades ago I heard Elisabeth Elliot share that after she learned of her husband's death she had spoken these words to herself while grabbing a broom and sweeping the floor. Ever since then, that story has stuck in my brain. And now I find myself sweeping, too. The heaviness inside me is lifting while I gather the dirt and leaves into a pile. My mind is slowly starting to work. I think I may be able to do the next thing—maybe even find a way to face the sadness and fear that sits like a brick in my stomach.

. . .

It's Friday—mid-morning. A week has passed since I learned that the cancerous tumor in my right breast has grown; in three days I will meet with the surgeon to discuss surgery and the possibility of a fast-tracked mastectomy. This possibility is one of the things that has scared me the most during these months of dealing with breast cancer and metastatic melanoma.

Since my doctor's appointment, I have wanted both distraction and quiet, to be with people and to hide. Folks have come over for dinner. All the windows on the first floor have been cleaned, inside and out. I have gone kayaking with friends down the Conestoga River. I've sat on my second-floor back porch, alone, intent on observing a yellow and black swallowtail that returns each day, playing around our butterfly bush, sliding across the air, then getting lost in the branches of the neighbor's maple tree. In these moments, I have gathered gladness and quiet into my heart.

But tears and prayers have sprung up easily in spite of the smiles. I don't feel ready for what might be next. My husband and daughters are woven into these prayers. It's not hard in this season to ask God for help and to make His presence known to us.

This morning my husband Ned sees me wandering around the house, unable to put my mind and hands to anything; he suggests a walk around the neighborhood. When we return, I get my broom and decide to "do the next thing." And it's while sweeping the patio and talking to God about my fears that I find my mind going over stories I know and love: *The Fellowship of the Ring . . . Hannah Coulter*.

. . Peace Like a River . . . The Chronicles of Narnia.

I remember Lucy following the lion Aslan, king of Narnia, in the woods. In *Prince Caspian* Lucy and her three siblings are on an arduous journey where their path is blocked again and again. At one particularly discouraging point, as the party turns back from an apparent dead end, Lucy sees Aslan and realizes that they need to change course and follow him. But the group did not see the Lion, so despite Lucy's attempt to persuade them they choose not to go Lucy's way. Later, Aslan tells her that he had called *her* to follow him even if others would not. After the sting of this revelation dissipates, he gives her a second chance, and Lucy chooses to submit and follow. Aslan goes before her.

There is so much to glean personally from this section, but it's what comes next in the story that my mind and heart need right now:

> For a long way Aslan went along the top of the precipices. Then they came to a place where some little trees grew right on the edge. He turned and disappeared among them. Lucy held her breath, for it looked as if he had plunged over the cliff; but she was too busy keeping him in sight to stop and think about this. She quickened her pace and was soon among the trees herself. Looking down, she could see a steep and narrow path going slantwise down into the gorge between rocks, and Aslan descending it. He turned and looked at her with his happy eyes. Lucy clapped her hands and began to scramble down after him.[79]

Aslan
Ned Bustard

Yes, in fixing my eyes on Jesus, just as Lucy's were fixed on Aslan, and in knowing Jesus' eyes are fixed on me, I discover a new resolve that comes from deep certainty. It is only natural then to follow Him when He says "Come"—no matter where that might lead. I feel this truth growing deeper within me, trusting that His presence not only goes before me but is also with me as He says, "Have courage! It is I! Don't be afraid!"

In John's Gospel, Jesus tells His disciples to get into a fishing boat to go across the Sea of Galilee though He is not going with them in the boat. At nightfall, a high wind swirls around them, and the sea throws itself against their vessel. This type of storm could very well cause their death. When they see something ghostlike coming towards them, they are terrified, but it is Jesus, walking on water. He says to them, "It is I! Don't be afraid!" (John 6:16–21).[80]

Walking on Water
Ned Bustard

Jesus sends them out into the impending storm. But He also comes to them in that same storm and tells them He is with them. Keith Winder, one of my pastors, recently noted about this passage,

> In this story, Jesus walks through the waves. He doesn't just appear on the boat. He walks through the same storm the disciples are experiencing. He shares our pain with us. Theologians call this presence of God in our lives, His immanence.[81]

God is always near to us. He is wherever you are at any moment. As it is written in Jeremiah, "Am I a God at hand, declares the LORD, and not a God far away? Can a man hide himself in secret places so that I cannot see him? declares the LORD" (Jer. 23:24).

The Gospel of Matthew expands on this in Chapter 14. After Jesus says, "Have courage! It is I. Don't be afraid," Peter replies, saying, "If it is you, Jesus, command me to come to you on the water!" And Jesus does, with a simple "Come!" (Matt. 14:28, 29) And then, this disciple-fisherman is walking on water —his eyes fixed on Jesus. This doesn't last long, however, as the strength of the storm frightens him and pulls his attention off his Lord onto his surroundings. As Peter is sinking, he cries out for Jesus to save him. Matthew chronicles this rescue by saying, "Immediately, Jesus reached out His hand, caught hold of him, and said, 'You of little faith, why did you doubt?' Then Jesus brought them both into the boat" (Matt. 14:31 CSB).

John points out that once Jesus is in the boat, they get safely to the other side of the sea. Matthew adds that once he and Peter are in the boat, the winds cease and the disciples worship Jesus by saying, "You are the Son of God" (v. 32).

Elaborating on this event, my pastor said, "God is there before the storm, God is there during the storm, and God will continue to be there at the end of the storm. Jesus has gotten in your boat, and he will safely take you to the other side."

Lucy grows to understand Aslan in a deeper way as she learns to obey him in the hard places. As each step of hers follows his, Lucy experiences more of his faithfulness and learns more about his purposes. In Scripture, Peter and the other disciples experience the reality and presence of Jesus—as the Son of God—when He walks through the storm to them, saves Peter from drowning, then gets into their boat and delivers them to the other side of the sea. He doesn't save them from the storm; He saves them *through* it. As I seek to trust and follow Jesus' lead in the midst of my own storms, I too will grow to know Him more fully, and this greater knowing of Him will strengthen my hope.

I can do the next thing.

I can go into this upcoming appointment with my surgeon, trusting in Christ's sustaining presence. Even if I am sorrowful and scared and struggling to keep my eyes on Him, I can move through this storm with Him present, with His eyes on me, while He says, "Have courage! It is I! Don't be afraid!"

silver spring lake

There are no two roads
that diverge in this wood,
just one uneven dirt path
heading through trees—
with the lake on the right,
   and blue skies in branches above.

You tuck my hand in yours.
We speak slow words
   of an uncertain future.

Up ahead,
I see a fairy house at a tree's roots
   and place an acorn cap by its door.
Further on, our path slopes
   slippery from Thursday's rain.

Your arm reaches around my waist;
my hand holds your shoulder.
We find our way to level ground.
At a clearing in the trees,
we come into an open expanse—
   lake in view, and
   clouds reflected in its stillness.

May I stand here long,
leaning against you,
until we have to move on,
until we have to reach
   the end of the road.

LIGHT I

The path of the righteous is like the light of dawn
that shines brighter and brighter until full day . . .
—Proverbs 4:18

As when it finds its way down around
a maze of hydrangea leaves—
    almost unseen and
landing soft on my garden bed floor;

Or when the last of the morning dew
glistens quietly in a patch of our yard
as the sun reveals itself through
topmost branches of our neighbor's tree,
brightening green maple leaves
above my head . . .

a reminder that sometimes a light surprises.

LIGHT II

Sometimes a light surprises . . .
—William Cowper

like tonight when I
stepped into the crisp night air,
then, looking up, was
startled by a trail of light
passing through the blue-black sky.

Rock Ford Plantation
Joshua Kiehl

He Who Began a Good Work

In my early days as a homeschooling mama of three girls, I searched for the snap of a finger that would help me guide my young students through a smooth day of learning and loving. I was convinced that if I could only plan the right schedule or read the right books, we would be transformed into a delightful family of learners in a day or two, without much trouble.

I could blame the reruns of *Bewitched* and *The Brady Bunch* that I watched as a child. In *Bewitched*, Samantha averted disaster with a twitch of her nose. In *The Brady Bunch*, Marcia's problems were solved in thirty minutes, give or take a few commercials. But God didn't give me a quick fix. Instead, He began to teach me how patiently He works His ways in us over a long period of time.

In the ups and downs of parenting and educating, I could not always see the good that we were already doing; I was too anxious over the things I was afraid we should be doing but were not. And piercing my heart deeply was the desire to help my girls grow in their love for God, for others, as well as for beauty, truth, and goodness. Becoming motivated students, focused on accomplishing their assignments in a reasonable amount of time each day would be "icing on the cake." Still, even on those days when the books, artwork, poetry, and history brought smiles to our faces and new ideas to our minds, I always felt a little worried that it might not be enough.

But God.

He is kind; He works His ways in us as we wrestle through our days. He has the long view in His sight; He goes before us, even as He is with us, while we, His children, struggle to walk the path on which He has put us. God is patient and compassionate; He knows we are weak and "made of dust." Over time I learned that "he who began a good work in [us] will carry it on to completion until the day of Christ Jesus" (Phil. 1:6 NIV). God is not surprised by our struggles, and, as we learn to pray and trust, He continues to accomplish in us that good He has planned for us.

Although this happened more than ten years ago, one family story continues to remind me of how impatient I was to see good results. I had to live through some ups and downs before I could see how God's patience and His long view brings about His ways in us.

This story starts with a love my husband, Ned, and I share for Chadds Ford, Pennsylvania, an area near where I grew up. Its rolling green land and woods have found their way into my imagination—this land is so steeped in history that when I was little I could easily picture Native Americans hunting around the trees and George Washington camping in the woods with his soldiers. The drive down Route 1 in Chadds Ford, near The Brandywine Battlefield and The Brandy-wine River Museum, is as familiar and beloved to me as my childhood backyard.

However, we live in Lancaster County surrounded by farmlands and Amish buggies. I have a great affection for the beauty of its spring-time planted fields and for the rows of tall corn stalks lining the back roads in summer. This is the land my daughters know well.

Yet decades of living here have not erased the unexplainable "something" that Ned and I love about Chadds Ford. We wanted our girls to know the feel of it, too.

So one year, when our daughters were 14, 9, and 7, Ned and I decided to create a fall where they could experience a little of the autumnal beauty of Chadds Ford without taking the long drive, while also making some family memories. Expecting laughter and good times, we planned Tuesday night picnics at Rock Ford Plantation, which is nestled in nearby Lancaster County Park. The land around this pre-Revolutionary War home looks much like Chadds Ford, and we decided the small green knoll facing the house and far off woods would be our destination to eat and play together.

I would pack our wicker picnic basket with favorite foods like chicken potpie, brownies, and apple cider. Hershey, our chocolate Labrador, would come along. Sometimes we would bring a book to read together or a Frisbee to throw.

Preparing for this picnic fit well with my vision of adding ordinary traditions into our family life—activities that made for memories of laughter and unity—as well as our hope to "hardwire" the Brandywine aesthetic into our daughters' psyches.

These picnics happened over the course of a couple of years more than a decade ago. I now remember these times with great fondness: we laughed, played Frisbee with Hershey, took walks around the fields, threw Pooh Sticks by a creek, and looked into the windows of the historic house. What I don't remember, thankfully, is the exact details of how difficult each girl was with each other as this new tradition started. I don't remember the grumbling or the prickly words. And I don't remember how deeply discouraged I was by the tenor of our family culture each week. But I was, in fact, very discouraged. I had assumed the girls would enjoy this new change in our routine without a problem, but my vision of fall nights and family fun had been dashed by their grumbling during our first several outings. Staying home on Tuesday nights began to seem like a better option.

Hershey

But sometime after our first month of picnics, when I was about to give up on these excursions, Ned wisely said to me, "We'll keep doing them. Eventually they will get into it and have fun. And one day, we will look back on these Tuesday picnics as one of the highlights of our life together."

And he was very right. We kept going to Rock Ford with dinner in the wicker basket and Hershey on her leash; eventually the delight I hoped for settled into our picnic routine.

The girls got older and weeknights got busier, and our picnic nights came to an end. But every now and then we would head over for rambles in the woods, walks around the open fields, or a "spell of sitting" on the old house's wide porch; we'd reminisce about our picnics (especially the time when Hershey, off her leash, ran after a deer, with all the girls screaming in shock).

Though the beginning of this Tuesday night picnic tradition didn't go just how I thought it would, now I see how sticking with it helped establish a beautiful tradition for us; the enjoyment we find in gathering together in a special way or with special foods has made its place in our family culture. Now when the girls come to visit us, we reap the harvest of those picnics at Rock Ford as we sit around our kitchen table and have a picnic of sorts. We have agreed that we love a spread of favorite cheeses and meats, crackers and chocolate, grapes and apples. With music playing and candles lit, we laugh and talk and relax.

When the girls were younger, I wished and worked for our family time to be easier. I wrestled with God, complaining that I was trying my best and was seeking to do what I thought would be pleasing to Him. Why did it have to be so hard? Over time I learned, as He patiently taught me, that He who began a good thing in us was going to keep working it out. There would be no snap of the fingers. And it wouldn't happen in a thirty-minute time period, like those sitcom reruns I watched as a child.

Gratefully I can also say that as He has been working His ways in my family, He has also been working His ways in me, helping me grow in wisdom and patience. I am learning to see by God's "longer view." And so, because of His steadfast love and faithfulness, I can say, with the psalmist, "Why, my soul, are you cast down? Why so disturbed within me? Put your hope in God, for I will yet praise him, my Savior and my God" (Ps. 43:5 NIV).

BLESSING

Every Sunday,
after receiving
bread and wine,
we hear,
"Listen to the Lord's
benediction."

We lift up our
hands; we open
our eyes. In front
of me with her
little arms out
wide and her palms
upturned, fingers
strumming the air,
is Jubilee.

The pastor's words
wind their way through
us like a fall
breeze stirring the
tall trees outside.

Holy Week: Cup
Ned Bustard

It moves in and
out, leaf-empty
branches stretching
up to take in
each ray of light,
while deep down roots
intertwine.

WHAT THIRTY-TWO LOOKS LIKE
(ON THE EVE OF OUR ANNIVERSARY)

An afternoon at the
kitchen table, creative work
and words—
   music, laughter.
Early evening lovemaking—
   attention and care.
Frozen pizza for dinner
   British spy movie
   chocolate-chocolate ice cream
      quiet traditions
then cleaning up the
kitchen, hanging laundry
   holding hands.
I never imagined life so sweet and good—
   but here we are
   living out our vows.
You are my beloved
   and I am yours.

my scar

The scar on my right breast and the empty space under the skin
are reminders of last summer's surgery.

A nurse shared that after the surgeon removed the growing tumor,
his tiny stitches would fade to a faint trace of a curve.

Yet I was willing to bear any scar if it could be a down payment
toward saving my breast or extending my life.

Like a delicate chain or
a thin, nearly invisible rainbow arching over my pink areola,
the scar is barely perceptible.

I want it to be a sign of hope, a symbol of a promise:
    all may be well.

Second Eve (detail)
Ned Bustard

one fall morning

The warm morning light seeps
through the closed curtains,
opening our room to the day.

Still in bed, I am wide-awake and aware.
    My knees are tight, and muscles, like rocks.
    My elbows are stiff and refuse to straighten out.
    And, new this morning, my thumb joints creak.

I pull my hands in front of my face
and move my thumbs back and forth.
These stiff joints and aching muscles
have been my months-long companions,
the side effects of meds—
    the names of which I barely can pronounce.

I hang my legs over the edge of the bed and
rub my calf muscles with a wooden roller.
Then positioning one foot with the other
on the floor, I set to hobble down the hall.

These steps may again be sturdy
after my medicines clear out this cancer,
    or when faith has become sight, and
    I'm dancing in the light of a brand new day.

LORD OF THE SABBATH

> And with that song the hobbits stood upon the
> threshold, and a golden light was all about them.
> —J.R.R. Tolkien

And so ends "The Old Forest," the sixth chapter of J.R.R. Tolkien's *The Fellowship of the Ring.* Each time I have read these books I have found myself entering into Chapter 7, "In the House of Tom Bombadil," anticipating all the good ahead for Frodo, Sam, Pippin, and Merry. My imagination fills with pictures of Goldberry and Tom's table spread with plates of heartwarming food and "drinking-bowls [which] seemed to be clear cold water, yet it went to their heart like wine,"[82] comfortable chairs and footstools, and a sweet-smelling fire in front of them. And all this before Tom Bombadil sang over the sleepy hobbits. The travelers would spend the next few days in this enchanted home where Bombadil would give them care and wisdom, which would strengthen them for the next part of their journey.

Throughout the stories o Tolkien's Middle-earth, starting with *The Hobbit* and following through the three books (or rather six, if one is being precise) of *The Lord of the Rings,* there is a pattern of rest and adventure. While guiding my eighth-grade students through these books, I discovered that after each adventure— whether walking through dark and perilous woods, trudging along snow-covered mountain paths,

Tom Bombadil
John Hendrix

or battling orcs—our heroes would eventually find themselves at a place of respite and renewal. And at this point I would remind them that although Tolkien was not seeking to create an allegory, his deep Christian beliefs laid a foundation for his storytelling. One of the ways we found this theological underpinning was in the cycles of rest and adventure which mirrored the command from God to keep the Sabbath holy by dedicating one day each week to respite from six days of work.

In *The Hobbit*, Bilbo and the dwarves found themselves in places of rest such as Rivendell with the elves, in the hall of Beorn and his animals, and in the nest of the eagles. In *The Lord of the Rings*, Frodo and his companions gained respite in Rivendell, as well as in Tom Bombadil's house, the magical Lothlorien, and the waterfall-hidden caves of Faramir. Some type of harrowing adventure usually preceded their arrival to these places of respite. And each break provided refreshment, renewal, and the ability to keep on the journey—even when the characters knew what lay ahead would be difficult.

My students and I discussed what rest looked like. We noticed that not only did the heroes sleep, they also ate delicious food, enjoyed stories and songs, made new friends, received words of wisdom and gifts, and left with provisions for the next part of their adventure. These elements were given at each place of rest.

Bilbo, the wizard Gandalf, and the thirteen dwarves in *The Hobbit* received excellent care while in the hall of Beorn, the shapeshifter. After making Beorn laugh and raising his curiosity, the travelers were invited into his place to be served a grand meal by his ponies, dogs, and even his sheep. (This scene is so fun to imagine.) The travelers spent several days in his place, eating, sleeping, and learning more about their host and the country they were passing through. The time they spent with Beorn illustrates the elements of renewal Tolkien wove into the rest and adventure pattern in *The Hobbit* and *The Lord of the Rings*.

That first night, Bilbo and his companions sat around Beorn's table, warmed and comforted by the fire. They ate a hearty supper and listened to his tales of the wild country; later the dwarves sang songs. They enjoyed cozy warm beds and a good breakfast in the morning. A few days later, Beorn gave them deeper knowledge of the land and how to travel through it, especially advising them what they were to avoid when they walked through Mirkwood Forest. At the company's departure, he gave them gifts of ponies and packages of food. Beorn also offered them his protection and friendship while they went onward.

Each rereading of these rich books has led me to a deeper understanding of Sabbath rest and the good work of offering this rest to others. I already resonated with Tolkien on the joys of a table spread with good food, surrounded by loved ones and laughter, and I enjoyed how he detailed these sections of his stories. But the more I saw the hosts of each resting place offering themselves to their guests through their listening ears, friendship, gifts, and strengthening wisdom, the more I saw biblical wisdom and truth spilling over in Tolkien's ideas.

In Exodus and Deuteronomy, God is didactically clear that the Israelites must keep the Sabbath holy—they are to work six days and to rest on the seventh. Psalm 23 brings this to life poetically, especially when connected with Tolkien's illustrations of rest.

The psalm begins with rest, provisions, and refreshment. Before any work or hardship occurs, the Shepherd gives His follower peace and fullness, as verses 2 and 3 say: "He makes me lie down in green pastures, he leads me beside quiet waters, he refreshes my soul" (Ps. 23:2–3 NIV). As the psalm continues, the Shepherd guides His follower in the right paths, though these paths include the darkest valleys and shadows of death.

These four verses are demonstrated throughout *The Lord of Rings*. Prior to Frodo's adventures, there are gatherings, food, long walks, and time with friends. As Frodo enters into his quest with the Ring, a fellowship comes together, and throughout their travels they are directed on good paths as well as through scary and sinister places. However, on the other side of these "darkest valleys" they arrive in friendly places and are given all they need for renewal and strength to keep going. Psalm 23:5 could be a description of these times: "You prepare a table before me in the presence of my enemies. You anoint my head with oil, my cup overflows" (NIV).

The psalm finishes, "Surely your goodness and love will follow me all the days of my life" (Ps. 23:6 NIV). Although a guiding force is never seen or heard in Tolkien's stories, one is alluded to when we hear Gandalf tell Frodo, "There was something else at work, beyond any design of the Ring-maker.... Bilbo was *meant* to find the Ring ... In which case you were also meant to have it. And that may be an encouraging thought."[83] Or think of what Galadriel said to Frodo: "Do not trouble your heart overmuch with thoughts of the road tonight. Maybe the paths that you each shall tread are already laid before your feet, even though you do not see them."[84] Finally, the hope of true rest in God's house finishes Psalm 23: "And I will dwell in the house of the Lord forever" (Ps. 23:6 NIV). The end of this epic story to save Middle-earth shows characters living in or heading to new blessings.

We are given a gift of grace in the commandment to make a day holy by resting from the six days of our work. On this day of ceasing from all that makes up our week—the creative good and the hard anxiety—we say, "I trust you God that you are taking care of me." This ceasing from work is not meant to be a legalistic duty. As theologian Marva Dawn says, "This is what we celebrate on the Sabbath day. We join the generations of believers—going all the way back to God's people, the Jews—who set aside a day to remember that we are precious and honored in God's sight and loved, profoundly loved, not because of what we produce."[85]

By making worship, community, and rest integral parts of our Sabbath, Sundays have been our family's day to make holy. (My husband, Ned, and I have jobs that no longer require us to work on Sundays; we know many who do, and they are purposeful in setting aside another day of the week for Sabbath keeping.)

More than a decade ago, Ned saw that although I enjoyed feeding friends or newcomers after church, it was also work for me and the family (no matter how I tried to simplify it). So, he made a change to our hosting plans. Even though we felt the call to hospitality and enfolding people, he decided we would not always have them at our house after church; instead we would invite folks out for lunch at Dominion, a neighborhood pizzeria. This started a fun tradition for us, which eventually grew into a church community tradition.

Several Sundays a month ,people from our church community—singles, teenagers, older folks, and families—headed to Dominion and gathered around long tables and booths, squeezing in next to each other and taking up more than half of the restaurant. Here we would talk, welcome visitors, eat delicious food, and drink soda or ale. We also got to know the people who worked there as we got to know each other better. Babies were held on laps, little ones ate together (or ran around), teenagers spent time talking with adults or with each other, and friends would get caught up with each other's lives.

As a result, many of my family's Sundays had the elements of Tolkien's illustrations of rest for his characters. These days included words of wisdom (sermons), songs (congregational singing), gifts (baptism and the Lord's Supper), feasting (pizza, cheese steaks, hard cider), friendship and stories (time with people sitting around the tables), and sleep (afternoon naps). On those Sundays when we experienced being in God's house and fellowshipping with his people— as well as the sheer fun of feasting with others at Dominion—we felt we had experienced what was the true gift of Sabbath: the goodness of the Lord in the land of the living. This was our provision for the coming week.

J.R.R. Tolkien wrote in *The Hobbit*, "If more of us valued food and cheer and song above hoarded gold, it would be a merrier world."[86] And how true! May we find ways to delight in making the Sabbath holy—even if it is only at a local pizzeria and with an afternoon nap. May we enter into the light of true rest, abiding in God's steadfast and faithful love for His people.

An Apple Pie Fit for a Hobbit[87]

For those wishing for an autumnal Sabbath Feast dessert (or for those who cannot wait for dessert), here is something that works perfectly for second breakfast or elevensies. *Note: The apple mixture for this recipe is prepared first and set in the refrigerator for 8 hours or overnight. It makes one (9-inch) pie.*

INGREDIENTS

1 recipe pie crust for a double-crust pie (see note below)
4 lbs. Granny Smith apples *(or a variety of sweet and tart pie-making apples)*, peeled, cored, and sliced
2 tbsp. fresh lemon juice
¾ cup plus 3 tbsp. sugar, divided
¼ cup plus 2 tbsp. all-purpose flour, divided
½ tsp. ground cinnamon
¼ tsp. ground nutmeg
¼ tsp. of ground allspice
⅛ tsp. salt
1 large egg, lightly beaten
1 tbsp. water

A note on pie crust: I have used Pillsbury piecrusts, and they work well. But my favorite recipe is Sister Pie's "All-Butter Pie Dough," which is available in their cookbook or online.[88]

In a large bowl, combine apples, lemon juice, ¾ cup sugar, ¼ cup flour, cinnamon, nutmeg, allspice, and salt; toss to combine. Refrigerate the mixture for at least 8 hours, and up to overnight. Strain mixture through a sieve; reserve apples, discard juice.
Preheat oven to 350°.

Bilbo and Sting
Ned Bustard

On a well-floured surface, roll out each disk of piecrust into a 12-inch circle. Place 1 dough circle into a 9-inch pie pan. Trim excess dough, having a ½-inch border.

In a small bowl combine 2 tbsp. sugar and 2 tbsp. flour. Sprinkle the mixture over the crust of the pan; spoon strained apples into the crust. (Sometimes I dot the top with unsalted butter.) Top with the remaining piecrust disk. Trim to fit. Using finger (a damp finger helps), lightly pinch the top and bottom crusts together to create a wavy edge.

For leaf decoration, roll any remaining pie crust leftovers out to ⅛-inch thickness. Use a leaf-shaped cutter to cut leaves, or use a paring knife to cut them out freehand. Brush a little bit of water on the top of the pie to adhere each leaf in place.

Using a paring knife, cut slits into the top crust. In a small bowl whisk together the egg and water. Using a pastry brush, lightly coat top crust with egg wash and sprinkle with 1 tbsp. of sugar (be careful not to let the sugar clump; you want an even layer).

Bake for 45–60 min. or until interior is bubbling and crust is golden. *If crust browns before filling is completely cooked, cover pie loosely with aluminum foil for remainder of baking time. (This is a point of disagreement with my mother; she says to put the foil on first then remove later.)*

NOVEMBER AFTERNOON ON MY PORCH

Over in my neighbor's yard
is a tree full of birds making a ruckus;
they are mad at each other or
mad at the weather.
The sky is white gray,
and the rain hums,
accompanying the fall of yellow maple leaves.
One leaf loops and loops again
to a soft landing.
And then another follows it,
pirouetting like a four-year-old on stage.
And another waves on by,
then another
and another slide back and forth in the air—
layering shades of brown and yellow
across my yard.
After a time, the birds stop
and the rain, too—
leaving me behind.

After Paul Cézanne's
MONT SAINTE-VICTOIRE

. . . beautiful in elevation, is the joy of all the earth, Mount Zion,
in the far north, the city of the great King.
—Psalm 48:2

To have not been left waiting and lonely
At the foot of the mountain would have been
Enough, but He led us to His holy
House, welcoming us in, His very kin.
Tears once flooded our faces; shaming night
Shadows filled our thoughts. Now His very hands
Wash us clean; each memory bathed by light.
He gathers multitudes of those from lands
Of every time and tongue. Yet more He shares
When He beckons us to enjoy fine wine
And meat of His table—He nothing spares.
With His invitation to *ask* and *find*,
We drink living water, gladdened by springs
Which offer us peace to rest and to sing.

DISCIPLINED BY HOPE[89]

Yesterday I stood in front of my church family and shared my testimony about this life in cancer-land and how God has cared for me in it. This was a sweet way to also thank them for their care, especially since it was during Thanksgiving weekend and the first Sunday in Advent. I share it here so that I can also say thank you to the people in my extended family, Lancaster community, Cultivating community, and Rabbit Room community (plus all the other folks that have prayed and been so kind).

Yesterday, during the sermon about Abram waiting on God, my pastor spoke on being *disciplined by hope* and said that that was what he saw in me—I was grateful for that idea. Today I read these words by T.S. Eliot and was again taken by the idea that faith, love, and hope are all in the waiting. But how to wait? What does waiting look like as I seek to be rooted in faith, with my eyes on Jesus, and to love the people and places God has given me to love?

> I said to my soul, be still, and wait without hope
> For hope would be hope for the wrong thing; wait without love,
> For love would be love of the wrong thing; there is yet faith
> But the faith and the love and the hope are all in the waiting.
> Wait without thought, for you are not ready for thought:
> So the darkness shall be the light, and the stillness the dancing.[90]

Here is my testimony:

My name is Leslie Anne Bustard. My husband, Ned, and I have been members of Wheatland Presbyterian Church since it started. We raised our three daughters—Carey, Maggie, and Elspeth—here in Lancaster City.

If I had been writing this testimony a few years ago, I would have shared my lifelong struggle to believe that I was a beloved child of God. I would have shared how places of inadequacy and insecurity in my heart led me to strive to feel secure in myself, with God, and with others. And I would share how God continues to be kind to me, and how I can see the ways God is keeping His promise to me that my life is hid in Christ. Because of this, He has never let me wander away from Him. He who began a good work in me continues to do that good work.

But my present story has a newfound richness about God in my life that I would like to share.

For almost two years I have been living in cancer-land. I have stage II breast cancer and stage IV melanoma. There won't be a time that I can say I've been cancer free for five years. This is more like managing a chronic disease: there is a sharp shadow—even on good days or long stretches of "normal"—that hangs around. When I found out about this cancer, a friend who had just finished her first year in remission from breast cancer said that those who would be praying for me would be like the friends of the paralytic who took their friend to Jesus by opening a hole in the roof of the place Jesus was speaking and lowering him down to Jesus. She told me I would not always be able to pray and that sometimes my faith would burn low, but my family and friends would carry me and take me to Jesus.

I don't know how God's sovereignty and my cancer go together. That is a mystery to me. But I do know He has called me and my family to walk this path with cancer in it. This suffering has broken my heart and my family's heart, but I believe God is close to the brokenhearted. I also know that He doesn't promise that those who put their faith in Jesus are exempt from hard trials and suffering. I know that God is good whether I am healed on this side of heaven or when I see Him face to face.

At the beginning of this battle with cancer, when I was realizing how much people were blessing me with prayers, cards, gifts, food, and help, I felt so undeserving—there was no way I should receive this much love, and I knew that I could never, even a little, pay it forward enough. As I was struggling with these thoughts God reminded me that this is what grace is—this is the grace God gives us in Jesus. We can never deserve God's abundant love and kindness is to us, but He delights to give it to us. I see now that I have, in a way, been a walking parable of His love to His people.

This fall friends who are connected with an artist and writers' group in Tennessee planned a trip for us to Northern Ireland. They also enlisted others from that community to help pay for the trip—the trip of a lifetime. Ned and I enjoyed every day of it.

Because I love poetry so much, on the first Thursday of our trip, when we were sitting on a ruined castle wall, I was randomly picking short poems to read out loud to Ned, and I stumbled on this one:

MIRACLE
Seamus Heaney

Not the one who takes up his bed and walks
But the ones who have known him all along
And carry him in—
Their shoulders numb, the ache and stoop deep-locked
In their backs, the stretcher handles
Slippery with sweat. And no let up
Until he's strapped on tight, made tilt-able
and raised to the tiled roof, then lowered for healing.
Be mindful of them as they stand and wait
For the burn of the paid out ropes to cool,
Their slight lightheadedness and incredulity
To pass, those who had known him all along.[91]

Reading this poem reminded me that this account in the Gospels had earlier been an important picture of God's grace to me exhibited through my friends' prayers. What a surprise to read it on this trip—yet one more picture of God's abundant ways of caring for us in cancer-land.

Although I may have a propensity towards smiling and laughing here at church, that doesn't mean these past two years have been easy. I have cried, been depressed, been worried and sad. But I have also felt a peace that surpasses understanding. There has been a lot to smile about and good projects to be involved in.

The Young Seamus
Ross Wilson

But the biggest question I have been praying about, meditating on, talking to Ned about is this: how does one live between the Now of ordinary Life and the Then of Death? I don't know when I'm going to die. It could be months or years. Maybe it will be longer than expected or maybe it won't. Maybe I'm in a season of feeling almost normal and that will last for a sweet long time and maybe it won't.

When did Jesus figure out He was walking towards His death? As He grew up and read the Scriptures and went to the Temple, when did it dawn on Him that His life was moving towards a horrific, painful death? And how did He keep loving, living, laughing, and doing all the good work God had called Him to before He went to the Cross?

I don't know for sure, but the Gospels seem to show that Jesus kept His eyes on the Father and stayed focused on His calling. I think that is how I am to live too. Between the Now of Life and the Then of a Death that I'm walking towards, I can live well, fulfilling the good works that were planned for me to do before Time began: love my husband, my girls, my family, my Wheatland family, and my friends—as a beloved child of God, with my eyes on the Father and my life deeply hid in Christ.

CLOUDS
(FOR WANT OF A BETTER TITLE)

I try to put words together about clouds,
    only *rolling billows* and
    streaks of pink
feel dull, over used.

The other day, clouds in our front window
looked like Michelangelo's voluptuous bodies.
Surprised, I called you over to see them with me.

At Saint Peter's Basilica three summers ago,
we stood together under the ceiling's panoply of
    shapes and colors and movement.
I leaned against you to support my head tilted
upwards as I corralled all those fleshy, floating
images into my memory.

While we were leaving the chapel,
    we stared at the high alter wall.
Frescoed blue circled around a cast
of bodies upon bodies watching Jesus intently
as He and Mary descended on a cloud.

I saw that blue this morning.
The sky was empty—
save for a small cloud, stretched out
like sheared sheep's wool that had been
carded and cleaned,
    waiting to be spun into white linen.

NO

Are we too quick to
say no to each other (like
toddlers who have
learned new words), forgetting the
yes and amen of Jesus?

AT Tea WITH a Friend

"I haven't written
in weeks," I said. "I think all
I can write about
are birds or trees." "Sounds like the
start of a poem," she said.

Luke 19:40

When words stumble slow
from my pen, when dark covers
day too soon, and leaves
have left behind their trees, still,
stones will cry aloud your praise.

A Way Forward

... forgetting what lies behind and straining forward to what lies ahead ...
—Philippians 3:13

While sifting through a pile of photos, I found one of me standing in my parents' family room talking with my brother. On a wall nearby hangs a framed Andrew Wyeth print. Seeing it in the photo gave me a satisfied "That's it!" feeling: I knew a Wyeth hung in my parents' home, but I couldn't recall which painting it was; all I remembered was how much it unsettled me as a child. The dark room with one window seemed cramped, and the empty chair with the little coat hanging on the armrest made me assume someone had died.

My early reactions to that painting are twined together with a pervasive feeling of melancholy that seemed to fill the air in my home when I was little. Looking at photos of me at four, five, six, seven, and older, I remember how often I felt uncertain or insecure. I didn't share these sad feelings with anyone because I did not know it was in the house and inside me—it just *was*. When I grew up, I learned that there was marital dissonance between my parents, and this must have been the heaviness I felt. Even though life would be full of much love and care, I carried this insecurity for years to come.

When I was older, my mom would often take my brother and me to the nearby Brandywine River Museum, home of the Wyeth dynasty of painters.[92] This museum—along with other historical landmarks along the winding tree-lined roads of Chadds Ford—was a regular part of my later childhood and teenage years. The contours and colors of the land, the way the light plays through the leaves, and the woods lining the roads still sit comfortably within me.

When my own daughters were old enough, we would visit the Chadds Ford area and wander around the museum with my parents. It was during these years, having forgotten that first Andrew Wyeth print, that I discovered my deep affection for his artwork.

Andrew lived his life among his neighbors and community in Chadds Ford, Pennsylvania. After spending his younger days playing in the fields and woods with his siblings and friends, his father—the famous illustrator N.C. Wyeth—tutored him in drawing and then oil painting. The land was Andrew's subject matter when he started painting professionally at the age of twenty. Eight years later, after his father's tragic death, he started including various members of his community, such as friends, nearby farmers, and boyhood companions, in his artwork. Many of Andrew's paintings ring true for me—he had both a realistic and mysterious way of conveying his deep care, curiosity, and honor for the people and places he loved.

These days, my favorite Wyeth paintings are of things I often pay attention to when walking around my neighborhood—old houses, trees, sunshine and shadows, drifting leaves, stone walls, the sky. I wonder how much my own love of these things and my affection for how Wyeth depicts them is connected. It doesn't even matter how many window scenes he has painted—opened or closed, looking inside or outside—I admire them all. I have even written poems about a few of his paintings, including *Wind from the Sea*, *Pentecost*, and *Pennsylvania Landscape*.

But though I love and have stood admiring (for longer than my daughters would have liked) many of Andrew Wyeth's paintings, *Trodden Weed* has captivated me the longest.

I don't remember what drew me to *Trodden Weed* , but I always feel the same when I see it: a desire to be walking outside, free and strong and belonging right there.

Those boots were first owned by Howard Pyle, N.C. Wyeth's art teacher and friend. I love how worn-in they look and the purposeful stride the owner of these boots is taking down the hill. The flapping coat adds to the energy.

My gaze wanders over all the shades of brown, the various lengths of grass, and the flattened weeds, and I marvel at his ability to paint like the German Renaissance painter Albrect Dürer. If I could, I would ask Andrew if the word *weed* in the title is about him? The idiom "well-trodden path" is used when referring to a course of action that has been followed by many other people. Is Andrew somehow reflecting on his path as a painter, following in the way of Howard Pyle and N.C. Wyeth?

Andrew Wyeth called this a self-portrait and painted it only weeks after he had a portion of a lung removed. If I were an artist painting my self-portrait, I would want something like this scene, but I imagine my feet bare, walking on green grass and crossing over the shadows of trees stretching along my path.

As I look back at my life, it is too easy to recall the sadness I felt as a child and the deep disappointments and inadequacies I wrestled with as an adult. But too much time has been wasted, and I'm weary of those memories. I want to remember and stand on the better stories of God's grace showing up to help me walk well in the places He called me.

After Wyeth's
Trodden Weed
Ned Bustard

Once I solved the
mystery of the print
the younger me found
creepy, I looked it up,
discovered its name to
be *The Writing Chair*,
and realized that it
wasn't scary at all.
And instead of serving
as a reminder of my
childhood melancholy, I now see it foreshad-
owing my love of good words and writing.
The verses "Goodness and mercy shall follow me
all the days of my life" (Ps. 23:6) and "The name of the LORD
is a strong tower; the righteous run to it and are safe" (Prov. 18:10
NKJV) often fill my imagination about God and me. With these words I
imagine Jesus kindly reminding me to stop looking over my shoulder at the times I
tripped, stumbled, and fell, and to face forward so I can fix my eyes on Him.

As I keep processing and seeking to understand the different parts of my life,
this Wyeth painting of the old boots and purposeful stride is a good reminder
of how grace and goodness have been at my heels, while the weeds of insecurity
have not overrun my path as I keep traveling into God's Eternity.

AFTER ANDREW WYETH'S
WIND FROM THE SEA

Sometimes you've got to open up the window
and let the wind blow through . . .
—Douglas Kaine McKelvey

The window had been left open during the night.
One could see beyond the wide expanse of yard
to dark tree lines and sliver of silver sea.
A lacey curtain hanging over ripped shade
was light enough to catch even a slight breeze off the water.
But today—this white-clouded day—
the wind came sudden and strong; and the curtain,
with its torn edges, flew into the room—
like a ghost: hovering, waiting.

Spirit, come.
Awake in us
all that is worn and weary.

AFTER ANDREW WYETH'S
PENTECOST

We've worked all night and caught nothing, but I will do as you say.
—Peter

Was Peter's mind racing when the net
was so full it almost ripped,
or when he hung it between the poles,
with the breeze off the sea
moving through its brown lines?
Did he run his hands over the frayed cords
as Jesus said, "Follow me and fish for men"?
What did he think when he saw twelve baskets of fish?
Or when night waves overwhelmed the boat,
and he stepped out, surrounded by high winds?

Days after the curtain tore in two,
what filled his thoughts in the still of the morning,
as he heard, "Throw your net to the right!"
What did he think when the net—
with a hundred-fold fish—did not rip?
And later, when the sound of wind roared
through the upper room,
what did Peter remember as he preached,
"It will be in the last days, says God,
I will pour out my Spirit on all people"?

Was it the net, fish-full, that did not rip?

cancer: ALMOST YEAR THREE

If we hope for what we do not see,
we wait for it with patience.
—Romans 8:25

Early morning autumn light—
loosened yellow maple leaves
float like flecks of gold on air;
My shadow lengthens long.

And the sun warms the crown
of my hair-empty head.

This, the feeling of hope.

TO MAKE VISIBLE

To make visible,
glory;
for a moment
see the mystery of eternity
in our ordinary.
To long for the light
and to let it sweep
through shadowed windows,
waiting hearts.
To listen.
To say yes,
let it be as you say it will be.
To wait till the word breaks in,
revealing grace
upon grace upon grace.

The Holy Family
Henry O. Tanner

THE SPACE BETWEEN
SORROW AND JOY

Let me learn, O Lord,
What it is to live so open to life and hope
That I might weep and rejoice
In the same breath
Without contradiction.
—Douglas Kaine McKelvey

The space between joy and sorrow is its own room in our hearts.

Joy—that mysterious movement of longing in the spirit. That feeling no words can adequately speak of but that is somehow wrapped up in delight, beauty, and hope.

And sorrow—more than the pain of a scratched knee, this is suffering that cuts deep into the spirit. Something that opens a void inside. Here hope seems a stranger.

In the opening chapters of Luke, as the story of the Messiah's birth unfolds, we witness Mary submitting to a hard, life-altering call. She learns she is chosen to carry and mother the Son of God; her community, including her betrothed, learns of her pregnancy; and later she and her husband travel to a faraway town to follow Rome's edict to be counted in a census. There she gives birth in a stable. Afterward, shepherds come to her and share their story of an angel bringing a message of a baby wrapped in swaddling clothes and lying in a manger. It is written that after they left to tell the rest of the town their news, Mary "treasured up all these things, pondering them in her heart" (Luke 2:19).

The word "treasure" is used in many translations of this verse. In my imagination, Mary has taken these words and put them in her heart, along with other memories connected to the foretelling of the birth of her son—as if putting keepsakes in a special box. She placed the astonishment of the shepherds next to Joseph's dream alongside the memory of her cousin Elizabeth's baby jumping in her womb and on top of the message she received from the angel Gabriel. These would be her treasures, ones she could take out, look at, and think about. These treasures could not be stolen from her, nor could they be destroyed by rust.

The second chapter of Luke tells of Mary and Joseph with baby Jesus in Jerusalem in the temple. An old man Simeon approaches them, and while he holds the baby, he declares that Jesus would cause the falling and rising of many in Israel, and that a sword would pierce Mary's own soul. Mary hears of a future pain connected with this little boy who has been the source of so much treasure.

Mary's joy and Mary's sorrow. Her treasure. Her sword.

And the space between.

Where is Mary's help—our help—in living in the space between the joy and the sorrow, the treasure and the sword?

The American painter Henry Ossawa Tanner (1859–1937) might offer us a glimpse at the answer.[93] Tanner used his brush and oil paints to create paintings of biblical narratives that portray the power of grace—grace found in a moment—and reveal God giving the gift of transformation to live between the treasure and the sword. As the art historian James Romaine asserts regarding Tanner's paintings of Mary, the artist sought to portray the visual power of grace and the power of its impact to highlight how Mary had been transformed by faith.[94]

The Annunciation, found in the Philadelphia Museum of Art, is Tanner's most famous biblical narrative. This painting was the beginning of Tanner's vision to paint stories of Scripture with integrity. Completed in 1898 after his trip in the Middle East, this annunciation captures both the realism and mystery wrapped up in this pivotal event in the God's great story of Redemption.

For six weeks in 1897 Henry Tanner visited Palestine and Egypt in order to experience its culture. He wanted his work to have both physical and spiritual integrity, so he sought to create a more authentic depiction of the biblical world. He brought actual household pieces back to his home in Paris to use as props in his paintings, as well as sketches he had made in the Holy Lands that included people and colors. *The Annunciation* includes an oil lamp, rug, and jugs. Not only does the environment of the painting look realistic, but Mary does as well: she is not an otherworldly saint, but a young girl who has been awakened from her sleep. Her blanket is half off the bed, and her dress looks slightly wrinkled.

The arches of the back wall, Mary's peaceful, tilted head, and the blue garment in the front corner allude to early Renaissance annunciation paintings. But aside from those details, this painting stands alone in its realism, its mystery, and the imaginative and startling way the angel is depicted. This is not a painting one easily confuses with Giotto's or Fra Angelico's annunciations. Neither is it easily forgotten.

Gabriel is a strange, radiating pillar of light. The moment Tanner captures on the canvas looks as if this messenger from God has already spoken "Do not be afraid, Mary, for you have found favor with God" (Luke 1:30). Although we do not know if he has spoken the rest of his message, there are several clues that help us see the transformative moment Tanner seeks to communicate to his viewers.

Once we have taken in the pillar of light, we look over to Mary and see that her face is illuminated by his light; the corner behind her is warmly highlighted. Our gaze lingers on Mary's expression; she shows no fear, despite the unexpected night visitor. She looks humbly yet intently at him. Her hands are peacefully folded in her lap. Within this story, the angel continues his message when he says, "You will conceive and give birth to a son, and you are to call him Jesus. He will be great and will be called the Son of the Most High. . . . His kingdom will never end" (Luke 1:31, 32 NIV).

This is the powerful moment where Mary is transformed by grace into a faith that is hers. Her expression of peace is our clue. Her words will be of submission: "I am the Lord's servant . . . May your word be to me fulfilled" (Luke 1:38 NIV).

Tanner's goal is not to say that Mary has worked up this peace and obedience by her own will. The work of faith is one of mystery and comes from outside herself. The strong vertical line of light—Gabriel—is perpendicular to the line of the shelf next to him. These two lines form a cross, a foreshadowing sign of Christ. Also, looking closely, one can see three jugs—in the left-hand corner, on top left shelf, and the right wall. When drawing a line from jug to jug to jug, they form a triangle—a symbol of the Trinity. These elements of the painting highlight that it is the cross of Christ and God's power that transforms Mary and gives her the faith to obey. And it is His presence that gives her the courage to live into the unknown of being an unwed mother, carrying a baby given to her by God for His purposes.

The Holy Family by Henry Tanner was created in 1909. In the ten years between his successful *The Annunciation* and this *Holy Family*, Tanner began to move away from the realism that characterized his earlier style, as influenced by his teacher, the painter Thomas Eakins, and to move toward a more expressive style, as influenced by the Impressionists. In the years following this painting he would still paint biblical narratives but with a wide variety and shades of blue and light. He would continue to pursue excellence, artistic integrity, and also spiritual integrity.

The Holy Family does not depict a specific Bible story. Joseph and Mary look like an ordinary couple in their home. James Romaine, in his commentary on this piece, highlights how this holy couple are made accessible to the viewer because Tanner has placed them in a room that is mostly in the shadows, making a table and other pieces in the background hard to decipher.[95] The room has a timelessness to it that helps us enter into the event.

The angle of the composition is a welcoming tool. We are not looking down at the couple from above; we are looking *into* the room and towards the couple. Joseph, leaning on the wall—partially shadowed, attentive to Mary—looks as if he could put his finger to his mouth, turn towards you, and whisper a gentle "shh."

The light moving into the space and onto Mary is reminiscent of Rembrandt's painting *Landscape with Rest on the Flight into Egypt.* In Rembrandt's painting, hills, sky, and shadows of trees surround the family, as they shelter under a cover of branches. A fire illuminates them just as we see the light illuminating Mary and Joseph in Tanner's painting. Another Rembrandt painting—*The Holy Family with Saint Anna*—is also a reminder of Tanner's holy family. Here, they are in an indoor scene of Joseph's workshop. Light comes in from the window, and Mary nurses Jesus. It is a common scene—one that makes this family familiar to us and that illustrates the way blessings and grace can come into our everyday lives.

The Holy Family with Saint Anna
Rembrandt Harmenszoon van Rijn

In Tanner's *The Holy Family*, the source of light in the right-hand corner is a mystery. Mary peacefully sits on a rug with her hands in her lap. Her veil glows in such a way it looks like a halo. Baby Jesus is sleeping next to Mary, and although the light is on Him too, He is barely visible. They both radiate this light. As James Romaine points out, she is facing towards a light from an unseen source, in an attitude of deep devotion, and with her baby. This light is symbolic of Christ's incarnation. And here, the ordinary meets the sacred: the transformative power of grace Tanner captures is the moment Mary is given is to see Jesus as her son and her savior. His presence in her life is a blessing and a mystery.

After 1900, Tanner did not experiment with any more new painting trends. He continued to work in his expressionistic style. And many of his paintings from this time are done with a dreamy deep blue, such as *Daniel in the Lions' Den* and *The Disciples See Christ Walking on the Water*. Some of this blue is prominent in his simply titled oil painting, *Mary*, which was completed in 1914 and has its home in the Smithsonian American Art Museum.

Mary sits on the bed, holding a light, which is almost in the center of the painting. Even when using expressionistic and impressionistic styles, Tanner still remained a naturalist—the light comes from a natural source, one we would recognize in everyday life. Notice how the light she holds lands on her stretched arm, and this leads us up to see her face. See how Tanner does not leave out the folds of her dress, the wrinkled sheets, and the softness of her veil. Behind her on the wall the shadows are dark and in various shades of gray and dark blue.

Mary's head leans slightly forward. The shadowed lines on the wall help our eyes follow her gaze out of the picture frame. We do not know for certain what she is looking at.

But between the dark and the light, she sits and waits.

Usually pictures of Mary holding a lighted lamp signify that Christ has come into the world. In the annunciation painting from 1898, there is an oil lamp on the shelf in the upper left hand corner. It is not lit. Christ has not yet come. Here in *Mary*, she holds a lit oil lamp: her courage and peace come from the Light of the World who is with her.

Here is the space between the treasure and the sword, between the joy and the sorrow.

By painting Mary between the dark shadows and the lighted oil lamp, Henry Ossawa Tanner suggests to us that the presence of Jesus and the transforming moment of grace entering into our everyday lives can make it possible to move in that space, whether with laughter or with tears, holding courage and peace in our hearts.

XI/MM

A found poem of Queen Elizabeth II

As a boy He learnt His father's trade,
then became a preacher,
   recruiting twelve to help Him.
His ministry lasted a few years.
   He never wrote anything down.
He was arrested,
   tortured, and
   crucified.
His death might have been the end,
… but then came resurrection.

I believe:
   Go in peace,
   be of good courage,
   hold fast that which is good,
   render to no man evil for evil,
   strengthen the faint-hearted,
   support the weak,
   help the afflicted,
   honor all
—a simple message.[96]

WHAT JO MARCH AND I HAVE IN COMMON

"Christmas won't be Christmas without any presents,"
grumbled Jo, lying on the rug.
—Louisa May Alcott

I read the opening lines of *Little Women* when I was in fifth grade, and I have not forgotten them since. Such truth for a ten-year-old found in seven simple words. But when I, as a wife and mother, reread this classic story of the four March sisters, it afforded me the opportunity to reflect on other truths—particularly the ideas found around this opening Christmas-time vignette.

Frontispiece from *Little Women* (1869)
May Alcott

After learning that there would be no Christmas gifts because it was wartime and money was scarce, Meg, Jo, Beth, and Amy March decided to spend their own money (one dollar each) to purchase gifts for their mother, who they lovingly refer to as Marmee. But when they woke on Christmas morning, they found *Pilgrim's Progress* tucked under their pillows, though they had not expected gifts. Following their eldest sister Meg's example, they pledged to read a little of the book every morning. They went downstairs happily to hug their mother and enjoy their warm and lovely breakfast.

But Marmee had just spent time with a poor widow who had many children, so Marmee encouraged her daughters to take their warm breakfast to this widow's family, as they needed it more than the Marches did. Although the girls did not want to do this, they followed their mother's lead. And after sharing their food with this poor family, the sisters realized that this was good, and they were glad.

Later in the day, as part of their Christmas celebrations, they staged a play for their friends. This very dramatic performance, written by Jo, included homemade costumes and props, with each sister playing parts. Much fun and laughter filled the attic theater. As they all came downstairs to the dining room, an abundance of delicious holiday foods and beautiful bouquets of hothouse flowers from their elderly neighbor greeted them. The March girls' Christmas Day ended with a great deal of festivity and gratitude.

Jo learned—as I am learning—that Christmas really can become a beautiful day, even when the traditions and expectations are not met the way we envision they will be. We hope for traditions that will fill our hearts with happy memories and root our loved ones in the goodness of the season, strengthening community bonds for the coming year. As Proverbs 24:3–4 says, "By wisdom a house is built, and by understanding it is established; by knowledge the rooms are filled with all precious and pleasant riches." The work that men and women do to cultivate and care for their people includes traditions and celebrations.

Intentionality and creativity—our plans detailed on paper or our purposes imagined while wide-awake at midnight—can bring both delight and disappointment to us, exposing our need for Christ's peace that surpasses all understanding. Without this gift of grace during the busy holidays, Proverbs 14:1's warning that "folly with her own hands tears [her house] down" may ring true.

Giving your family and friends what you have to offer—whether in foods, gifts, traditions, or surprises—is a heart pull to be followed. But we need to hold it all loosely, offering it with open hands, waiting in love; this should temper our enthusiasm. Sacrificial love is our starting point and the reason we continue to plan and provide for others. When our plans are for the sake of "all that glitters," we learn that it may not really shine for those we are serving.

One December more than two decades ago, when our oldest daughter, Carey, was three or four, I had envisioned making a lovely Christmas morning breakfast. I set the table with shiny plates, good silverware, and holiday napkins, and then decorated it with candles, maroon ribbons, and fresh greens. In my mind I was setting the stage for Christmases to come, when we would all say, "Oh good! Christmas breakfast, when we eat the pineapple egg casserole Mom discovered in Cape May …" Can you tell where this is going?

Carey and Ned did not like the pineapple casserole at all. I got mad at them and let them know it. Because I would not shake off my anger, I squashed Christmas joy for the next hour or two. I regret my actions and attitude of that morning. Looking back, I can see that I responded this way because I did not hold my plans loosely or with love, but instead made them all about me and what

I wanted. I was trying to live out the sparkly scenarios in the magazines I had read for holiday inspirations. Creating traditions around a table set with delicious food is what I loved then (as I do now). Somehow, though, I had mixed up the "glory" of a perfect table with the goodness of offering delight out of the love I had for my family. Since then I've learned, baby step by baby step, how to offer joyful Christmas activities with open hands and heart.

He Tabernacled Among Us
Ned Bustard

Several years later, when our third daughter was still a baby, we spent much of November and December supporting my mom and caring for my dad after his open-heart surgery. When we headed back home to get ready for Christmas, I asked Carey what kind of cookie we should make. I was too tired to do a large assortment, but one batch of a favorite recipe seemed doable. Maybe my grandmother's oatmeal raisin? Maybe chocolate chip cookies? Or sugar cookies with sprinkles? Any of those would be fun to make with Carey and Maggie, our two-year-old. I could picture us standing at the kitchen counter listening to Christmas music and stirring the ingredients.

Carey replied quickly: "Those cookies at the store with the picture in the middle, and all you do is put them on a cookie sheet and into the oven. I even like them not cooked." And that's what we did. In the twenty years since that one, we've made and decorated other cookies. But we still buy those refrigerator Pillsbury cookies with Rudolph or Frosty in the center—we may bake them or eat them cold.

And although my daughters enjoy making and decorating Christmas cookies, they really enjoy their dad's custom-made Christmas Music Mix CD. He includes old favorites and new songs, and sometimes he asks for input. This CD is his secret project—he always has it ready for us to listen to after Thanksgiving dinner, and we continue to listen to it in the car throughout December. In the past few years, the girls have added their own twist to the tradition by creating Christmas playlists online and sharing these lists with us.[97]

But our Christmas breakfast tradition? For many years we either had Christmas breakfast at Ned's mother's home or at my mother's. But one year, to ensure that the Bustard family had a day to be at home doing Christmas together without heading off to out-of-town family gatherings, we started a new tradition and designated December 24th our Christmas Day. It was our no-rush day to enjoy new gifts, take naps, eat food, and watch movies. This meant that we had to decide what to have for breakfast.

After much discussion, we chose bacon and sausage, hash browns or roasted potatoes, scrambled eggs, Pillsbury biscuits, and Pillsbury cinnamon rolls (notice the lack of breakfast casseroles). To add to the holiday festivities, I set the table with our good silverware and Christmas dishes, holiday serving dishes and candles; I bring out Christmas poems to read over breakfast. After we open presents, Ned cooks the bacon, sausages, and eggs (because he is a master at not burning them), and I make sure the biscuits and the cinnamon rolls are baked and the table is sparkly. This breakfast makes everyone happy. Because I am still drawn to those lovely photos of gooey homemade sticky buns or French Toast casseroles, I had never envisioned biscuits and rolls from tubes as part of our breakfast traditions, but they are stress-free, and we all like them. As we gather together around the table, we read Scripture, poems, and prayers, and then we dig in.

There are other Bustard traditions that add to the joy of Christmas, but as Jo learned that Christmas would still be joyful even without a pile of presents to open, I have learned that Christmas is still Christmas without a pineapple egg casserole. And as Jo and her sisters received the extravagance of neighborly generosity, I have received the good gift of my daughters, now adults, adding their creativity to our Christmas traditions. Extending to me and their dad the goodness they received from us in their childhoods—a batch of Pillsbury biscuits, a beautifully set table, a mix of Christmas songs—they get in on planning and cooking holiday meals and offer new ideas for our Christmas times together. They add to the precious and pleasant riches that fill our home.

.

HINTS OF A LONGED-FOR, FAR-OFF COUNTRY

I pulled out the tree
we spotted in a row of freshly cut Frasers
at Frey's and breathed in—
as if for the first time—
its sweet pine scent.

We set it up by
our front window, with its hundreds
of twinkling lights
reflecting back in the darkened glass.

Peace Tree
Ned Bustard

ISAIAH 35:1

A fir tree's fresh scent—
a hint that one day streams of
living water will
flow through the wilderness and
the deserts will blossom bright.

A prayer for the new year

O good-giving God, you generously offer us perfect gifts. They are like rivers of light cascading down from you, the Father of Lights.

Praise you, Lord. No scarcity is found in you—you give us our daily bread. You offer us abundance, in ways we were looking for and in ways we didn't expect. Forgive us for those times when we thought we knew how our needs should be met and didn't see how you were providing for us.

Help us, Lord, as we traverse this New Year, facing a wintered barren landscape, to recollect how you lit our way in the past and removed the shadows that brought fear or loneliness to our hearts. May the Holy Spirit and your words give us wisdom to keep on your way, so we can see the light shine as a full day, warm and lovely.

Although we wrestle with winding, maze-like paths, this will not be forever. One day, when you return and restore all things, we'll dance along paths unencumbered by valleys or rocky hills. The ground beneath our feet will feel firm and the grass lush. Our way through new creation will be eternally lit by your presence.

Lord, we pray this year will begin with your promises alive in our hearts. May the hope that you will bring forth the fullness of our salvation be our treasure. May we remember your faithfulness in bringing forth the fruit of our hands, trusting that these will be good gifts to those in our lives and will be glorifying to you.

Praise you, from whom all blessings flow.

Amen.

NEW YEAR'S DAY AND TOP TEN LISTS

New Year's Day ranks up there as one of my favorite holidays of the year, right behind Thanksgiving and Christmas Eve Day. I would not have said that when I was a teenager—back then, New Year's Day meant no presents; vacation was officially over and school would start in the next few days. In my family it also meant pork and sauerkraut—a tradition I did not embrace as fully as my parents did. Each year the first of January was quite the disappointment.

The status of New Year's Day changed for me over the years, though, as my husband and I began a new tradition of gathering people in our home for a time of simple feasting and sharing. Our long-time friends Tom and Becky Becker have been constants at this get-together, as we've squeezed our family of five and their family of seven—plus an eclectic mix of any teenagers and young adults currently in our orbit—into our narrow row house. Some years we have hosted over twenty people.

But though the guest list has changed from year to year, the menu and activities have stayed the same. For dinner, I have always made a couple of big pots of soup and set out leftover Christmas cookies; friends bring drinks, salad, and bread. We eat dinner sprawled out around the downstairs—at the kitchen table, on the floor in the library, or on the chairs and couch in the living room—each of us with a pen in hand, busily filling in a Top Ten Lists handout.

The food is always yummy and filling, but I think these Top Ten Lists are what have kept people coming back. Teens who came to our New Year's Day gathering years ago still try to come now that they're adults. If they can't, they email requests for a PDF of the handout so they can share it with their friends.

The Top Ten Lists consist of five categories and a final comment: Music, Literature, Movies/Shows/TV, Events, and Miscellaneous. The goal when filling out the handout is to name ten things that were important to you from that year for each category. At the end of the sheet there is room to enter one Personal Hope (a desire, not a resolution) for the new year.

Once everyone has finished eating and filling out their lists (there is no consulting other people during list-making time), we gather in the living room, where the rules are read out:

1. One person at a time shares one category. Then the next person to the left shares their list for that category, and so on, until everyone has shared. Then the first person shares their list for the next category.
2. If an item is shared that also appears on others' lists, those people raise their hand and cross the item off their list.
3. Love your neighbor (there shall be no mocking of items on other participants' lists).

And here is where the wonder of the season occurs. We all love sharing and we all love being heard. But we also love hearing what other people like and what has been significant to them. Each person gets a chance to share the things from the past year that were good, hard, enjoyable, and memorable. Every year, a Harry Potter book or movie is inevitably referenced, as is *Parks and Rec* or *The Office*. A Bustard will most likely list a Marvel movie or a British show, and a Becker will mention an obscure indie musical recording. Learning about new music or books and sharing common likes adds to the fun. This time of list-making and sharing has created sweet bonds of care and memories between children, teens, and adults. We all get to peek into each other's hearts and offer our gladness that we have arrived together at the beginning of a new year and a new season.

Cheesy Wild Rice Soup

We like to keep New Year's Day dinner simple, as most people are still feeling stuffed and weary from Christmas holiday celebrating. This soup is both simple and a crowd pleaser. (It serves six people—I usually double it.)

INGREDIENTS

1 6–8 oz. pkg. long grain and wild rice mix
4 cups milk
2 cans condensed cream of potato soup
8 oz. shredded cheese (*I like sharp cheddar and Monterey Jack*)
½ lb. crumbled bacon

Prepare rice per package instructions.
In a soup pot, combine, rice, soups, and cheese. Mix well. Cook and stir until the cheese is melted and the soup is a pleasing warmth (but be careful the bottom of the pot doesn't scorch). Garnish with bacon.

CULTIVATING THE EYE TO SEE

Imagine a child squinting up at the bright blue sky while she names the cloud formations. Or discovering a still yellow finch lying on the ground and shedding tears for the death of this little creature. Or sitting on the porch swing, listening to the rain and watching as the lightning and thunder make her jump and squeal.

The way a young child can meander through the day welcoming new sights, sounds, and experiences is one of those mysterious grace-upon-grace gifts that God gives us. And this grace is compounded for me when I am in on it, when I accept the in-the-moment invitation to experience it with them—getting to see their big eyes and quick laughs as they run around glad for whatever has caught their attention.

Those wonder-filled children are like the many artists and poets throughout time and in every culture who, having caught a glimpse of the world in its beauty or in its suffering, generously give us their sight. Whether through shaded lines, or stirring words, or notes that shape sound and silence, these artists generously offer their vision and creation to the world and give us the reason we need to wipe clear our own smudged glasses.

I like how Calvin Seerveld speaks of artists:

God's Spirit calls an artist to help her neighbors who are imaginatively handicapped, who do not notice the fifteen different hues of green outside the window, who have never sensed the bravery in bashfulness, or seen how lovely an ugly person can be—to open up such neighbors to the wonder of God's creatures, their historical misery and glory.[98]

Following in the steps of the God who voiced creation and saw it was very good, we are made to be cultivators of sight—of what we see, and how we take in and name for ourselves what we have seen. We glance; we glimpse. We linger; we observe. We behold; we discern. As Jesus says, "Your eyes are windows into your body. If you open your eyes wide in wonder and belief, your body fills up with light. If you live squinty-eyed in greed and distrust, your body is a musty cellar. If you pull the blinds on your windows, what a dark life you will have!" (Matt. 6:22–23 MSG)

But we need not cultivate our sight without help. The Holy Spirit is given to be our counselor. And He offers us allies—like children, poets, and artists.

Some allies seem to find us by happenstance, and some come to us by choice. But reflect on your own life, and you may find the Holy Spirit has been guiding you and helping you to see and grow in wisdom and in love.

Reflected Glory
Leslie Bustard

Last summer, while re-reading *The Gift of Asher Lev* by Chaim Potok, I noticed that the main character carried with him a copy of Rainer Marie Rilke's *Letters on Cézanne.* Since Cézanne has long been a favorite artist of mine, I bought my own copy of Rilke's book, wondering, "What will I learn about Cézanne from Rilke?"

As I read about Rilke's love for Cézanne's paintings and about the things he saw in them, I began to see Cézanne's paintings in ways I never had before. Despite many years of enjoying Cézanne's water scenes and mountain vistas on canvas, I realized that my "seeing" had been shallow.

I underlined many of Rilke's words and ideas as I read, such as,

> Although one of his idiosyncrasies is to use pure chrome yellow and burning lacquer red ... he knows how to contain their loudness within a picture: cast into a listening blue, as if into an ear, it receives a silent response from within, so that none outside needs to think himself addressed or accosted.[99]

Despite all the times I had sought out Cézanne's paintings in my museums, had I really *looked* at the colors he used? Did I see how they played with each other in a picture? How is Cézanne's blue a "listening blue"? How does Cézanne's work welcome me in, instead of attacking me? These ideas fascinated me as I looked at his still life paintings. I found his classic piece of oranges and apples on a table covered with a white cloth and thought about colors, reality, and "thereness." And I wrote a poem in response to what Rilke had shown me.

AFTER PAUL CÉZANNE'S *APPLES AND ORANGES*

As if these colors could heal me of indecision once and for all . . .
—Rainer Maria Rilke

Cézanne arranged his still life with much thought,
having planned each detail of the table
with its white cloth, jug, and bowl. The apples
and oranges placed in their own spots. He
took pleasure in seeing the reds with the
greens and the blues with the yellows, and how
these colors conversed quietly among
themselves. Painting was a simple act of
love, one that held on, continued. His work
came from here. Oh Lord, how to live like that.

Through the late spring months and early summer, the Square Halo Gallery, an intimate gallery run by my husband Ned, hosted a show of the French Expressionist Georges Rouault. Each time I walked into the gallery and paid attention to Georges Rouault's paintings, I saw his lament as well as his hope, and I held onto this vision of his. Cézanne's vibrant use of colors came to mind as I looked at Rouault's vivid swathes of orange, green, and blue.

Rouault was concerned for the downtrodden and their suffering, and he painted them with compassion. His hope was rooted in the life, death, and resurrection of the Suffering Servant, which he also spent years painting. Whether illustrating the humbled, bent head of Jesus on the cross or Christ with hands outstretched toward a kneeling woman, Rouault captured the loving heart of God's Son for his people. He lends viewers his sight so we too can see Christ as the light in a world that was rife with trouble and sorrow.

"Life moves pretty fast. If you don't stop and look around once in a while, you could miss it," the sage Ferris Bueller once observed.[100] So how can we cultivate eyes that see in this age of scrolling and swiping—eyes that see deeply, with love and compassion and hope? For me, the answer has come through finding community with others who are also paying attention to their world. Rouault, Cézanne, and Rilke have been among my guides as I seek to keep my eyes open to all the colors, details, joy, and sorrow in the world around me.

THE WORD OF THE LORD CAME TO US

You say we are
   stars
   sand
   salt.

You call us
   living stones
   living sacrifices.

We are made ready by you
Living Water.

You name us
Oaks of Righteousness
   grounding
   rooting
   building us
into the House of the Lord,

so we can declare you
Good.

Water
Hannah Claire Weston

A wee drop in your hand

This—
   perfect cup of tea
   laughter at your table
   miles of rolling green land—

this is worthy of hours
venturing through dark night skies,
over deep ocean waters, and even
fog-filled roads.

Rain

The unceasing sound
of midnight rain on the roof
wakens me; I close
my eyes—its pitter patter
ebbs and flows into my dreams.

Writing Practice

Each morning I see the same tree out the
same window; I look
out of habit. Today, its branches are bare;
not one bird sits
or sings. All the limbs criss-cross each other,
some long and straight
and some bent; the tip-top ones seem to reach
up to touch the clouds.

Psalm 126:1–3

God has made laughter for me; everyone
who hears will laugh with me.
—Sarah

"And the Lord kept his
promise," we'll say, our laughter
like Sarah's when she
was barren no more and all
her sadness had come untrue.

February 4th

The snow is in piles, lining the street—
an outcome of neighbors digging out
after a day-long snowfall.
Already it is tinted gray, corners mushy.

But out my back door, sun is bright,
and patches of ice on stone glitter.

Shadows of tree branches stretch long and
crisscross the pristine white of my yard.

And a thin layer of snow sits still
on dry vines hanging along our back fence.

Air feels crisp.
Birds chirrup above me,
as if to say hope had touched down.

THE GOODNESS OF POETRY IN MY LIFE[101]

I am grateful to be here sharing with you—several beloved faces have been in my mind as I prayed over this and wrote. Thank you for inviting me to speak tonight; thank you also to those of you have been praying for me and for my family as I have been dealing with cancer these past few years.

I love teaching about the different aspects of being a woman, about the importance of imagination and stories, and even about wrestling with cancer. There are many ways these things are connected for me, but the main one is how the pursuit of beauty, truth, and goodness through discovering, reading, sharing, and writing poetry has been a means of grace for me. I wanted to share this with you, in hopes that delving a little into the goodness of poetry in one's everyday, even busy, life may be a refreshing gift for you—one that might encourage you to add more beauty into your own lives.

I have heard people say that poetry isn't their thing—mostly because someone made them analyze poems that really didn't make sense to them. Or because they've tried to find poems that they might enjoy, but there are so many out there, they don't know where to start. When we do find poetry we appreciate or that speaks to us, it is usually because someone has shared it with us and that connection draws us in.

Poetry, or verse, is the oldest form of literature. It is really, as the poet Dana Gioia says, the primal form of all literature.[102] Poetry was flourishing as an oral art before the invention of writing. It is pre-historic. Verse stood at the center of cultures as the most powerful way of remembering, preserving, and transmitting the identity of a tribe, culture, or nation. It was, he says, humanity's first memory and broadcast technology—and the only way it was transmitted was by the human body.

Robert Frost—that most important American poet that you learned about sometime in school (or perhaps you had to memorize one of his poems)—says that poetry is a way of remembering what it would impoverish us to forget.[103] It enriches human consciousness; it protects things of common value from being lost.

One reason poetry has found its way into my life is because, as Dana Gioia explains, poetry is a distinct category of language—a special way of speaking that invites and rewards a special way of listening. At its foundation it is a form of oral communication, so poetry needs to sound different from ordinary speech.

It has in it a form, a demand/invitation to attention and to response. This is why there is meter (and different types of meters), rhyme (and different types of rhyme schemes), alliteration and assonance.

If done right, these elements, enchant (or heighten the attention of) the listener.

I keep referring to Dana Gioia—he has been one of my mentors and heroes in my pursuit and understanding of poetry. He says,

> Poetry offers a way of understanding and expressing existence that is fundamentally different from conceptual thought. . . . [Conceptual language] primarily addresses the intellect. It is analytical, which is to say, it takes things apart . . . Poetic language, however, is holistic and experiential. Poetry simultaneously addresses our intellect and our physical senses, our emotions, imagination, intuition, and memory without asking us to divide them.[104]

There are many truths we cannot understand except through poems, stories, songs, and images. Because, mysteriously, they touch on each aspect of being human.

But the way we interact with poetry is not the way ancient cultures interacted with it. Today, poetry is much more for the individual—maybe as a writing vocation or as a hobby or favorite reading material. Poetry doesn't move whole communities or bind people together as it once did.

For example, when America officially became the United States, many writers realized that we didn't have a mythology—like that of England, Greece, or Rome—that made us "us," so they started writing different stories and poems. This is why we have something like "Paul Revere's Ride." It made a fantastical story that everyone could know and use as a way of saying "that's our story, that's our hero." Another example: Hannah More, a friend to William Wilberforce, wrote poems against slavery and the slave trade that were shared throughout the upper classes and society of England. Her words were part of what helped end the slave trade in England. Before people and Parliament decided against this evil politically, they needed to be moved in their hearts. Hannah More's words did this.

In the past few years, poetry has taken up a larger part of my heart and mind. I would say it has been a means of grace—a way that God has sustained me—through this time with cancer. But even before I had cancer, poetry was something that interested me. Words and how they are put together has always been something that grabbed my attention. I remember when I discovered Micah 5:4: "He will stand and shepherd his flock in the strength of LORD, in the majesty of the name of the LORD his God. And they will live securely, for then his greatness will reach to the ends of the earth." I was a teenager when I read that. I didn't know exactly what it was about, but I had enough background in Bible learning to know this was Jesus. And I loved the picture it gave me of Him—my imagination was enlarged. That same year I also discovered "[cast] all your care upon Him, for He cares for you" (1 Pet. 5:7 NKJV). That picture of casting—throwing—what worried me onto God because He really did care for me made God seem so personal and close. This also enlarged my imagination.

And then—the psalms and proverbs. They are poetry, and the poetic language and metaphors have also drawn me closer to God. I realized this when I read "The name of the LORD is a strong tower; the righteous run to it and are safe" (Prov. 18:10 NKJV). I love history and I love architecture. And thinking of this idea, of crying out to God in His name because He is for me and will help me—that He is a strong tower—is comforting, even if it is mysterious. It is poetry. It speaks to me and my mind and heart even when I don't get it all. I'm in my fifties now and have spent much time throughout my life in Scripture, and the more time I spend in it the more I've come to see that the poetic nature of Scripture is how God communicates. He speaks, and it is good; He sends us Jesus, the Word of God made flesh. Then He calls us to be His workmanship—His *poeisis*—poem.

Words spoken for creating life, beauty, goodness, and truth started with God; they are rooted in our DNA as humans made in His image. These ideas about words and poetry and story have formed me as a follower of Jesus.

I enjoyed reading poems in school and having discussions about what they meant—I liked getting to the idea of what the poet was saying and how he got to his point. I liked seeing how one word or phrase built on another and the surprising ways poets used words.

In college I discovered Anne Bradstreet—the first American colonist to have her poets published. She was a Puritan—a hardworking wife and mother. Her poems married her love for God and His glory with her love for her family and home. I saw the struggle she had to rightly order her loves. I was excited to read her words and to see that her struggle was like my struggle, and I was encouraged in my young heart to keep trying to love God.

BY NIGHT WHEN OTHERS SOUNDLY SLEPT
Anne Bradstreet

1
By night when others soundly slept
And hath at once both ease and Rest,
My waking eyes were open kept
And so to lie I found it best.

2
I sought him whom my Soul did Love,
With tears I sought him earnestly.
He bow'd his ear down from Above.
In vain I did not seek or cry.

3
My hungry Soul he fill'd with Good;
He in his Bottle put my tears,
My smarting wounds washt in his blood,
And banisht thence my Doubts and fears.

4
What to my Saviour shall I give
Who freely hath done this for me?
I'll serve him here whilst I shall live
And Loue him to Eternity.

Years later, as a young mom, I loved reading poetry to my daughters when they were little. I found good poetry anthologies and enjoyed adding poems into our days. A few poems, like this one by Langston Hughes, became part of our ordinary life:

WINTER MOON
Langston Hughes

How thin and sharp is the moon tonight
How thin and sharp and ghostly white
is the slim curved crook of the moon tonight.

I also had an old book of Japanese poetry that I read to them during the week, and then we tried writing some haiku together. I love the simplicity of haiku and the way these Buddhist poets from centuries ago spoke words that I can still relate to and take delight in.

Stubborn woodpecker
Still hammering
At twilight
At that single spot[105]

As the girls got older they knew that, even if they were not into poetry like I was, poetry was part of our family culture. I read Billy Collins to them often because he made me laugh, but we also loved Aaron Belz's funky poetry—his absurd but somehow truthful short poems. Sometimes we still take them out to read to each other.

CRITIQUE
Aaron Belz

That's not very good
Try doing that differently
That's not very good either
You are not very good at this.

And one daughter would stand in the kitchen and read from *Now We Are Six* by A.A. Milne because that made her so happy.

When they were older, I would make pancake breakfasts and set the table with nice plates and silverware, and while we ate I would read poems by Luci Shaw and Malcolm Guite. Or we would read their poems together on other church calendar special days. I liked adding meaning to these days by sharing poems of these two writers that I love.

These are happy memories of a few of the little seeds that made us the Bustards. This is how poetry has been communal for me.

But it has also helped me grow as a person—to move beyond my anxieties, my discontentment, and my lack of trust in God. Luci Shaw's poetry has been a gift to me from God that has helped me in so many ways. By reading her poems I have learned to pay attention to how words work, how they move inside of me; her poems have helped me to see Scripture and the gospel and God's love more clearly. In some mysterious way, she has helped me pay better attention to the world around me. I started looking even more closely at trees, flowers, butterflies, grass, and clouds because of the way she talked about them. And by paying more attention, I have grown to love the world around me in a new, lifegiving way.

Marilyn McEntyre, one of my other favorite writers and poets, says this:

> Poems demand we slow down, notice patterns, reckon with ambiguities, consider subtle distinctions between one term or image and its alternative, and recognize the relationship between techniques and purposes. But we take this work on, if we practice finding paths through poems, staying with them as we tease out their possibilities, follow where they point us by allusion and suggestion, and unpack their metaphors . . . they teach us to listen more attentively . . . they restore to us what the noise and haste of commercial culture dull and destroy: being attuned to subtleties of sense and feeling, being awake to the possibilities of "an ordinary moment on an ordinary day." They train and exercise the imagination.[106]

I have found this to be true, especially with the work of Luci Shaw. This poem helped begin it all when I first discovered it twenty-five years ago:

I GAVE THIS DAY TO GOD
Luci Shaw

I gave this day to God when I got up, and look,
look what it birthed! There up the hill was
   the apple tree, bronze leaves, its fallen apples
spilling richly down the slope, the way God spilled
   his seed into Mary, into us. In her the holy promise
came to rest in generous soil after a long
   fall. How often it ends in gravel, or dry dust.
Blackberry patches thorny with distraction. Oh,
   I pray my soul will welcome always that small
seed. That I will hail it when it enters me.
   I don't mind being grit, soil, dirt, mud-brown,
laced with the rot of old leaves, if only the seed
   can find me, find a home and bear a fruit
sweet, flushed, full-fleshed—a glory apple.[107]

One aspect in which I've grown as a wife, mother, homemaker, caregiver, and friend has been learning that all of life can be an act of worship to God. All of life is sacred. And poetry has helped me enter into the beauty of even ordinary life and find ways to love it more deeply. Peter Peteira's poem "A Pot of Red Lentils" has done this for me (and I'm not even a fan of red lentils), as has Julie L. Moore's "Joy." But while there are so many poems I want to share that have moved my heart to love more deeply and have enlarged my imagination to love more deeply too, there are also poems—like Anya Silver's "Just Red"—that have helped me lament and be angry.

As I've grown in my love of other people's words, I have wanted to write my own. In October of 2020 I asked God to help me with this—I had written many poems when I was younger, but I felt rather embarrassed by my teenaged self and how dramatic she was. But I felt God's grace on her one day: I said to myself, like it was some new epiphany, what did I expect? Most teenagers are dramatic. So that helped me move on. I started to grow in courage—courage to be vulnerable even to myself, courage to ask for help and input, and courage to write about things and work on words and phrases and to say things that might feel hard or silly or too much. It's been a good journey during this time with cancer, and poetry has helped me work through things.

And as I write and as I have read poems, my cancer journey has been filled with creativity and beauty, so that the goodness and nearness of God was real, and the truth—even lots of hard truths—could be born. I don't know why this is—it is a mystery. But as I read the poets, I think they would agree.

12 noon, mid-February

Quiet morning snow gave way
to the patter of ice rain
on our roof and window sills.

When it stopped,
a faraway chatter of birds
filled the silence.

I could picture them in a tree
all bunched together,
feathers fluffed up.

Their beaks opening and closing,
their words incessant—
possibly a cheer for a reprieve from rain.

A thought of April floated through my mind—
of green and birds and flowers,
of spring showers and umbrellas.

Rain started again,
but the birds kept chattering.
And above them,

the caw caw caw of a lone blackbird,
and the peals of an old church bell
chiming noon.

THURSDAY

Sunday night when I learned there was more cancer,
that a year of fighting had not held off another tumor,

the place inside me where I imagine my emotions reside
was a yawning cavern, empty.

I decided it was denial, and let myself sleep long
and nap and wander around.
I thought of other people praying.

But today,
with the expanse of blue sky above me
and the silver drip of icicles I passed while walking the dog,

I know I must be waking up.

For, as I walked into the kitchen,
I thought of soups I want to make and
cookies I want to bake.

I looked for the Dickens book packed away in the basement.
I thought of pencil and paper and images and words.

I even hung the wooden red-and-white heart sign
from last Valentine's Day and
made dinner for you and me.

Stephen Crotts

A Hidden Life

For you have died, and your life is hidden with Christ.
—Colossians 3:3

Most years the Lenten season comes and goes without me giving up anything. One year I successfully stayed off Facebook for forty days . . . or maybe I did not eat chocolate? Or maybe I just made it into a memory. But this year I am beginning to understand Lent as a time to pay attention to which things I rely on more than I rely on the Holy Spirit or Christ's righteousness. And so I have spent these past forty days learning more from God about what He has for me—a hidden life.

When I find myself dissatisfied with being seen and known by only those who love me and instead want affirmation from people "out there"; or when I am anxious that the work of my hands won't be noticed by enough people to make it feel worthwhile; or when I forget the miracle of this past year without tumors and instead fixate on how unhappy I am about the weight I've gained (as a side effect of the medicines I take to fight cancer), I am learning to I say to myself and to Jesus, "A hidden life . . ."

I feel a whispered peace settle me.
And it is like the start of spring.

As we come out of winter, we begin to wake up to more sunshine, blue clouds, and bird song. Light seems to escape from the within the baby green leaves. Pink and purple crocuses carpet green yards. White-flowered branches and cherry blossoms spill over the sidewalk. Forsythia with its wild yellow explodes in hedges lining the roads. Life that was hidden in the ground and in the trees comes out into the open.

> My frame was not hidden from you,
> when I was being made in secret,
> intricately woven in the depths of the earth.
> (Psalm 139:15)

I think I will order a butterfly kit from Insect Lore just to watch caterpillars turn into butterflies. A cup of caterpillars and their food will arrive in the mail. Caterpillars will eat and grow and grow, and then one day each of them will form their own chrysalises. Eventually, butterflies will emerge, ready to wing their way out into the world. Hidden life becomes new life.

Just like winter turning into spring, the caterpillar's transformation is such a good metaphor for what happens in hidden places. I have been thinking of other examples.

Like each one of my babies, when they were still in my womb. The magical experiences of their first flutters, feeling their hidden presence inside. I loved how each time I was pregnant I could feel a tiny pushy foot, my daughters' hiccups, or their somersaults. Life was growing, but it was hidden from my sight.

Or my tumors hiding deep inside my body—one grew so big it made a huge lump under my skin. A couple grew in places I could not feel. I take my meds every day, and they work into the dark parts of my body, keeping melanoma or breast cancer cells from growing. It's a hidden work that only God can see. Learning to

Greatest in the Kingdom
Ned Bustard

trust God in all the dark places is part of the new life He is growing in me.

What else is hidden? Treasures in our hearts. The promise of heaven, vouchsafed by the Holy Ghost. Living water springs out of our hearts and flows to other people. Finding shelter in God as our high tower. Grace upon grace. The deep calling unto deep. Dying. Being buried. Resurrection and new bodies.

Faith. Our eyes cannot see Jesus, and our hands cannot touch Him. But He makes Himself known. God's words are deep inside of us.

> In him was life, and the life was the light of men. The light shines
> in the darkness, and the darkness has not overcome it.
> (John 1:4–5)

Christ's life was hidden—Eternity taking up space in a body. Jesus lived in a small village before it was the time to bring the kingdom of God out of the shadows. Sometimes He directed people not to tell anyone He was the promised Messiah; they were to keep this truth hidden—that He was the king and high priest who loved those most people did not care to see. Then His death tore down the curtain that hid the Holy of Holies from the world. Now we do not need to hide our faces from God. We are hidden in Christ and united to Him; we'll live in the presence of God for eternity, without shame covering us. His dead body is no longer hidden in a grave. His resurrection brings light and life to us and to the world.

> When Christ who is your life appears,
> then you also will appear with him in glory.
> (Colossians 3:4)

And as I hide His word in my heart, I will learn what it means to be a tree planted by streams of living water, with roots deep down in the soil, leaves shining light from the inside out, flowers spilling over, and fruit bursting with sweetness.

THE WAY THINGS ARE

I
Cancer hides in darkness—billeted inside.
If not dealt with, tumors will wreak havoc
in unknown places around my body.

II
The other day, as I turned onto Barley Mill Road,
I caught a glimpse of a single tiny ash leaf.
Its yellow glow skimmed a breeze.

III
Each afternoon this week,
a monarch returns to my butterfly bush.
Its orange wings flirting with the flowers.

IV
Rays of light dispersing through green-filled
branches, flowering morning glories, and
quick flights of swallows in the early night sky,

and Jesus.

BE STILL

The LORD will fight for you; you need only to be still.
—Exodus 14:14

My drug of choice is Benadryl—
pure, in its liquid form, and
shot straight into my port.
I can count backward from ten,
and then find myself
disconnected from my head,
heavy and sleepy.
I need a multitude of drugs
to attack this cancer,
ones I can hardly spell or pronounce.
There is Anastrozole and encorafenib
and binimetinib.
But Benadryl puts me to sleep
while Kanjinti courses through me—
so that I can say to God,
    I was still while you fought for me.

Naturografia di Lago
Roberto Ghezzi

CAPTURING BEAUTY: THE ART
OF ROBERTO GHEZZI

I look and look.
Looking's a way of being: one becomes,
sometimes a pair of eyes walking.
Walking wherever looking takes one.
The eyes dig and burrow into the world.
—Denise Levertov,

Like a young child in need of attention, the natural world around us demands our gaze and delight. As Denise Levertov highlights in her poem "Looking, Walking, Being," the habit of really looking is like allowing our eyes to take us for a walk around the world and root us in it. And in this looking, we see the world bearing witness that "beauty is goodness made manifest to the senses."[108]

It seems almost cliché to ask, "What is beauty?" Throughout the twentieth century, the art world mocked the idea of creating beauty; serious artists did not pursue it. Daniel Finch, painter and art professor at Messiah University, once commented that when he was in art school, the worst thing that could be said of someone's work during a class critique was "Oh, your piece is very beautiful." In contrast, Makoto Fujimura, an artist seeking to revitalize the place of beauty in the arts, helpfully elaborates, "Beauty is the quality connected with those things that are in themselves appealing and desirable. Beautiful things are a delight to the senses, a pleasure to the mind, a refreshment for the spirit."[109]

The Italian artist Roberto Ghezzi's sublime work helps us to see the goodness and glory of beauty made manifest to the senses. His vision is to capture beauty by partnering with nature. He is known for artistic research that remains in close contact with water and earth. Instead of calling what he does "art work" he calls it *Naturografia*. Roberto's work seems to embody Fujimura's words: "I wanted to help recover a view of beauty as a gift we discover, receive, and steward."[110]

Nature is that gift worth discovering. Roberto shows us an example of stewarding it well as he works with natural materials and within natural settings. An accomplished, classically trained painter, he states, "Man has always created works of art by painting nature, or using elements of nature, or in nature: *Naturografia* is a living work where artist and nature collaborate together."[111]

He elaborates: "My research has been enriched with extraordinary experiences, and I have been able to dialogue with different environments, from the brackish lagoon to the mountain stream, from the man-made port to the river park."[112] Traveling the world to find environments to collaborate with, and using specific techniques and tools, Roberto partners with the light, land, water, vegetation, minerals, and living organisms to create a portrait of that area. Instead of painting what he sees in the wild, he dialogues with the elements to create a visual testimony of its life.

A recent issue of *SEEN Journal* explained Roberto's technique:

> Ghezzi specifically places the canvases in sites selected due to their environment—chemical, physical, and biological characteristics. Landscape elements include weather occurrences that will give back a different stratification of sediments and traces on each support prepared to accommodate them. The differences in water level due to tides and rain, wind, soil and sand, insects, and other small animals, but also molds, algae, leaves, and twigs, each will leave their footprint and create a kind of identity card.[113]

It's this residue that is captured on Ghezzi's finely woven materials or wooden boards and then displayed in art galleries.

During a trip to Italy in early December 2019, I experienced *beauty as goodness made manifest to the senses* in Roberto's collaborative work with nature. While attending an opening night for new artwork in a local gallery with my husband and friends, I found Roberto's piece in an outside courtyard, hanging between two sturdy poles and illuminated by a bright light. Its dreamy appearance beckoned us forward, and we found we could walk around it and view both sides. When seen from afar, it initially reminded me of a Rothko painting with its swaths of light browns

Installazione per la Creazione di Naturografie
Roberto Ghezzi

and pale purple-blue whites. But as we moved closer and examined it carefully, I could see sediment and the small debris of twigs, insect body parts, and other unidentifiable detritus. Sandwiched in the center of this work was a branch, as if rooted in the light-brown bottom and stretching into the blue, sky-like, upper half of the piece. I had never experienced such beauty and innocence in a piece of art. Several times during the rest of the evening I found myself returning to the courtyard to re-examine and enjoy it.

The next day, we traveled to Cortona, the ancient hilltop city in Tuscany, Italy, to have lunch with Roberto, who is a long-time friend of one of my traveling companions. Sitting together in one of his favorite restaurants, we talked about his work while enjoying our house-made pasta and local red wine. When we asked Roberto about his vision for his work, he said, without a pause, "I want to capture beauty." Having just experienced his work in person the night before, I knew he was fulfilling this goal.

Makoto Fujimura writes, "Beauty invites us in, capturing our attention and making us want to linger."[114] I see this invitation in Roberto Ghezzi's work, as he invites us to look and to look again. In his *Naturographia*, Ghezzi captures these moments of natural beauty and gives us an opportunity to see them differently—to pause before them, to linger. And to say, in wonder, "How many are your works, Lord! In wisdom you made them all; the earth is full of your creatures" (Ps. 104:24 NIV).

A Poem for Lent

With February full of family birthdays
and Valentine's Day,
Lent usually finds me unprepared.
I've spent my energy on presents and chocolate.

I realize the season of repentance has begun
when I see smudged crosses on my neighbors' foreheads
and hear what friends are giving up for forty days.

But me, my hands are empty,
and I'm already repenting of forgetfulness.

It's a little like heading to my tool shed on a Saturday morning,
ready to prepare for spring planting,
only to realize I've forgotten to replace the rusty, cracked shovel
and broken green hose.

What a grace to arrive Easter day singing
Alleluia.
And what a glory to see the yellow of forsythia
and tulips blooming red.[115]

THE END OF WINTER

Leaf-empty oak trees—
their profiles resting
on blue-dusky skies—
invite a lingering look
over their lines, their stillness.
They ask us to consider our
souls, exposed to this wide world,
and to make space for coming
birds and their nests,
to listen for the wind's hum,
and to capture light
as it makes its way
down to our taproots.

Tracery
Leslie Bustard

ASH WEDNESDAY

For thus said the LORD God, the Holy One of Israel, "In returning and rest
you shall be saved; in quietness and in trust shall be your strength . . ."
—Isaiah 30:15

This Ash Wednesday, Ned and I actually made it to the 7 a.m. service at church to receive the ashes on our foreheads. This is only the second time in my life I've made the effort—the first was years and years ago when I walked with a young friend to our neighborhood Catholic church's evening service. It was all new to me, and I enjoyed it. But this Ash Wednesday felt different.

There was a short time of responsive readings and prayers. At the end we went forward the way we do every Sunday for communion. We shuffled out of our pews, and in two single files slowly made our way to the front where our two pastors stood. As I stood behind my friend Rebecca, I could hear Pastor Keith say, "Remember that you are dust and to dust you shall return." And I thought, "Oh dear, this is a little too real for me now." I don't know how to describe the tiny, electric, uncomfortable-under-my-skin-feeling I had while I waited, but I was aware of it. When I stepped up to Keith, I had not noticed a few pieces of hair hanging over my forehead. Pastor Keith smiled at me while he pushed my hair aside to put the sign of the cross with the ashes on my forehead; the twinkle in Keith's eyes caused a slight snort-laugh to escape my lips. I thought, "Oh, so this is how I'm going to respond to this solemn moment of getting the cross put on my forehead by my pastor—like an uncomfortable middle school girl?"

When we got home, I fell asleep on the couch and slept for a couple hours. When I woke up, I mindlessly rubbed my forehead, mussing up the sign of the cross that Keith had placed earlier that morning. Now I looked like a little kid with a dirty face. I didn't wash it off until the evening—I thought it was poetic to have some black smudges above my eyes.

This Ash Wednesday felt like a comedy of sorts—the comedy of being a needy, messy human in a holy moment. Here I am, Jesus. Please keep making all things new, me included.

. . .

The day before Ash Wednesday, I had a PET scan and happily learned there are still no tumors taking up space in my body. It was a clear and clean scan. I was given my own little resurrection.

On Ash Wednesday, I spent most of the day in the kitchen, trying out a new potato soup recipe and baking banana bread and apple muffins. White whole wheat, apples, oatmeal, dried cherries, maple syrup—just my kind of perfect. (Ned's banana bread has chocolate chips in it—just his kind of perfect.) Since I haven't had a lot of desire to be creative in the kitchen, this time was a way for me to live into that little resurrection.

...

The day after Ash Wednesday, Ned and I went to the memorial service of Fay Goddard. Fay was part of the core group of people who started Wheatland Church. Ned and I were in our late twenties and Carey was two when we met her. With her housemate Dorcas Simpson, Fay was in our first care group at Wheatland. She had become paralyzed by polio while serving as a missionary in the Philippines over twenty-five years ago, but being in a wheelchair didn't

Fay Goddard, 1954

slow Fay down. She was full of life and served and loved the Lord and people wherever she was and in many creative and rich ways. When Carey heard Fay had died, she said, "Fay was one of those church people who are at the core of who I am."

During her memorial service we all sang Fay's favorite hymns—"The Old Rugged Cross" and "All the Way My Savior Leads Me"—old gospel songs I hadn't sung in decades. But they were good ones to sing at the beginning of Lent, while thinking about Fay and the hope we have in Jesus and His resurrection.

A Prayer For Morning Time

Dear Heavenly Father,

Here we are together before you,
about to listen to stories,
sing songs, and enjoy pictures.
These are part of your big beautiful world.
You have given us such an abundance
of goodness to learn about.
Thank you.

Today, may we learn a little more
and enjoy a little more,
so that we may keep adding to
the treasure that is in our hearts and minds.
Help each of us to find something new to
remember and to be glad about.

Even though we sit together,
we each have our own ideas and dreams
rolling around in our minds.
Help us to remember them later today,
so we can pay attention to
what we are doing right now.

Thank you for giving us each
a whole day to learn more of your love for us.
And thank you for helping us learn
how to love you in our learning
and in our playing.

Lord, you are good and kind.[116]

PENITENT MAGDALEN

So teach us to number our days
that we may get a heart of wisdom.
—Psalm 90:12

Bruce Herman

Bruce Herman, a long-distance friend and respected artist whose work I have admired for a long time, recently sent me a piece of original art. It is a sketch, its lines and shadowing rendered in orange colored pencils, after Georges de La Tour's *The Penitent Magdalen.* His gift arrived during a time when I was wrestling in myself and talking with God about the mystery of the length of my days, so the timing of this gift, as well as the subject matter, felt very much of the Lord.

French Baroque artist Georges de La Tour actually painted four versions of *The Penitent Magdalen,* each one of Mary at a mirror. Bruce Herman based his piece on the one done in oil on canvas that is found in the Metropolitan Museum of Art.

Mary was one of the women followers of Jesus. After Jesus removed seven demons from her, Mary joined with other women in providing for Him and His disciples out of their own means. Mary appears throughout the Gospels; it is easy to imagine that she was with Jesus and the disciples as they traveled around Galilee. Mary Magdalen was with Mary, Jesus' mother, when He was crucified on the cross. After Christ's death, she went with other women to the garden to take care of His body with spices, only to discover that the tomb was empty. My favorite story is about how Mary stayed in the garden, where Christ's tomb was, crying and asking the gardener where He had taken the body of Jesus. When the gardener speaks her name, "Mary," she suddenly knows she's speaking to Jesus, resurrected (John 20:11–18).

The first thing I am drawn to in La Tour's painting is the gilded frame with the mirror and double image of the candle. From there my eye follows the invisible line toward Mary's head and her upper body. I see the light shining in the mirror and onto her white skin exposed by the V-shaped drape-y white blouse. My eyes follow down to her red skirt and to her hands folded on the top of the skull resting on her lap. The painting loosely fits into a triangular form, helping my eyes take in the other elements in this scene.

This painting speaks not just through her contemplative face but also through symbolism. The candle sitting on the table and reflecting in the mirror represents the Light of Christ. See how the light shines both in the darkness and in the mirror, illuminating Mary's face and her upper body and white blouse? The real candle and its mirrored image give off a double light.

As Mary may have heard Christ say "I am the light of the world" (John 8:12), as well as "let your light shine before others" (Matt. 5:16), I am drawn to the double-lighted image of the flickering candle. In many Rembrandt paintings, the light comes from the outside, such as an upper right corner, and flows down and across the painting. "With La Tour," Christopher P. Jones writes, "his lighting is nearly always *inside* the picture. It is often the very focus of the attention, glowing like the nucleus of the work, so that all the other features tend to be arranged around this light source, creating a bubble of light and an extreme 'vignette' around the outer edges."[117] It makes sense to me that this light, representing Jesus, is what my eye is drawn to first.

The skull represents death. It brings to mind Shakespeare's play *Hamlet* and the famous speech "To be or not to be . . . that is the question." In this soliloquy, among other thoughts, Hamlet is meditating on death. Many times when the play is presented he is holding up or looking at a skull. Here Mary has the skull on her lap and her fingers are intertwined together, resting on the skull.

The gilded mirror and the jewels on the table (and also on the floor) are said to represent the vanities of the world. Notice how the jewelry is not easily seen. Mary seems to have put aside the vain treasures of the world.

Lastly, I wonder why La Tour chose a white blouse and a red skirt. This could symbolize how Christ washed her in his blood and covered her with his righteousness.

What also grabs my attention is how Mary gazes above the mirror and the candle. Is someone coming into the room? Is there a noise somewhere? Can we imagine what she is thinking about? Is she pondering death? The length of her days? The knowledge that one day death and the vanities of the world will be no more? Is she remembering the Light of the World who walked with her? Or looking forward to the day when she will see Jesus again and be fully known?

Although art historians have written or discussed what La Tour may have been seeking to communicate through this painting, *The Penitent Mary*—especially the piece Bruce Herman made for me—offers different thoughts to me.

When I think of the skull, I am reminded to keep praying Psalm 90:12: "Teach us to number our days that we may get a heart of wisdom." But the light of the candle reminds me of the good promise in John 1:5: "The light shines in the darkness and the darkness has not overcome it." And then I remember 1 Corinthians 13:12: "For now we see in a mirror dimly; but then face to face. Now I know in part; then I shall know fully, even as I have been fully known." The shadow of cancer and death is a reality, but it is not the final reality. Jesus' light and the hope I carry of seeing Him face to face and fully knowing whatever there is to know—that is the final reality..

During my first year of cancer, which also included the shadow of COVID, a small painting of a badger served as a reminder to actively remember that Jesus was with me and that He is faithful to me. This was my reminder because, as Trufflehunter explains in *Prince Caspian*, "[Badgers] don't forget."[118] This year, I have been looking at this piece by Bruce Herman as a reminder to turn my heart and thoughts to Scripture and to Jesus and to ask Him to help me rest in Him.

Psalm 90:12 has always been a favorite verse of mine. I love this prayer—that God would help me grow in wisdom. I have also loved the last

Trufflehunter
Jamin Still

verse: "Let the favor of the Lord our God be upon us, and establish the work of our hands upon us; yes, establish the work of our hands!" As I am living days whose number only God knows, I want to live well, even when I'm weary of the unknown or anxious about tumors. I want God to keep giving me good work to do. And I want His light to shine in my darkness and out into the places where He has put me.

Easter '57

Easter '57
is scribbled on the back
of a torn black and white—
her Sunday dress blown by
a breeze, his face caught
between a squint and a stare.

My mom was ten then.
In a few years the farm
they labored hard for would
fail, the cows would be sold
and a house in town bought.
Her mother would fall sick
and her dad grow weary.

Thirty years later, we
headed down south to find
their gravestone, like their farm,
well-tended and tidy.
The house in town was lost
to wild weeds and decay.

William and Pauline Carey

Mom once told me she saw
her dad in my brother—
both dark-haired and lanky.

And me—I don't have much
else but a few stories
and my love for a black
and white of two people
standing straight and tall on
a sunny, windy day
of Easter '57.[119]

QUIET I

A robin's egg in a nest,

a row of yellow tulips, petals closed,

the last few shadowed moments
on the eastern horizon,

and Holy Saturday,
as Christ was lying in the sealed tomb,
   and angels were waiting.

QUIET II

That moment before sleep takes over,
I slowly free fall
into a yawning, empty space,

and for a few minutes,
all I hear is whir of wind
as it rattles old window panes,
the ring of a neighbor's chimes,
and rain on the porch roof.

I'll keep falling like Alice
who tumbled into Wonderland
then land shoeless on the street
in front of my childhood home.

Here God and His angels sit
behind clouds,
the moon hangs low and brightly amber.
I'll find a hiding place
near flowering honeysuckle,
where only the Holy Ghost can find me.

courage

Courage can overcome despair.
—Charlotte Brontë

Early morning drizzle, hard and gray . . .

Primroses on my windowsill are yellow and bright,
a promise of spring days ahead.

Outside, a mourning dove sighs.
A patch of snowdrops, green and white,
clump together, trying to keep warm.

Chattering birds flit from tree to fence to grass.
Their heads bob up and down,
poking around for food.

A red cardinal appears, and
a sweet sense of courage rises in my throat.

tonsure

Like me, with my skin
and scar exposed, did newly-
vowed monks think of rain
and wind on their bare heads as
reminders of Christ with them?

courage for the now, now, and now and now

> Here I am, still present
> in this place and time, alive to live this
> day that is *today*, still moved by beauty,
> stirred by song and story, yet comforted
> by the good company of friends, still capable
> of rich conversation and laughter and
> moments of joy and right sorrow . . .
> — Douglas Kaine McKelvey

It's been seventeen months since I learned I had both stage II breast cancer and stage IV melanoma. I know that my length of time is not the longest any one has had to endure; it is just the length of my valley of the shadow-of-death story so far. During this time I have learned what it means to be sustained and cared for by God. And now it has become the time for me to learn what it means to abide in Christ, the one who also walked in the valley, as I learn of His courage and fortitude.

When both cancers were confirmed last January, I was sad and tired. Simultaneously, I felt a real sense of God's sustaining presence. The words in Joshua 1:9, "Do not be afraid . . . for the LORD your God will be with you wherever you go" (NIV), had already been rooted in my heart from years of meditating on Scripture and seeing this beautiful promise repeated over and over throughout the Old and New Testaments.

I tried to pay attention, with a seeking heart, to how God's presence was real in my life. Along the way, I was given a multitude of prayers, cards, gifts, encouraging messages, time with family and friends, and faithful words. God used the Body of Christ to show His tangible presence in those sorrowful days. My friend Katy, during her hard breast cancer fight, found community, listening ears, poetry, psalms, music, and writing to be a means of grace for her. This was true for me, too. Although I knew what was happening had a real heaviness to it, I felt wrapped in a cocoon of on-going goodness. I sought to follow the words of Walter Wangerin Jr. as he reflected on the winter walks he took while battling cancer: "Maybe this is my last opportunity to walk in a winter's snowfall. Not to make a memory of it, but to know it now."[120]

Paying attention to and delighting in what I saw around me became a daily goal; I loved the beauty of blue skies, the music of birds' songs, and the vibrant pinks, yellows, and greens in the flowers and trees. On my long morning walks, I particularly loved watching the sunlight shining through leaves and through leaf-filled branches . Like Walter Wangerin, I wanted to do more then make a memory of the world around me, as if storing up experiences before I died; I wanted to know this beauty now. "However short or long my personal journey hereafter (a year, years, or half a year) time present remains for me what it always was before: an opportunity to pay attention. Time doesn't become more intense. Time is . . . time. I am now. It is enough."[121]

Being sustained was the theme of my first year of cancer—sustained through all the tears and tests, the waiting for results, the medications' hard side effects, the ongoing fatigue, as well as surgery and recovery from surgery. If someone asked me how I was doing, one quick (and truthful) answer would be: "I feel sustained by God. I don't know how God's sovereignty and this cancer He has called me to go together. But I know He is good and He has it in hand."

Shadows of Glory
Leslie Bustard

As a dear friend who has also battled breast cancer said to me, "I think of the friends that brought the paralytic to Jesus through the roof. They carried him on a mat and lifted him down to the feet of Jesus. In Mark it says that 'when Jesus saw *their* faith, he said to the paralytic, son your sins are forgiven.' When you have cancer you are on the mat. And it is those who surround you with prayer and love who are carrying you to Jesus." I learned this to be true in my experience as well. When all I could pray was the Lord's Prayer, Psalm 23, or just "Lord, have mercy," I rested in being the paralytic on the mat, with my friends taking me to Jesus.

. . .

At the start of this new year, my heart and mind are stumbling along this path I have been given to walk. I am not doubting God's goodness or presence, but questions have been tumbling around in my mind. In March a new, aggressive tumor showed up in my left arm. A couple of weeks after surgery to remove it and twenty-four lymph nodes, two more tumors showed up on a PET scan. At one point I said to God, "I figured more tumors would come, but so soon after surgery? I thought I would get a chance to recover first."

The reality of the mystery of my days loomed larger in my head, especially after my oncologist reminded me that the word "remission" would not be part of my vocabulary in the years ahead. I would need to get my head around living with cancer the way one lives with a chronic disease. My doctor said we would be playing whack-a-mole—when something comes up, we would deal with it. I had been told this last year, but the reality of it is becoming more concrete in my mind now.

How can I live well in this, not knowing how long I will have? Stage IV melanoma patients usually live for five years. And when I add to that knowledge the complications of fighting stage II breast cancer, it's suddenly easy to get stuck in the quicksand of sorrow. My length of days is a mystery. As folks will remind me, "We all know we will die—you just have that knowledge hanging over your everyday life." How does Jesus help me through this? What does courage and fortitude look like now?

Timothy Keller, in an *Atlantic* essay, shared his thoughts on learning of his pancreatic cancer:

> But as death, the last enemy, became real to my heart, I realized that my beliefs would have to become just as real to my heart, or I wouldn't be able to get through the day. Theoretical ideas about God's love and the future resurrection had to become life-gripping truths, or be discarded as useless.[122]

This had been my reality, but I need more of the hope of the resurrection in my everyday life, so I don't obsess over how long God knows I will live.

My favorite band gives voice to my plight as they sing,

> I'm lost in the waves that crush me . . .
> I see the light but never find the surface
> I don't know if I can swim no more
> White knuckles and wild horses
> One day we'll wash up on mercy's shore[123]

. . .

I am asking God to help me dig deeper into the "now" of my days, but for this, I need courage and fortitude. Brad Littlejohn defines fortitude as "not just the gutsy determination to stare death in the face and laugh ... [but] the long slow fortitude of bearing up under the recognition that life may never be quite the same as it was, the recognition that some hopes and dreams will need to be painfully and persistently rebuilt."[124] When did Jesus first realize that He was walking a road to a gruesome death? Was it when He was young, standing among the religious teachers in the Temple? Perhaps it was when He heard the Suffering Servant passages in the writings of Isaiah? Did His mother Mary tell him? Or did He remember the whispers of a faraway conversation before time began of the plans to redeem a people through a great sacrifice? I wonder about this often.

XXIII
Ned Bustard

Christ walked as one who knew He was living for love and for death and for resurrection. I want to be like Him, loving well the people God has given me, sharing my gifts with those around me, enjoying all the good things that come to me, and not ruled by the questions of the future. Wendell Berry's character Hannah Coulter says it well: "And so you have a life that you are living only now, now, and now and now, gone before you can speak of it, and you must be thankful for living day by day, moment by moment, in this presence."[125]

I want to live now, now, and now and now. The hope of seeing Jesus is real, and I look forward to eternity in His New Creation, but before then, I want to grab hold of my family and friends, and love, laugh, dance, travel, read books, go to museums, and sit on the beach.

The presence of Jesus in my days gives me courage and the desire to keep going; knowing He loved and served His people as He walked toward a violent death on a cross means I have a sympathetic high priest hearing my prayers and making available to me all that I need to live like Him. The promise to be strong and courageous because He will not leave me or forsake me is still true, even if my struggles with this cancer grow harder and heavier.

Still, every week I am reminded of the reality behind the reality I see. Each Sunday, my pastor proclaims "The gifts of God for the people of God" and "This Table is a place of nourishment for followers of Jesus Christ. All baptized Christians who trust in Christ alone . . . and seek strength to live more faithfully are welcome to eat this meal."

After taking in the bread and the wine, in unison we pray, "Everliving God, thank you for feeding us with these holy mysteries—the spiritual food of the Body and Blood of your Son. Heavenly Father, please assist us with your grace, that we may continue in holy fellowship with you, and do all such good works that you have prepared for us to walk in; through Jesus Christ our Lord. Amen."

Communion each Sunday has been a reminder that God is present in my life. He is the source of my strength and my courage to keep living in the *now*, no matter the mystery and the shadows, while still hoping in a forever future of living before Him. How good God is to not only sustain me in this time, but also to give me gifts like these to enlarge the growing fortitude in my heart.

> For all these blessings I give you praise.
> Knowing that today—this day—is a day
> you have decreed I should live; and so I can
> trust it is also a day in which you will supply
> every grace that is necessary for my soul to
> flourish, though my body weakens.
>
> Even when I stand at that utter edge of mortal life,
> I would . . . praise you for your long faithfulness.[126]

THE BOUNDARY LINES HAVE FALLEN FOR ME IN PLEASANT PLACES[127]

810 Woodsdale
Joshua Kiehl

We sat in the driveway of my mom's home, looking at its gray and wheat-colored stone facade. I could sense that my mom was silently absorbing all she could as she sat next to me in the car; I was remembering what every room looked like behind each of the windows. The "For Sale" sign positioned at the edge of the yard, just outside my view, nagged at me.

After a while I took her hand and, looking her in the eye, tearfully said, "You did a good work in there. It was hard, I know, but you loved us well."

My mom squeezed my hand and said, "I did, didn't I?"

That was the last time we saw the house before the buyers signed the papers; that was the goodbye I didn't know was a goodbye to the place my mom had made her home for fifty-two years—my whole life. Within a week, COVID exploded and we were both required to quarantine for health reasons. The next month, the keys to 810 (our nickname for the house) were handed over to strangers.

. . .

How could I say goodbye to my childhood home without the opportunity to walk through each room, taking that last look out the front window, running my fingers down the smooth wooden banister, or standing in my old bedroom, remembering where the Duran Duran poster hung?

These days, I have been wandering around the house in my mind, trying to attend carefully to all the details, trying to settle the memories of this home— what has been part of the filling of my years—into a place in my soul, and trying to honor the woman who put her heart and hands to making one place *very good* for her family.

THE BOUNDARY LINES HAVE FALLEN FOR ME IN PLEASANT PLACES. PSALM 16:6

The street, flat and long enough for bikes with training wheels, red wagons, roller skates, and skateboards . . .

The split rail fence, made by Dad's hands, marking the east, west, and south perimeter of a less than half-acre plot . . .

The old trees standing in each corner of the backyard, for the tree house, the gathering of holly greens, and even the rescue of a stray, gray cat . . .

The backyard, a green expanse where dogs could run and children could play *Star Wars* . . .

The stone, locally quarried, paired with the Williamsburg blue front door and wooden shutters . . .

The smooth, honey-colored wooden floors reflecting the sunlight in the living room . . .

BY KNOWLEDGE THE rooms are FILLED WITH aLL precious anD PLEasanT riches. proverbs 24:4

The living room carpet, positioned in just the right place for spreading out new Legos each Christmas afternoon . . .

The warm brown sheen of the simple dining room table, its leaves facing down and waiting to be put up for a holiday meal . . .

The antique corner hutch, displaying the dark green lemonade set with pitcher and glasses, treasures of never-known grandparents . . .

Speakers in the living room and the family room, connected to one stereo system, to play the Christmas music loud . . .

The family room's green plaid couch, long enough for three young granddaughters to crowd around their Mum-Mum . . .

A bedroom-turned-office, with a typewriter and keyboards, for little girls to clump around in Mum-Mum's shoes, playing secretary . . .

The double-oven stove, cooking two pies on Thanksgiving morning and several dishes and a turkey later in the day . . .

THE WISE WOMAN BUILDS HER HOUSE. PROVERBS 14:1

My mom, from the age of twenty-one, learning the ways of commitment to one man and one place . . .

Working hard at home for a family of four and giving years of conscientious attention to working outside the home . . .

Inviting people in and keeping the screened-in porch available for long chats and tall drinks . . .

Planning carefully for each all-the-family-comes-home holiday meal and always ready for loved ones to walk through the door . . .

Preparing my brother's old room, "the dormitory," with crisp sheets and clean towels, so it's ready when family arrives . . .

Snuggling grandbabies in her arms, making crispy scrapple when grandchildren sleep over, and caring for teenage joys and sorrows . . .

Keeping a calendar for home upkeep and repairs so she knows when the furnace needs to be serviced and the roof inspected . . .

Lending a ready ear, supportive words, and serving hands—a stubborn love for each of us.

. . .

Even though my mom's maple-colored dry sink now stands in my living room, piles of family photos have been divided up, and boxes of cherished miscellaneous items have been placed on shelves in my basement, it does not feel possible that we won't return to 810 for Thanksgiving—to watch the Macy's Day Parade in the morning, to eat Fritos and laugh with my brother and his family in the afternoon, and then gather around the dining room table for our traditional meal.

My goodbye to 810 is incomplete. I spend time during this pandemic free-writing details of each room and asking questions of my life in this place, hoping that writing will give me some answers. Maybe I will re-watch the movie *A Ghost Story*—I can relate to the ghost, wandering unseen in a white sheet through his house, looking at the new lives in his home. But in my daydreams, I am a ghost observing all the younger selves of me and my family. I don't know where all this mind-meandering will lead.

BUT I, THROUGH THE ABUNDANCE OF YOUR STEADFAST LOVE, WILL ENTER YOUR HOUSE PSALM 5:7

But by God's kindness, as I look back, I see abundance—years of abundance, spilling in and out of a Williamsburg blue front door and binding a family together. Following are two recipes that remind me of home.

My Grandmother's Cookies

INGREDIENTS

Annie Travlis Symons

1 cup golden raisins
½ cup margarine
½ cup Crisco
1 cup sugar
2 eggs
2 cups flour
2 cups regular oatmeal
½ tsp. salt
½ tsp. baking soda
1 tsp. cinnamon
½ tsp. allspice
½ tsp. cloves

Preheat oven to 350°. Cook raisins in boiling water for five minutes (save six tablespoons of the water). Cream margarine, Crisco, sugar, and eggs together. In separate bowl, combine flour, oatmeal, salt, baking soda, cinnamon, allspice, and cloves.

To the shortening mixture, alternate adding the flour mixture and the raisins in reserved water. Mix well.

Drop by teaspoon-full onto greased cookie tray, and bake.

Bake at 350 for ten minutes.

Brown Sugar Cinnamon Rolls

INGREDIENTS *(for the dough[128])*

2 cups whole milk
1 cup vegetable oil
½ cup sugar
1 pkg. (2¼ tsp.) active dry yeast
4½ cups all-purpose flour
½ tsp. baking powder
½ tsp. baking soda
½ tbsp. salt

Leslie's mom with her granddaughters

In a medium saucepan over medium heat, stir together milk, vegetable oil, and sugar; keep from boiling. Remove from heat and let sit until lukewarm.

Sprinkle the yeast on top of milk mixture and let sit for 1 minute.

Measure 4 cups of flour into a large bowl, then add liquid-yeast mixture. Stir until just combined, cover with a clean kitchen towel, and set aside in a relatively warm place for 1 hour; it will spend this rising and doubling in size.

Remove the towel and add the baking powder, baking soda, salt, and remaining ½ cup flour. Stir thoroughly to combine. Use the dough right away. (Or you can place the mixing bowl in the refrigerator for up to 3 days. The dough will rise during this time, so punch it down when it rises to the top.)

INGREDIENTS *(for the filling[129])*

⅔ cup dark brown sugar
1½ tbsp. ground cinnamon
½ cup unsalted butter, melted *(or more if you want!)*

Mix together the brown sugar and the cinnamon in a bowl and set aside.

ASSEMBLE THE ROLLS

Remove dough from the pan. On a floured baking surface, roll into a large rectangle—not too thin and not too thick.

Spread melted butter all over the rectangle, then sprinkle sugar mixture on top of the butter so that it covers the surface. (If you want more butter and more sugar, go ahead and do it!)

Starting on the long side, roll the rectangle tightly toward its other side. Use both hands and work slowly, being careful to keep the roll tight. Pinch the seams together.

On a cutting board, with a sharp knife, make 1½-inch slices.

Melt a little more butter and pour all over the bottom of your chosen baking dish (I use a 13×9 baking dish).

Place the sliced rolls in the baking dish; try not to overcrowd them (though I always seem to crowd them and they still turn out okay).

Preheat oven to 375°. Cover the baking dish with a kitchen towel and set aside to rise on the countertop for at least 20 minutes before baking. Remove the towel and bake in the oven for 13–17 minutes (pay attention: they may need more baking time; but don't let them get overly brown). Use a toothpick to make certain the rolls are thoroughly baked inside.

Once the rolls are out of the oven and are still warm (not too hot), drizzle icing over the top—as much you want and all over!

INGREDIENTS *(for the icing[130])*

2 cups powdered sugar
2 tbsp. butter, softened
1 tsp. vanilla
3–4 tbsp. milk or half-and-half

In a medium bowl, combine all ingredients until smooth, adding just enough milk to reach desired glaze consistency.

A Prayer for the Graduates[131]

Holy and Heavenly Father,

You created the world by your word
with love and imagination.
We know you are good
when we see what you have made
and how you fashioned humanity in your image,
giving us the call to be creative makers and
dedicated caretakers like you.

You show more of who you are
through your Word—
drawing your people to yourself
and shepherding them with Grace and Truth.
And in your written word we learn of
 your righteousness, justice, love, and mercy.

And your heart is more fully revealed to us
through the life, death, and resurrection of Jesus.
He is the Word made flesh and the Good Shepherd.
And because of Jesus, we know you see us
and you will not leave us.

Lord, here we are,
a group of graduates and their loved ones.
These women and men have worked hard.
They have learned more about themselves and the world.
We are grateful they have been taught and shepherded
by godly and thoughtful professors and administration.

Yet we confess that we have struggled with
fear, anxiety, anger, and judgmentalism,
as COVID and societal strife
have marked this recent season.

Still, we are thankful.
Thank you for your faithfulness to The King's College.
Thank you for your mercies new every morning.
Thank you for being a God of restoration and new creation.
Thank you for being a strong tower to run to.

As these men and women graduate from this place,
teach them to be still;
quiet their anxiety and worry
.

Let them know you are God.
May they know your presence and your provision.
Through your Spirit and Word, be real to them.
Help them to grow into your wisdom and ways.
Help them to love and desire what you love.
Help them to move into the callings and
places you have for them.

Who are we to be loved by you?
But we *are*, Lord.
We praise your name for your holy kindness.

O Father, enlarge our hearts.
O Spirit, expand your vision.
O Christ, establish your kingdom among us.
May your will in us be accomplished.

We ask all these things
in the beautiful and strong name
of Jesus, our king.
Amen.

Roller Coasters

You know that late August day
when you and I made plans
to go to Hershey Park after 5?
(The tickets would be half off.)
I said I would go on the roller coaster rides
with you. You looked at me funny
and said, "You get sick on roller coasters."
But you tried to believe me
when I said I would be okay.
I really was trying to be spontaneous and
show you love,

since I'm not very spontaneous

but love you so much.

You were right. I do get sick on roller coasters.
And that night, I rode two with you.
You loved them but
felt guilty that I was sick
(even though you were right).
And you had to deal with me
almost throwing up in the middle of the park.

You still like to remind me of that day.
And I still don't like roller coasters.

And this year,
having cancer, and all the
tests and meds and waiting,
and learning of a tumor
that might not be a tumor,
makes me motion sick
and tired.
I'm sorry you have to live through it, too.

Hopefully we will get back to Hershey Park.
We'll drink peanut butter chocolate shakes again.
And, we'll bring your sisters.
I'll watch you all ride the roller coasters.

After Andrew Wyeth's *AIRBORNE*

The wind . . . you cannot tell where it comes from or where it is going.
So it is with everyone born of the Spirit.
—Jesus to Nicodemus

Those feathers came on the air,
tumbling and sliding: wind
underneath and around them—
filling space above the long yard,
moving on to someplace and somewhere.
The breeze without a path;
the anemometer broken.
White and gray curiosities flying forward
from nowhere we could see,
then landing on the rock wall,
dipping in the pond,
and hiding in the tall rushes.

A poet once asked, "Who has seen the wind?"
Jesus reminded a Jewish scholar,
"The wind blows wherever it pleases."
And what if these windows were opened,
and those feathers blew through, settling
on the old wood floor and crumbling mantle?
If our glance slanted sideways for a moment,
we might witness the mystery of angels passing by
or the Holy Spirit's work
of awakening all that is dead to new life.

GRATITUDE: THE FOUNDATION OF HUMAN CREATIVITY

It is a Sunday evening in January 2020 and I am sitting with my husband and friends at a local restaurant. My oncologist had already confirmed that I have stage II breast cancer, but now we are taking in the devastating news that I also have melanoma. One friend leans close and asks me, "Can you keep looking for beauty in this time? Will you share with us what you find?"

These questions might seem heartless when one is staring at a long death sentence, but to me—and my friend knew this—they were right on the mark. This was the real core of the matter: how would I, who has continually sought after beauty in my everyday, ordinary life, continue the quest when the road turned into the valley of shadow?

Look at This Pretty Leaf I Found
Leslie Bustard

The philosopher Josef Pieper said, "To be conscious of gratitude is to acknowledge a gift."[132] That is a beautiful saying, because it calls us to look at our lives through a lens of gift, to cultivate attention to what we have been given. It does not let us take things for granted.

But there is a dark side to this saying, one that every person in the world has experienced. So often, in our lives in this fallen world, we are given things that we don't want. What are we to do with those things? How can we live with gratitude when our path turns in a direction that we do not want to go?

Walking through that shadowed valley of cancer and seeking after beauty— everywhere from my backyard to my doctor's office—became a journey of discovery for me, a life-lesson of how attentiveness leads to gratitude. This is the means of grace God offered me. He offers this means of grace wherever He calls His children to go.

THE STORY STARTS WITH GIVING

In the beginning and since the beginning, God has woven stories, songs, and poems together, showing us His eternal plans for uniting heaven and earth and humanity to Himself. And lest we be surprised by the outcome, He has also illustrated for us the way our hearts turn and twist and how we follow our hearts' desires and loves—sometimes toward Him, but more often in a circuitous, tortuous path away from Him, so that we must be won through tremendous sacrifice.

The Creation Story in the first two chapters of Genesis is our *telos* story. If we pay close attention, we learn for whom and for what we were made—and the key to the story is *gift*. This world, all of it, is God's gift to us. As Saint Paul says to the Ephesians,

> Be filled with the Spirit, addressing one another in psalms and hymns and spiritual songs, singing and making melody to the Lord with your heart, *giving thanks always and for everything* to God the Father in the name of our Lord Jesus Christ.
> (Ephesians 5:18–20, *emphasis added*)

That gives us the key to our identity: we are created and made to live in joyful reception of what God gives.

As Brian Brown reminds us,

> In the beginning was God, Father, Son, and Holy Spirit, a hierarchy of mutual love who was the perfect form of everything good and true and beautiful... He looked into the disordered nothing, and He spoke mean-ing—extending His nature to create matter reflecting that nature.[133]

And after all this glorious creation—from heavens to seas to mountains to trees to birds—God created man and woman, to image Him into His world as cultivators, caretakers, and subcreators, doing all in His name and for His glory. God gave the man and the woman a place and a work, and He told them to go out into the world and, in a spirit of gratitude for all He had made, make *more*.

At first, that is what we did. But then we lost our way. Adam and Eve lost sight of creation as God's gift given freely, and instead saw it as something that must be grasped and wrenched. The Tower of Babel account, found later in Genesis, illustrates how Adam's disobedience and sin (as seen in Genesis 3) distorts humanity's motivations and work. Genesis 11:4 says, "they said, 'Come, let us build ourselves a city, with a tower that reaches to the heavens, so that we may make a name for ourselves; otherwise we will be scattered over the face of the whole earth'" (NIV).

Apologist William Edgar writes,

> Here, the city, with its ziggurat [a tower with steps meant to invite God and the gods down to earth] was created for the purpose of making a name for its builders apart from the name of God.... Here the name is an attempt for autonomy.[134]

Sunk in sin, humanity craved autonomy as an "escape" from gifts and the gratitude they merit. The Babel story hearkens back to the story of the Fall, where Adam and Eve rejected gratitude in favor of grasping; taking, rather than receiving what God makes for us.

Obviously, these efforts to escape from gratitude did not work out; the Fall introduced death into the world, and Babel shattered our human community. The story of how God set out to reunite heaven, earth, and humanity to Himself through the life, death, and resurrection of Jesus is woven through the rest of Scripture. As we wait with all creation for Christ's return, we know we cannot live and create in perfect love like God did at Creation. But we can live and create in a way that rejects being formed by a Tower-of-Babel vision for making.

SLOWING DOWN AND RECEIVING

The first spring and summer of my time in cancer-land were marked by late morning walks and mid-afternoon quiet time, usually spent sitting outside. We initially fought my melanoma with an infusion of two types of immunotherapy. The side effects of this left me with swollen ankles and knees, and with pain in my legs and arms that made it almost impossible to walk or move well. Large doses of steroids eventually reduced the inflammation and pain; as soon as I was able, I started walking to keep the swelling down. And afterwards, tired out, I would sit on my second-story back porch, looking out into my little corner of the world.

The quiet of this time and the uncertainty of my cancer led me to pay close attention to what was all around me. I determined that beauty would be my companion and God would be my sustainer, and I sought, in the midst of all the uncertainty and pain, to receive His gifts with open hands.

Blue skies and trails of clouds above me, bird song to the right and to the left of me, and the shadows of branches stretching and playing across the grass in front of me—ordinary life began to shine out in a way I'd never seen before.

There were times my daughters had to remind me to pay attention to their conversations because I was easily distracted by the sun stretching down through tree limbs and leaves.

Poems and poets became my friends. I craved words to help me name how raw and vulnerable I felt and the hope I needed in the face of suffering. As I begged for trust in God, no matter what He called me and my family to walk through, I sought to rest in His promise to never leave me or forsake me, and to remember that to keep my eyes on Jesus was a real way to be sustained.

Clouds Are Round About You
Leslie Bustard

But how to fix one's eyes? How to grow in knowing God's reality in my own mysterious, troubling days? How to cultivate the heart of thankfulness in all things, when "all things" were hard with an unknown end?

The only way I could answer these questions was by trying to pay attention—closer attention than I had ever paid before. God speaks; He speaks through nature, through other people, through the liturgy, through His Word. But so often, we are barely paying attention. For me, these days of pain and darkness became days of quiet, days of depth, where I could truly begin to cultivate the skill of paying attention to all the ways God speaks.

Before I had even read the words of Pieper in *Happiness and Contemplation*, I had begun to learn what he meant when he wrote,

> Who among us has not suddenly looked into his child's face, in the midst of the toils and troubles of everyday life, and at that moment "seen" that everything which is good, is loved and lovable, loved by God! Such certainties all mean, at bottom, one and the same thing: that the world is plumb and sound; that everything comes to its appointed goal; that in spite of all appearances, underlying all things is—peace, salvation, gloria; that nothing and no one is lost; that "God holds in his hand the beginning, middle, and end of all that is." Such non-rational, intuitive certainties of the divine base of all that is can be vouchsafed to our gaze even when it is turned toward the most insignificant-looking things, if only it is a gaze inspired by love. That, in the precise sense, is contemplation.[135]

It was in the contemplation of the sustaining love of Jesus that I learned to rest in gratitude.

Flannery O'Connor once prayed to God that He would "please help me push myself aside"[136] so she could know Him better. I stole that prayer from her, and by a miracle of grace in the midst of suffering, God answered it. He allowed me to recognize that wisdom meant receiving His ways and words. It meant allowing Him to make my days be what He deemed right and glorifying.

And then He sent another gift, one I had heard others speak of but could not have believed fully until I experienced it. In this submission and in this resting, my days in cancer-land overflowed with creativity through writing and making that I never would have imagined on my own. I recall especially this poem I wrote during that time, which tries to capture the juxtaposition between my own shifting life and God's constant provision.

The ground is still solid.
Grass is still full of green.
Squirrels still keep running along high wires.
And bees—still searching for clover.
Trees are still playing shadows with the sun.
And the neighbors' flowers, planted last year,
    are blooming white, spilling over their trellis.

Pieper again captured my experience of attentiveness, gratitude, and making when he wrote,

Out of this kind of contemplation of the created world arise in never-ending wealth all true poetry and all real art, for it is the nature of poetry and art to be paean and praise heard above all the wails of lamentation . . . No one can obtain felicity by pursuit. This explains why one of the elements of being happy is the feeling that a debt of gratitude is owed, a debt impossible to pay. . . . To be conscious of gratitude is to acknowledge a gift.[137]

Daily attentiveness and gratitude became my way of seeking to "cooperate with holy grace in every moment of my existence."[138]

DEEP GRATITUDE

Glory be to God for dappled things—
For skies of couple-colour as a brinded cow;
For rose-moles all in stipple upon trout that swim;
Fresh-firecoal chestnut-falls; finches' wings;
Landscape plotted and pieced—fold, fallow, and plough;
And áll trádes, their gear and tackle and trim.

All things counter, original, spare, strange;
Whatever is fickle, freckled (who knows how?)
With swift, slow; sweet, sour; adazzle, dim;
He fathers-forth whose beauty is past change:
Praise him.

Gerard Manley Hopkins in his poem "Pied Beauty" shows us how to pay attention, and then how this attentiveness bears the fruit of gratitude. His words help us focus on the variety found in nature, like a multi-colored sky, spotted fish, finches' wings, as well as how man adds to this variety through how he cultivates the land. Hopkins is not pointing out beauty that has "clean lines." He wants us to see the differences and be glad for them, as well as to know the God who saw fit to fill the earth with all that is "fickle, freckled . . . swift, slow, sweet."

Living *coram deo*—before the face of God—includes being attentive to and acknowledging the blessings that go beyond our imagining. The God whose beauty does not change makes all of life a gift. His gifts may be found when contemplating a surprise of swallows swooping low in the early evening, experiencing the spark of an artistic vision, or receiving the bread and wine with one's church community each Sunday. Gratitude flows out of this living-before-the-face-of-God life.

With the priest-poet Hopkins and other artists, we can learn to enter into the raw grandeur of the world; we learn to use words and images to help others see as well, and then we learn to return the glory to God. When we care how our work affects others, our experiences will show how our attention, imagination, and materials assist our neighbors in beholding and becoming. However, to make for the sake of the world and to the praise of God, we must put aside whatever philosophy pulls us into a Tower-of-Babel mindset. To do this, we need to practice the spiritual discipline of gratitude.

The last line of the first stanza in "Pied Beauty" says "all gear, their tackle, and trim," referring to the tools used by farmers to work with the "plotted and pieced" land. We are reminded that to plough the land or to let it lie fallow, one must have the right equipment and know-how. So it is with all work that requires experience and expertise to achieve success. Wise artists, those submitting to God's ways of work, will view their materials and tools with gratitude. Tools, even simple ones like a well-sharpened Blackwing pencil, are gifts. Wisdom calls us to hone them to fit our hands and minds well.

In the movie *Babette's Feast*, based on a short story by Isak Dinesen, Babette, an acclaimed Parisian cook living as an émigré in a small seaside Jutland village, is an example of what can occur when an artist knows her craft well and then lives into life as one of gift giving and receiving.

Arriving sick and worn out at the doorsteps of a small home, Babette is taken in by two sisters who live there. They lead an old religious community left to them by their father that is rife with small and large unresolved grievances. Babette serves these two sisters, and their home and community life are blessed by this care. Later, when Babette wins the lottery, she decides to prepare a magnificent feast for her people. Here the sisters, and the readers, learn the great depths of Babette's talents: Babette knows how to pick perfect wines and prepare delicious foods—foods her friends had never experienced due to their spartan life.

The sisters are fascinated by a turtle that Babette purchases, yet taken aback when they learn that it will be put into a soup; later, at the feast, they taste the soup and realize they have never eaten anything so exquisite. Each aspect of the feast softens the guests' hearts to the goodness of the food and forgiveness toward each other. Out of gratitude and love for this small religious community, Babette the artist uses her talents and her tools to create a meal that brings wholeness to her people.

When we place ourselves at the center of our ambitions, it becomes easy to compare our gifts with others', "desiring this man's art and that man's scope, with what I enjoy contented least."[139] But living rightly before God calls us to take gratefully the materials we have been given—imagination, paints, cameras, pencils, vocal cords—and learn to use them with excellence, for others.

Artist Theodore Prescott says of the inspiration and the work,

> I am often grateful for the "idea," the inspiration. But then comes the hard task of finding the form, the pursuit of which can literally take years. The initial gratitude is long gone, and it's only when the necessary form is found that gratitude returns. Then all that wrestling and the dead ends are seen as necessary and good.[140]

But what of these "wails of lamentation"? How do we "cooperate with holy grace" and live a life of attentiveness and gratitude when our road goes through valleys darkly shadowed?[141] Or when the work goes too long after the inspiration? Our days are filled with joy, love, and creativity, but also with sorrow, brokenness, fear, and anxiety. In the midst of horror and death, how do we even attempt to "[give] thanks always and for everything to God the Father in the name of our Lord Jesus Christ"? (Eph. 5:20)

TEACH US TO NUMBER OUR DAYS

Since the day my doctor confirmed I had stage II breast cancer *and* stage IV melanoma, the psalmist's words have been shaping my prayers: "Teach us to number our days, that we can gain a heart of wisdom" (Ps. 90:12 NIV).

In November 2021, close to the two-year mark of living with cancer, I had been tumor-free for six months. I found myself ready to know a specific detail about the BRAF inhibitors that had been keeping the melanoma from spreading again. These meds are powerful and fast-acting, but they are not proven to be durable, so I asked my oncologist how long they are known to work. According to different studies, he said, patients have lasted two to five years on these particular meds. Although the doctor assured me that we would try other treatments when the BRAF inhibitors stopped working, my understanding of the shadowed mystery of my life was brought into sharp focus.

That Christmas season, God showed me how Mary, the mother of Jesus, could be a guide for how to live the days given to me. Her faith in God and her submission to His plan showed me how to pray for these things for myself.

Luke 1 and 2 hint that Mary knew that difficulty and death faced her in the wake of the angel's message. Gabriel, the angelic messenger, revealed that God's plan was for her to bear God's Son, a message Mary received with faith and humility. After this, despite being pregnant, unwed, and facing a long road of hardship, she visited her cousin Elizabeth, where she bore witness to God's grace through a song of gratitude and praise.

Law and Grace
Theodore Prescott

My soul magnifies the Lord,
 and my spirit rejoices in God my Savior,
 for he has looked on the humble estate of his servant.
 For behold, from now on all generations will call me blessed;
 For he who is mighty has done great things for me,
 and holy is his name. (Luke 1:46–49)

After giving birth to Jesus, and in
accordance with God's law, she and
Joseph took the infant to the temple
and offered their sacrifices. Simeon,
a prophet, greeted them, and taking
Jesus in his arms, gave thanks that
God had fulfilled the promise that
Simeon would not die until he saw
the Christ. But it is Simeon's words to
Mary—that a sword would pierce her
soul—that touched my heart. Only
God knew when this sword would
pierce her heart, just as only He
knows when my cancer will no longer be held back by treatment.
Like Mary, I crave the sustaining grace found in her son Jesus. Here is a poem
where I reflect on Mary and what she was experiencing.

Annunciation
Ned Bustard

AFTER REMBRANDT'S
SIMEON AND ANNA IN THE TEMPLE

. . . and a sword shall pierce through your soul.
—Luke 2:35

Maybe Mary missed those shocking details
Simeon spoke as she looked at Jesus in
his ancient arms. With her memories of
angels and shepherds, one could understand
any weariness at unexpected
words. Except, she was in the habit of
listening to astonishing and strange
prophecies—as if she knew the ways of
the world were revealed through donkeys and old

men. (I think I would have asked one or two
questions and maybe for a timeline.) Yet
young Mary had been learning that even
as a small candle breaks the shadowed dark,
hard paths are lightened by sustaining grace.

Jesus, the Son of God, is the light on our hard paths and the Good Shepherd
in our dark valleys. He is the teacher who guides us into a life of obedience and
gratitude. Jesus is trustworthy—although He knew He was walking to His death
on a cross, He still loved people, performed miracles, taught about God's king-
dom, celebrated weddings and festival
days, and worshiped the Father.

Just like Jesus, weeping in the
garden and begging the cup of death
to be passed by Him yet still submit-
ting to the Father's ways, we submit to
how God plans our days even if they
are filled with sorrow. And we know
that in the death, resurrection, and
ascension of Jesus, our life is hidden
in His, and we have more than we
know for which to be grateful.

When we learn to root ourselves
deeply in the soil of gratitude and
when we speak words of thanksgiving
and sing psalms to each other, we

Simeon and Anna in the Temple
Rembrandt van Rijn

proclaim true wisdom to all in the heavens and on the
earth: "God is God and he is not mocked. This is God's world . . . Thanksgiving to
God in the name of Jesus Christ announces that death and sin and sorrow have
been defeated and Christ is making all things new."[142]

Praise Him.

RAÐLJÓST[143]

Van Gogh's light washed
   across his canvases,
while Rembrandt's angled—
   shining in one place.
And I see light behind all
   Rouault's paintings.

Today, this little one shines
   enough to find my way by
with enough of a promise
   that it won't get extinguished,
   even on a gray day.

ISAIAH 41:19

We should have a land of trees.
—Langston Hughes

When the banquet is
set high on God's mountain, I
hope our view is the
trees—the cedars and cypress
planted by springs of water.

Stephen Crotts

A LITURGY FOR A WALK IN
MY NEIGHBORHOOD[144]

Heavenly Father,
as you walked with Adam and Eve
in the cool of the day,
    walk with me.

Holy Spirit,
as you walked with Enoch and Abraham,
guiding them to their next destinations,
    walk with me.

Lord Jesus,
as you walked with your disciples
through valleys and hills,
    walk with me.

As I open my front door,
remind me that I follow in
the footsteps of others who
have kept their eyes fixed on you.

As I walk down my front steps,
remind me that you have put me in this
particular place for just a time as this.

As I turn up my block, mind wandering ahead
to where I might go, remind me of the places
you've gifted people to call home:
    the Garden Between the Two Rivers,
    the Land Flowing with Milk and Honey,
    the Land of Exile,
and remind me that in each home, you told your people to cultivate
and care for the land, to plant gardens, and to pray for its prospering
even though it would include weeds and sorrow.

Good Shepherd, thank you for this ordinary
walk through my neighborhood. And as I
walk, Lord, keep me attentive to what is
around me. Even though I have passed these
homes a hundred times, help me to pay
attention and discover some new life or beauty:
    overflowing flower boxes,
    the stretching of shadows,
    a freshly painted front door,
    birds chirping on a wire,
    a green maple sapling,
    a busy squirrel hurrying across my path,
    children racing their bikes.

Awaken my senses and my imagination to
these pleasant boundary lines.

The following lament may be added as needed:

> Forgive me, Lord.
> As I am walking through
> this good place you have given me,
> I confess to coveting
> my neighbors' homes and goods.
> I confess to being complacent
> at the familiarity of my own home,
> discontent and wanting one newer or shinier.
> Teach my heart to be glad
> for the goodness my neighbors enjoy,
> and grateful for the gifts
> you have given me.

Jesus of Nazareth, you had a neighborhood
  but you didn't have a home to call your own.
Thank you for giving me this place to call home.
When you healed people, you sent them
back to their homes and families,
to live lives restored to ordinary,
  everyday life.
And you promise us that one day
we will walk with you
on streets paved with gold,
everything redeemed.
May this short walk today be a
reminder that I will walk one day
in the New Jerusalem. Thank you
that you are preparing for your people
—even for me—
a home that will far exceed
any of the houses I admire.

Help me to treasure this hope.
Help me to be a good steward
   of my home and my neighborhood.
Help me to remember that I live
   in both the Now and the Not Yet.

As I turn this new corner
or walk down a strange street,
remind me keep my heart open
to care for neighbors I don't know.
Help me to look for opportunities
   to reach out to them,
     to listen to their stories of joy and sorrow,
     or to offer a cup of cold water.

May my heart not only rejoice in the beauty
of this neighborhood around me,
but also lament when I see its brokenness.
Show me where I need to act for restoration.
Help me to pray for wholeness
   here in my neighborhood.

Lord Jesus, I ask that you would tune my
heart and sharpen my sight to see what you
have placed in my way:
the sparrow on the wire—a reminder to
trust you to provide for my
needs and my daily bread;
the stump of a chopped down tree—a
reminder that Jesus was the Shoot of Jesse;
fences covered with ivy—a reminder that
Christ is the True Vine;
my neighbor sweeping their front step—
a reminder of your image in us all and your
call to love my neighbors as I love myself.

In a tree-lined neighborhood one might add:

> Creator God, of all the things
> I love in my neighborhood,
> I think that it is the trees
> you have given me—these elms,
> maples, and sycamores—that I love
> the most. I love how the sun shines
> bright through their green leaves
> in the summer, how they change
> their colors in autumn and weave
> through the air like dancers, how the snow
> glistens on bare branches, and how the
> raindrops on flowering buds
> capture the early morning light.
> Their beauty makes me ache with longing
> for the beauty of New Creation. Lord,
> please form me and my people to be
> pictures of your goodness like those trees,
> to be Oaks of Righteous, offering life
> and loveliness to this place,
>   and keeping us rooted in you.

> Holy and Blessed Trinity, as I walk
> through my neighborhood today,
> open my eyes again to see
> how the boundary lines
> you have given me
> have fallen in pleasant places.

> Amen.

(penultimate) verse

In my backyard
the snowbells
cluster together
wrapped in white,
heads bent
as if in prayer

and the crocuses—
a Pollock-riot
of purple, yellow, pink
each one's head tipped
toward the sun
in praise

the daffodils nod,
still green cocoons,
slight sliver of yellow,
whisper of promise
that soon—soon they'll open
wide awake and ready

but it's the forsythia I'm waiting for—
each blossom a spark
that flames out wild
into my winter life.
Each year they return,
inviting me to linger, to not pass by
until I've taken off my shoes—

PART II

...

Field Notes from
Cancer-Land

THE WAITING PRAYER[145]

Help me to wait, Lord, on you.
May my longings stretch out to you.

May my hands be empty
   —of the regular work of teaching
   (even if it was hard and I struggled with it)
   —of the rhythms of community
   and projects and planning and creative energy
   —of grocery shopping and errands
   and having people in my home.

May my hands be filled to the full with you.

You know these things.
You give and you take and
bless your name
because you know
the beginning and the end

so help me—
to wait.

To wait now and
   trust right now
for today and
   tomorrow
for after the cancer.

To not fight it.

Help me to quiet
my head and heart
of all you know I struggle with.

Help me to be content
and grateful
   and filled somehow
   mysteriously
   with you, Jesus,
whatever that looks like—

Help me to grasp
your word quickly
and fill my mind with it:
   helmet of salvation
   sword of the Spirit
   breastplate of righteousness
   belt of truth
   feet shod with the gospel to stand

Let these truths
abide in me and
be my anchor
   and
Jesus, you are my
sympathetic high priest,
my living intercessor—
your kindness leads me to repentance.

Help me to wait—as you
save me through and work
your ways in me.

I am scared of breast surgery and of recovery—
shepherd me and help me
through it.

How do I give life-giving words to Maggie?
How do I guide Ellie?
How do I support Carey?
Help me to love Ned well.
Help me to pray for
   my friends and be faithful—
   by your Spirit.

Help me to
   return and rest
   repent and trust
   and wait

I don't always
know how to
spend my days

I know you know
all my thoughts
and you are keeping them
and somehow completing your work in me.

FIELD NOTES

JANUARY 30, 2020

Before Christmas break I discovered a lump in my right breast. The next day I headed to my doctor, who sent me for a mammogram and an ultrasound, which confirmed that I have cancer in my right breast. We started off hopeful, because it was small and it looked like the lymph nodes were clear. But a biopsy revealed that it is Invasive Duct Carcinoma and is Triple Positive (on the hormone receptors). The prognosis is very good for recovery but the journey will still be hard, including chemo, surgery, and radiation. It's been a long month of tests and visits to the doctors.

This is an email I sent to friends yesterday, describing what this week was like and where I am in the journey:

> So here I am, home and on the couch, recovering from today's port surgery. I will gratefully say it again—thank you for your prayers, for your emails, your texts, your cards, your kind offers to help. Whether you told me you were thinking of me or not, somehow all these prayers and good words have mysteriously kept me sustained. That doesn't mean these past three days have been easy, but somehow I got to the end of today and am okay (and yes, on pain meds from the surgery— that helps so much!).
>
> Each procedure went well. Each person doing their job was very friendly and kind and attentive—that made it all so much better. Even the two people working at the cafe at the cancer center were sweet and gave me free food (I think I looked pretty pathetic). I felt yucky all day yesterday—I think it was stress. Monday I had a mole removed from my back. So once all the lovely painkillers wore off, the sutures made walking and sitting and generally moving around on Tuesday very hard. We are waiting to hear back from pathology to see if it is okay.
>
> Today was the port surgery, which went well. Sleeping under anes-

thesia was amazing. Oh my—I was out and then I was awake. I think I was dreaming, but maybe not. Grateful for a 45-minute deep sleep.

Here is the deal: the right side lymph nodes show no cancer cells, but there is a little concern about something in the left side lymph nodes. MRIs always show everything—causing undo concern. So it may be nothing or it may be something. The surgeon did a biopsy on the left where there is concern and he also felt a lump. He is a breast cancer surgeon but before that he worked in lymph node cancer surgeries—so hooray for an experienced surgeon.

Next Wednesday is my appointment with the oncologist about all the results and what happens next.

Grateful for you all and your prayers and care for me. It is rather overwhelming. During this time of waiting to learn what will be next, I have been learning to rest in God and to trust Him. Only He knows what is ahead. And He promises His presence will never leave me. So even if I don't know what living through this fight with cancer will be like, I know He will somehow provide, because He keeps doing it right now. I am going to learn the reality of Psalm 23.

Warmly,
Leslie

...

February 13, 2020

Dear friends and family,

I know it has been a while since I updated this, but I have been waiting to update until after I had a chance to share with our daughters. The past week-and-a-half has brought harder news: last Sunday, Ned and I learned that I have metastatic melanoma. The mole on my back turned out to have melanoma in it, and the cancer somehow ended up in my left lymph node(s). So in addition to the stage I breast cancer in my right breast, I have at least stage III melanoma in me.

Last week I had the brain MRI, and thankfully (!!!!) that was clear of any cancer. I also had a PET scan. Although all my major organs are clear of melanoma, there is something sketchy showing up where my colon meets my small intestine. Tomorrow I have a a series of tests to see if there is anything on top of the intestines.

I have chosen not to freak myself out over how dangerous and crazy melanoma is by not doing any research on it. I know from talking to my doctors that this is not good. I am grateful, though, as they have told me about immunotherapy and how successful this treatment is for those fighting melanoma. It has its own set of risks and ways to take care of those risks. I am grateful for the success stories of this treatment, though.

I really am so grateful for my surgeon (Dr. Bleznak), my oncologist (Dr. Brennan), my nurse navigator (Julie Justice), and my plastic surgeon (Dr. Bast). They are very caring and are working hard to figure out the best path for my treatment. Please pray for them. (Dr. Brennan even calls me just to check on how I am doing.)

For now we need to confirm the absence or presence of more cancer. Then, surgery (to remove the lump) and immunotherapy. Also, meds to starve the breast cancer of progesterone and estrogen. Radiation at some point for the breast cancer.

Thank you for praying for me and for my family. Breast cancer is awful, but we've moved into a whole new realm of awful.

I don't know what to say as to how I am feeling. Yesterday I shared with a friend that I am meditating on and trying to grasp what it means to really hope and rest in the Lord, and to trust him even though He has called me and my family to walk through this valley of shadow and death. To believe that even now I will see the goodness of the Lord in the land of the living. So every day I am either peaceful and quiet, or I am crying and feeling really overwhelmed.

I know that Jesus is the Good Shepherd who will guide us to the next destination. Please pray that there is no more cancer. Please pray for me and my family as we keep having more tests, which means more waiting. Waiting is what God has been calling us to, but it is hard. Pray for my husband and girls, who I love so much, as they each have their own responsibilities and now also have to carry this burden and sorrow that I have cancer.

My mom is in an assisted living place in Wilmington, DE. She is doing so much better. I praise the Lord daily for my brother David and his girlfriend, Sharon, and all the good they have done for my mom. I have not told her about this second cancer. Knowing about the one is enough for now, until I know what exactly is going to happen. So if you see her, please don't speak of it.

Thank you for your care and your prayers. They really do mean so much to me. Much love,
Leslie

. . .

FEBRUARY 18, 2020

Ned and I are about to travel to Philly to meet a specialist there—my doctors arranged this meeting so we can get an official second opinion. It is also a way for the specialists to meet me, and for us to get "a foot in the door" for any possible clinical trials I could try, in addition to the treatment I will have for both the melanoma and the breast cancer. I should be having a CT scan soon—to see if there is any cancer from the metastatic melanoma on my intestines or hiding out deeper in my intestines. I humbly ask you to keep praying that the cancer has not spread to my intestines. Everything else seems clear right now, which is so helpful!

Today I woke up singing Ellie Holcomb's "Red Sea Road"—it's a good song to have running through your heart and mind. I'm praying that God will part the Red Sea for me, my family, and everyone on this journey with me.

Gratefully yours,

Leslie

...

FEBRUARY 19, 2020

Just updating you about yesterday: the doctor we met was great. We had a good talk, and he affirmed that what my doctors are planning is good. He said Lancaster and Penn Medicine is a solid place for fighting breast cancer.

The two spots that showed up on my PET scan in my intestines could be indicative that there is cancer in my intestines, but he said it is curious that I haven't shown any symptoms that would indicate that it is cancer. I did share with him that throughout the day my stomach does a quick flare up and makes itself known, but nothing that causes lots of pain. This happens often. It started the day after I heard I had breast cancer, so I thought it might be stress. He thought it could be. (Now I'm feeling even more aware of these flareups, so I'm trying not add this to my worries . . .)

The CT scan will hopefully be the last test. Please pray that there is no cancer anywhere else, especially in the intestines. If there isn't any cancer in the intestines, then the melanoma is at stage III—and that is just better than moving to stage IV.

I hope to see Carey and Maggie this weekend in NYC with Ned—hoping for some sweet time with them.

Warmly,

Leslie

...

FEBRUARY 24, 2020

Thank you for your kind words and for all who are praying.

That CT scan is tomorrow, so please pray that there isn't cancer in those places in the intestines where the colonoscopy couldn't reach. This Thursday we'll meet with Dr. Brennan, my oncologist. I hope that will be the meeting that gives us a plan for what is next.

My weekend in NYC had so much goodness in it: time with dear friends, time with The King's College community, quiet time in a friend's apartment, *To Kill a Mockingbird* with Maggie (the play was gut-wrenching and beautiful), time with a dear friend I trust deeply who has also fought cancer, time with Carey and Ned at the Strand Bookstore and a great little bar restaurant, time laughing and talking with Carey and her friends, and then time with Carey and Maggie in the UWS, at another bookstore, and then church. It was all very life-giving. While we were gone, friends started painting a bunch of rooms and the hallway at our house. The color is a buttery yellow and it's just perfect.

I am learning that your prayers and your faith are holding me up—there are no words to share how grateful I am. This is all hard, but God is faithful in ways that I am learning each day.

Leslie

. . .

FEBRUARY 27, 2020

Dear family and friends,

Today, as you know and have so kindly been praying for, was the meeting with Dr. Brennan to review my CT scan and to talk about treatments.

They were not able to confirm that there is cancer on top of the intestines, but they are 95% certain that it is. So they are planning to treat the metastatic melanoma as stage IV.

Next week I will start the most aggressive of the immunotherapy treatments. I will be getting a combination of ipilimumab and nivolumab every 3 weeks. There will be 4 doses of it, and then scans to evaluate how the cancer is responding.

Using these two drugs gives the greatest "rewards" but it also carries the greatest risks (compared to just getting nivo alone). Side effects can happen to 30–50% of the people on this treatment and can happen anytime (even after treatment has stopped). Some side effects can be mild and some could land me in the hospital and on steroids. But this is the treatment with the best rate of cure.

But what about the breast cancer? Because it is stage I, slow growing, and not as aggressive as the melanoma, I will be on two meds (one oral and one injection) to stop estrogen and progesterone. This will starve the cancer and jump start menopause (hooray for not being able to sleep at night and all the other things that happen). This summer, after a round of immunotherapy and an evaluation as to how the melanoma is responding, there will be breast surgery. Although I am hoping for a lumpectomy with radiation, there may be a need for a mastectomy. (To be honest, a mastectomy makes me feel really anxious ...)

My heart feels weary and sad, although I know will be receiving the best possible treatment for this melanoma. The doctor said that there is a history of cure with this treatment, and that he is working with patients now who are doing well and getting to remission. He says, based on 10 years of immunotherapy work on cancer, that this treatment is the most durable, long term.

But it seems I am back to a life of waiting—waiting to see if the treatment is working, waiting to see if I will have those risky side effects, and waiting to see if I will have a mastectomy. It seems this treatment will leave me fatigued, but I will most likely be able to do regular life stuff, like care for my family and friends as best as I can (while they care for me!) and be involved with the school play and keep working on the Square Halo conference.

Next week I take a class on immunotherapy and its side effects/risks, and then at the end of the week I will get my first treatment.

So what do I need prayer for?

- That the side effects won't happen.
- That I would wait on the Lord as He has called me to.
- That this treatment will give me a cure.
- That God would part the Red Sea and crush all the enemies—cancer, fear, distrust, Satan's lies (I don't know what that would look like, but I am looking to see what God is doing).
- That the Lord would be gracious to my family and make Himself known as their Good Shepherd.
- That in the midst of the valley of the shadow of death, we would know Him to be faithful, so we could be courageous.
- That in our weakness, He would be our strength, even when we don't know what that might look like.

As we learn more, I will keep sharing. Ned and I are still processing and still thinking of questions. My heart does feel heavy and sad, even though there is hope for this treatment.

Warmly,
Leslie

FEBRUARY 29, 2020

Just a note to say thank you all—I have read each one of your messages and been so grateful for your prayers and good words. They truly are a blessing to me. The past few days have not been without tears, but I am beginning to see the Lord pointing the way since I learned about the stage IV diagnosis .

Dear friends from The Rabbit Room (an organization Ned is connected with through his illustration and design work on the lovely book *Every Moment Holy*) came together and sent me a painting titled "I Go Before You" by one of my favorite singer-songwriters and friend Eric Peters. I love the painting, and I love the title.

Yesterday, I was reading Walter Wangerin's *Reliving the Passion*, and I read Mark 14:27–18 and Mark 16:6–7, which basically is Jesus saying, "But after I am raised up, I will go before you to Galilee." Wangerin writes, "The dearest comfort in this promise is that precisely by taking the Way of the Lord, we will meet the Lord himself. In suffering is he revealed! In the experience of our own crosses he is made manifest."[146] At the end of the short meditation, Wangerin wrote this prayer: "Master, Grant me, in the study of your story, both love and faith. Love will make me attentive to all you do. Faith will make me bold to follow."[147]

I share these things to remind myself and to encourage you that the Lord does not leave us (me) comfortless on the hard road He is has called us (me) to walk. John Newton says Jesus has experimental sympathy. He knows our sorrows not merely as He knows all things, but as one who has been in our situation and who, though without sin Himself, endured, when upon earth, inexpressibly more for us than He will ever lay upon us. He has sanctified poverty, pain, disgrace, temptation, and death by passing through these states; and in whatever states His people are, they may by faith have fellowship with Him in their suffering, and He will, by sympathy and love, have fellowship and interest with them in theirs.[148] (I recommend you get your hands on *The Letters of John Newton* and slowly meditate on his writings. He was a truly gospel-centered and grace-rooted pastor with a shepherding heart.) This is what I yearn for: to know the realness of Jesus' love for me and to love Him more deeply than I ever have. I am grateful the Holy Spirit has been kindly pointing these comforts out to me and that He is rooting them in me.

I am grateful that He daily reminds that I can take refuge in Him; that when I want to escape and hide, I can run to Him. I am learning to do that each day. May you, too, know that He is our strong tower, the place where we find shelter.

Thank you for praying for me. The Holy Spirit works His strengthening ways in me through your words.

Love,

Leslie

MARCH 3, 2020

Just connecting to let you know that my immunotherapy treatment starts this Thursday. It takes 4 hours for the infusion, so I'll take my books and journal and read, read, read…

The biggest thing on my mind is learning to wait and trust the Lord as we see how my body will respond to this treatment. Many people don't have the severe side effects and just deal with extra fatigue and decreased appetite. But others deal with riskier things such as colitis (inflammation of the colon) and pnue-montitis (inflammation of the lung).

I've been told to call my doctor if I have any symptoms different than my baseline when it comes to coughs, pain, or shortness of breath, and to call if I have a fever of 100.4°, vomiting or diarrhea uncontrolled by medications, new numbness, extreme pain, severe sudden headache, or a rash that doesn't go away with meds.

O Church Arise
Ned Bustard

Basically, I could look like I'm not even on cancer meds because my body is responding so well, I could have a mild reaction, or I could land in the hospital. The nurse said most people respond well, and since I was young (happy to know 52 is young), strong, and (otherwise) healthy, I could do well. But no one knows why people respond the way they do to their immunotherapy meds.

I will do 4 doses of these meds—once every 3 weeks. At the end of the that, there will be scans to see how things are going. After that, discussions and decisions about breast surgery.

Thank you for praying for me and for praying for my family. I am really grateful. We sang "O Church Arise" (a Getty hymn) in church this Sunday, and I was taken by the last verse:

So Spirit, come, put strength in every stride; give grace for every hurdle, that we may run with faith, to win the prize of a servant, good and faithful. As saints of old still line the way, retelling triumphs of his grace, we hear their calls, and hunger for the day when with Christ we stand in glory.[149]

Leslie

MARCH 5, 2020

Today is the day my treatment starts. Blood work and then 4 hours of infusion time. I have a pile of books, new colored pencils and a coloring book, and my computer to keep me going. A friend gave me a lovely soft blanket yesterday. So off I go at 10 a.m. Thank you for your kindness in praying for me. I truly am humbled by it all.

Although there have been physical and emotional storms rolling around in me, I am learning what it means to have Jesus as my Good Shepherd and to be His beloved. This, in the midst of other verses and prayers, has been coming to my mind (excerpted from "Saint Patrick's Breastplate"). I am grateful for these truths:

Christ with me,
Christ before me,
Christ behind me,
Christ in me,
Christ beneath me,
Christ above me,
Christ on my right,
Christ on my left,
Christ when I lie down,

Christ when I sit down,
Christ when I arise,
Christ in the heart of
every man who
thinks of me,
Christ in the mouth
of everyone who
speaks of me,
Christ in every eye
that sees me,

Christ in every ear
that hears me.
I arise today through
a mighty strength,
the invocation of the
Trinity, through belief
in the Threeness, through
confession of the Oneness
of the Creator of creation.

As before, my desire is a cure (which my doctor says is very possible) and no risky side effects.

...

Thank you for praying. The first round of meds is in me. I will seriously be learning Exodus 14:14 where the Lord says, "[I] will fight for you; you need only to be still" (NIV). The nurses and aides in the infusion center were wonderful. Light was happily bright in my little corner of the world. The infusion did not take 4 hours; I misunderstood—I was just going to *be* there 4 hours. So I didn't get to read, but I did listen to music

and color. And I ate two of these tasty peanut butter sandwiches that they kept offering to me.

Ned was wonderful and good to me, as always. I listened to "Beyond the Blue" and "Farther Along" by Josh Garrels—I have loved those songs for so long. The words speak volumes to me.

Then I listened to Sandra McCracken's *Steadfast Live* album because that, too, has been very helpful to me these past few years. Also, Jon Foreman's "Your Love is Strong"—the Lord's Prayer is woven throughout. Grateful for things like iPhones and earbuds.

But even more grateful for all of you and your care. The Lord upheld me and shepherded me today as an answer to your prayers.

Warmly,

Leslie

...

MARCH 6, 2020

Good morning—today is my first full day with meds in me to fight melanoma. I am grateful that my doctor has said there is much hope for a cure, and that even though there could be risky side effects, these two meds offer the greatest rewards. So now I wait. I don't know when I will post here next, because I don't know what will be happening through the week. Next week I only have 3 appointments at the cancer center, and not one is a test.

But I do know I woke up today, and the day felt almost ordinary. I made housework plans, Ellie-coming-home from England plans, and writing project plans. The weariness in my heart is not as heavy as it has been. I imagine I will still be on a roller coaster of emotions and my body will be tired, but today, even though it is gray outside, shines a little brighter in BookEnd, our little home.

Thank you for praying and for all the prayers you will say in the future. I am the paralytic being taken to Jesus by his friends. You have opened the roof and brought me down to Him—I couldn't do this alone. The abundance of everyone's care is overwhelming—I am truly thankful for each of your posts, messages, texts, email, or mail. Every time you offer your attention to me it is a gift.

Much love,

Leslie

...

MARCH 9, 2020

Halfway into the first week of immunotherapy meds and no side effects, except feeling tired midday. Naps are still an important thing. Today I had an iron infusion (for anemia) and an injection (of something for the breast cancer). I also did something incredibly normal that I have not really done in 2 months: a real grocery shopping trip with actual ideas of what to feed Ned and Ellie (who came home from England Saturday night!). So that seriously made me happy. When I came home there was a box of soup, rolls, and cookies sent by long-time friends through Spoonful of Comfort. Play practice was a delight. It all feels sweetly low-key and ordinary.

Finally reading *On the Road with Saint Augustine* by James K.A. Smith. I loved these lines from the first chapter: "It's not just a matter of finally settling down or coming to the end of the road. We find rest because we are found; we make it home because someone comes to get us." And then, "God is not tapping his foot judgmentally inside the door as you sneak in, crawling over the threshold in shame. He's the father running toward you, losing his sandals on the way, his robes spilling off his shoulders, with a laughing smile whose joy says, 'I can't believe you came home!' That's what grace looks like." And lastly, my favorite: "Jesus is the shout of God, the way God runs out to meet us."[150]

This song has been playing on repeat in my mind and heart: "Sweet Comfort," by Sandra McCracken. The words are hard but just right.

Thank you for praying—always thankful.

Warmly,

Leslie

. . .

MARCH 12, 2020

Today I am officially one week out from the first infusion. Yesterday I met with Dr. Brennan's PA. It was a good visit and she confirmed what I had been noticing: my side effects were the normal ones. I feel tired and my knee joints ache sometimes. My stomach still flares up with a weird ache, which is uncomfortable but doesn't stop me from doing anything. This week has had its sweet ups—it helps when the sunshine is out and I can drive to play practice with the windows down while playing a favorite song. But sometimes I feel tired and somewhat down.

Yesterday started as dreary day, and my energy and mood seemed to match it. The PA said that was normal, too, as I transition out of such an intense time of waiting and into my new ordinary. So I'm learning to take steps toward getting into good rhythms, working on responsibilities that I love, and being patient with myself.

Thank you for praying—there is no end to my gratefulness for it.

Love,

Leslie

. . .

March 16, 2020

Just asking for prayer, as my knees have swollen up, and I can barely walk. I have a call in to the nurses and hope to see someone soon about this.

The end of last week and this weekend was hard—I am extra tired (I can seriously take a solid 2+ hour nap), which leads to feeling extra emotional. Last week I felt this hard egg shape on my right side and realized that it was the cancer on my intestine. Feeling that and having these symptoms has somehow made this cancer thing even more real, in a scarier way.

There have been sweet things going on—a nice, spring walk with Ned by a stream, where we heard birds and saw green buds on trees and enjoyed the blue sky. Also wandered around Frey's Greenhouse and enjoyed how wonderful they made it all look.

Wrote a couple of essays for *Cultivating* magazine and baked Irish soda bread.[151] Listened to a friend, Dru Johnson, speak at The Row House on rituals.[152] Also listened to a sermon on Sunday that Carey sent to us, and it was really helpful. Set up the big TV that Ned's dad got for us. Ellie and I watched the super sweet *To All the Boys I Loved*—that was what my brain could handle. It was cute.

Ellie has a rare autoimmune disease, so she and I are quarantined, and we are figuring out some life/spirit sustaining daily rhythms. This week my favorite song has been "Lover of My Soul," by Jeremy Casella.

Right now, I am concerned about these knees and how I cannot walk without Ned's help. Thank you for praying—will let you know about my knees.

Warmly,

Leslie

. . .

March 20, 2020

Hello friends,

How are you all? How is staying home and social distancing going for you this week?

We have hunkered down, as both Ellie and I are immune compromised. We have been blessed by friends who are going grocery shopping and providing meals for us. Also, grateful for texts and messages and emails from people checking in on us.

I wanted to share that my knees are so much better. The only issue I have is my right knee usually needs to be "popped." Until today, my left knee still felt tight, but I could still walk. I'm so grateful that I didn't need steroids. Thank you for praying. Right now, do please pray for my appetite—I'm back at that place where not a lot of food is appetizing. Or if I do eat, I'm not interested in a lot. This morning I realized that I have lost about six pounds in the past two weeks. People have been giving us good meals and snacks, so our fridge is full. I'm grateful for that! I am trying, really I am!! This Wednesday I get my 2nd cycle of immuno-therapy.

This week, I started to incorporate some daily rhythms for the three of us—eating meals together, with prayer, poetry, and read aloud time. I've decided to read Billy Collins poetry to Ned and Ellie. His poems make me smile, and I hadn't read them in a while. I have spent more time watching TV than I have in ages—I'm so grateful for the huge new TV Ned's dad got for us.

We had to cancel our Square Halo conference. I have been planning this for so long—I'm really sad, but I'm grateful that all the presenters are up for trying it again next year.

It is hitting me that in this time of fighting cancer and being quarantined all the things that I love and that make me "me" have been taken out of my hands—time with the whole family, time with friends, time at church, teaching, producing a play, planning a conference . . . and with the loss of so much physical and creative energy, I also have little energy to do much housework or to cook and bake (which I like) or to read for long stretches (which I really love). Ugh—I am probably spending too much time on Facebook—although I do like seeing so many friends from around town and the country.

I think I'm starting to figure out how to pray and to focus on Jesus; I hope during this time I will learn to be satisfied by the love of Jesus in deeper and truer ways. Because in the end, it really is all about Jesus.

Ned reminded me how much we loved the 77s and their album *Sticks and Stones*, so we have been listening to it while making lunch. Our first summer married, we would play this CD really loud while doing the dishes. I can picture the sun streaming into our kitchen, which was covered with big pink and blue flowered wallpaper. We lived on the third floor; our first apartment (which was almost a dive), felt like a tree house. Their song "MT" was/is my favorite.

Ned and Leslie in their first apartment (1990)

This week I read "Fishing on the Susquehanna in July," by Billy Collins. Although his poem "Litany" is laugh out loud funny and is the one that introduced me to him, this is probably the poem that got me interested in reading more of his stuff.

Leslie

. . .

MARCH 24, 2020

My knees are still hard and swollen. Maybe a little better, as I can put weight on them, but not enough to walk by myself. Dr. Brennan sent this message:

> We try not to have you on steroids while on immunotherapy but if you are on <10 mg daily of prednisone it might not be an issue. I'd like to see you tomorrow and examine what is going on before determining about steroids and next steps. This is not an expected side effect of immunotherapy (although it can happen, it is very rare). Depending on what we see, we might drop the ipilimumab and continue just the nivolumab for now; might consider steroids, imaging, or rheumatology evaluation.

I do hope my knees clear up today, because I like the idea of taking both immunotherapy meds—more to fight the melanoma. So this message felt a little discouraging.

Today I found this quote from Augustine in one of my commonplace scrapbooks (I cut it from a bulletin at least five years ago—it must have gone with a sermon), and I found it very strengthening:

> By delaying [His gift] God strengthens our longing, through long-
> ing he expands our soul, and by expanding our soul he increases
> its capacity. So brethren, let us long, because we are to be filled . . .
> That is our life, to be trained by longing; and our training through
> the holy longing advances in the measure that our longings are
> detached from the love of this world . . . . Let us stretch ourselves out
> towards him, that when he comes he may fill us full.

Oh, I like the picture of stretching myself out towards Jesus, waiting for Him to fill me full. I don't know what that looks like, but I like the poetry of it. I want to be satisfied by my union with Christ and by His love.

Several friends this week have encouraged me by saying that it might be hard to hold onto Jesus right now because I'm so tired, but that Jesus is holding on to me, and my friends and family can do the work of faith on my behalf. And it doesn't matter if I don't feel Jesus holding onto me—He is. He is the one carrying me. They also remind me not to be discouraged by my need to sleep; sleeping is my job. I'm so grateful for these reminders. Much love to you all. Thank you for your prayers, your messages, and your care. I read all the messages and am grateful.

Leslie

. . .

MARCH 25, 2020

My knees are still swollen—not as big as before but I still cannot walk, really. My right calf is really tight and my right ankle's swollen, too.

The doctor decided today not to do the immunotherapy treatment so I can go on a low dose of steroids. He is also discussing taking me off one of the two immunotherapy meds (because that would be the one that gives me the risky side effects) or putting me on another med. He is concerned that this knee reaction points to me being at risk for the other side effects that involve my lungs and liver. So I feel rather sad at this news, because the combination of the two meds is the best fighter of the cancer. But the doctor said a cure can still happen with the one med or with the pills.

I was so tired today—I think I was sleep-talking almost. I fell asleep on the ultrasound table. Then I came home and slept some more. I think I will be okay for the rest of the day. Trying to hang out downstairs because I am bored of my bedroom.

My dear friend Lynette told me today was the 50th anniversary of Simon and Garfunkle's "Bridge Over Troubled Water" making it to number one on the Billboard Charts. I have loved them since 8th grade, so I think I will spend some time listening to them today. Two of my favorite songs are "The Only Living Boy in New York" and "Keep the Customer Satisfied" (which I think is about selling drugs? But I love the horns a lot).

Thank you for your prayers and good words—I'm very grateful. Please do pray for my mom as she is in assisted living, and is, of course, quarantined. She is trying her best to stay positive, but she misses seeing us. We talk every day, which is sweet.

Love,
Leslie

...

MARCH 26, 2020

Hello all,

The sun is shining outside, and I see blue sky. I talked to my Maggie this morning, which makes me glad.

Ellie is working on turning Ned's old office into her bedroom. I'm glad she has a project. I imagine we are all finding projects to work on in the house and in the yard. I don't have the energy to do house projects, which makes me sad. But I'm hoping to enjoy some podcasts or to listen to Bible Project stuff—I need to keep my brain going. I was grateful I got to read some poetry that I have loved for several years to friends in my Cultivating Project community. It made my people- and poetry-loving heart very happy.

Today I am grateful to say the knees feel a little better. My calf is still swollen, as is my right ankle. But I can hobble. (I will not show you a photo of them because they are yucky.) After some x-rays and lab work, my doctor said I'm showing signs of "immunotherapy induced arthritis," so it sounds like I'll be starting steroids. But I don't remember what this means about next cycle of meds . . .

I'm so grateful to be able to hobble. A friend made the most glorious loaf of wheat bread, and I had enough happy energy to make it into French toast topped with blueberries and maple syrup. It made me happy to hobble around and work on brunch. Ned helped, too. We also prayed the morning prayer from the Daily Prayer app that our Pastor Luke introduced us to. Ned, Ellie, and I had teatime around 3 p.m. and talked to his mom and then his dad on the phone. So good. I want to have some good rhythms in our day, but then I get tired or I can't walk. I'm grateful that God is not demanding these things of us, as we stumble along trying to figure out these upside-down days. He is compassionate and gracious and filling us up with Himself. I'm holding on to those things.

Today I was reminded of a very favorite verse: "But I, through the abundance of your steadfast love, will enter your house" (Ps. 5:7). I have always loved the words "abundance" and "steadfast" in reference to God's love for me. I really didn't believe that He loved me for so long, even though I grew up in the church and went to a Christian school. I was aware of all the places I fell short and didn't understand that He was compassionate, welcoming, and full of grace. God has been very persistent in teaching me that He does love me, and His love comes from His choice and stays on me and His people because He wants it to. He is always welcoming us into Himself. Even on this cancer roller coaster, where my heart and spirit are wavery and weak, I'm learning to rest in this truth (and if I forget, friends lovingly remind me). I hope you can be encouraged, too, by His abundant steadfast love for you—His love brings us to Him and into His presence.

Love,
Leslie

. . .

March 27, 2020

Just to keep you in the loop as you think of me to pray:

Because my left knee is still not better (I can bend it but not straighten it out when walking) and my right foot/ankle/calf is still swollen from the immuno-therapy meds, the doctor is upping my steroids to 80 mg for two days. After that we'll decrease it by 20 mg each day so that I will only be on 10 mg by Wednesday and can have the immunotherapy treatment. The hope is that this will set my legs straight so we can keep doing the immunotherapy. If not, we will keep me on steroids till this is fixed and put me on BRAF pills for a while to fight the melanoma.

I really want this to work. Some of it is vanity—long-term steroid use will cause me to gain weight, and I just worked hard to lose 25 pounds and keep in healthier shape. But the worst really is that it can cause bone density loss and cataracts and weird reactions on the skin. So that seems more important than weight gain. Also, steroid use can cause one to get hyper, which might explain why yesterday, with only 20 mg of steroids in me, I was so happy and actually wanted to eat food. I can't imagine being more happy/hyper.

What a thing to be living through.

Last night, I listened to The Gray Havens album *She Waits*. So good. Many of the songs are about longing for heaven and eternity and restoration. I've loved these songs for a while—I like how The Gray Havens put words together and how they sound, but now their lyrics seem a little more poignant, and they hit a little closer to home.

Much love,

Leslie

. . .

MARCH 31, 2020

Hello friends,

Yesterday was the best day with my knees and my right calf and foot. But I woke up today with both kneecaps feeling bulgy and tight. I can walk okay, but I can tell they are not right. My right foot and toes have much more definition and less swelling; my right back calf feels like it needs a really good stretch; it's tight.

Tomorrow I would have gotten my immunotherapy treatment. But the plan now is to put me back to 60 mg of steroids or more to get my joints and muscles back to normal, or at least to where I only need 10 mg. Next week Dr. Brennan will put me on the BRAF therapy treatment, which are pills. These are also known to fight and work against the melanoma. I'll be on those until he decides to put me back on the immunotherapy.

There has been discouragement in my heart over this, but as I was praying and confessing this to the Lord, I started to come to a clearer realization that He is in this. He knows it all; He knows what is needed for now and what lies ahead, and He has it all in hand. And that truly is where I am called to rest and hope and trust. My head and heart could actually put words to this, and I was glad.

The upside to steroids: I haven't felt so clear-headed and -hearted in months. I told Ned that it feels like a fog has lifted. And even though I know God has been in this the whole time, and I have felt sustained with an overabundance of care, there has been an aspect of feeling like I'm in no-man's land, wandering about. But for the past week, things have cleared: I have creative and thinking brain cells; I've cooked and read and taken care of home life. I'm so glad and grateful to feel this. (Downside: it's hard to actually sleep straight through the night . . .)

I want to get my legs back to normal, so I can walk outside and go to a park or walk downtown and help Ellie with her room and do house projects. I miss that a lot. I am grateful I don't need to take two naps a day. And for now, I truly am glad to have a clear mind and heart.

Thinking of you all as I write this, as I know you all are going through your own upside-down world with this pandemic and all its consequences. I hope you are finding comfort and strength and rest and hope in the Lord in this time. He who began a good work in us will complete it, even during (and because of) our time sheltering in place.

A friend, Eric Peters, and his family have been living through their own awful, awful situation: when the tornado went through Nashville, they lost their home. He wrote the following words on his own CaringBridge site. I found his words really strengthening:

> But if only one thing is left of me standing in all of this, it's an entrenched, rooted faith within my battle born soul urging quiet, confidence, stillness, and rest. Cry if you need to. Do not be afraid. Laugh and find humor.[153]

Quiet, stillness, and rest are truly what I am called to, but I want to dig deeper into confidence—confidence sustained because Jesus is going before me and Jesus is holding me. I have been held by the confidence of my praying friends and family. Today, I am glad to have a clear mind and heart to hold some of that confidence myself, right now. Eric has a song "Fighting for My Life" that I like a lot; I like the honesty and the hope in what he sings and how the music plays along.

Much love. I cannot say it enough—your words and prayers are gift. Thank you for caring for and remembering me, even as you go through your own life and struggles. May Jesus be real to you, as He holds all things together.

Leslie

. . .

APRIL 3, 2020

Good afternoon,

The saga of my knees and steroids continued this week. I thought they were on the mend, but then they started to flair up again, so the doctor put me back on 80 mg of steroids yesterday and today with the hope of them getting better. Today is a much better day, and I'm grateful.

I will be starting the BRAF therapy (taking two types of pills at home) in a few days. One I take once a day on an empty stomach, and two I take twice a day. One stays in the refrigerator, and the other in a cool dry place. Looking forward to having a nice little chart that will help me keep track of it all. I am trying not to worry over the side effects, as any side effects I have will not really start till after I am off the steroids; both medications will overlap for the next week or so.

Although I really did cry and feel sad over some of this the other day, my mind has felt clear, and I have been able to pray, mediate on Scripture, and practice quiet. And the past two days have been a gift of peace and sweetness. I can't go anywhere, but I've been able to do things that make me glad in my cozy library chair (like read, pray, journal, write, text friends, talk on the phone). I have also been able to do things around the house and cook and be creative.

One side effect of steroids: an uncontrollable desire to reorganize all the books in your house

Last night as my head hit the pillow, I thought of my "things I would like to do" list and felt so glad for these days when I can actually do things I love. This has all felt like a real gift from Jesus to ease my tired heart. I don't know what the next chapter on meds will look like, but it looks like it won't be easy, so now is a time to cultivate some inner and outer goodness. I'm so grateful I could almost burst.

Today, a melanoma nurse navigator called me, and we talked for about an hour. I needed to talk, and I needed her wisdom, and she gave me the help I needed. She had a wonderful soothing voice and a patient listening ear. She offered comfort and good ideas; we covered many topics. We talked about managing food on steroids (my appetite is up and that is new, and I am mourning the idea of gaining the weight I just lost this fall). One thing she shared: usually her patients on steroids get cranky and moody. I told her I haven't felt this good (except for lack of sleep) since Ned and I were in Italy four months ago. I hope these good feelings stay. She also encouraged me to remember that this road will be bumpy and there will be hiccups—it will not be smooth. I will get some treatment in, and then I may have a reaction and need to go on a meds holiday to deal with that reaction.

I have been imagining treatment as an easy road with the treatment just doing its thing—isn't having cancer enough? But there will be issues that come up because of the medications. What I heard her say is that I should look at this like living with a chronic disease—we are working for stability, a cure, but this is a long-haul thing. This helped me put some things in perspective.

I wrote a blog post for my beloved Veritas Academy community called "Why We Should Travel to Narnia When We Can't Leave Our Homes."[154] What a gift to me to get to write about Narnia and C.S. Lewis and put together something that combines my love of teaching, encouraging, and pointing people to Jesus and beauty. It came at just the right time.

Yesterday, one of my favorite contemporary poets, Luci Shaw, wrote this poem about this COVID time. I hope it encourages you as it did me:

virus
Luci Shaw

The absurdity of a world
on its knees, behind its doors,
whose fingers, even, may be traitors
and whose breath, created for living,
may breed death. Its instruction:
Split up. Stay apart. This is now
the ultimate act of friendship.
Like the moon of light at the bottom
of the well, hope shines small,
but if we stay, head over edge,
we may watch the deep water shimmer
with small possibilities. At noon,
a pale sun shines, telling us
we may still live in the light.

Grateful for you all and for how you are taking the time to care for me by listening in, praying, and offering good words. I know this time is not easy for you, so the minutes you take to pay attention to me is a gift.

Warmly,
Leslie

. . .

APRIL 11, 2020

Dear family and friends,

This Saturday will be my first full day on the BRAF meds, trametinib and dabrafenib. Right now, I am also on 20 mg of steroids. My knees are doing 95% fine—hooray. Over the next week the steroids will taper off to nothing. Once that happens, the side effects of the BRAF treatment will start. Right now I'm feeling pretty much all me (except for the insomnia)—I have more energy than I have ever had, plus a bigger appetite and a very real scatterbrain-ness. It's been a gift to be living in my own skin and to feel like who I was before this all started.

I am trying not to worry about the next part of this story—side effects. They don't sound fun. There will be ones the doctor said I will get—such as fever, some type of rash, major fatigue, sun sensitivity, loss of appetite, maybe intestinal issues, maybe thinning or loss of hair—and then maybe even worse internal ones (I don't feel like listing those—the papers that came with my pills certainly covered all the bases). Thank you to those who have been praying that the side effects would be mild. Let's keep praying that!

This week, having a clear mind and heart, I spent lots of time in the new study that Ned and Ellie helped me put together last weekend. Sitting in my overstuffed, cozy chair, in a room with lots of sunlight, I focused on some of the psalms. I have been greatly encouraged by meditating on Psalm 36 , 37, and 38—those chapters are full of God's abundant love to us and what it looks like—many word pictures, which I love. Psalm 36:5 says, "Lord, your faithful love reaches to heaven, your faithfulness to the clouds," then verse 10 says, "Spread your faithful love over those who know you ... (CSB)." And I started picturing that God's steadfast, faithful love, which reaches to the heavens, is actually like the heavens, filled with all those glorious stars shining down and spread widely over us. I could see the black night at Laity Lodge in Texas, perfectly overcrowded with small and large bits of light reaching up and over, left to right. All that to me was the beauty of God's love spread over us.

This week has been full of the ordinary, home-life things I have loved doing over the years. So again, I have been gifted these days with such goodness—gathering Ned and Ellie together for each day's meal, making cinnamon rolls, trying to dye Easter eggs the natural way, working on getting the third floor (Ned's office and Ellie's new bedroom) all pulled together, talking with friends and family on the phone or texting or messaging, and gathering books to share with other friends. Friends are still helping us stay quarantined by going grocery shopping for us. This coming week, more friends (real gardeners!) are coming to help me with my garden. Other outside house projects are in the works, all made possible because two friends set up a GoFundMe page.

This week, a dear friend posted a video of one of my favorite hymns—performed by church friends a decade ago. I didn't even know this video existed. Matthew Monticchio wrote this song for our church, and it has found its way into our family culture and into my heart; its words come quickly to mind. And it is just right for Easter time:

> Christ is risen, sing,
> fear not death's strong power nor sting.
> Tune your heart to joy,
> our strong God will death destroy.
> Wake my soul to sing,
> you alone cause praise to ring.
> Soul recount the ways
> that your God sustains your days.[155]

I am looking forward to Resurrection Sunday tomorrow. Looking forward to what our church will offer us, virtually. Then Maggie and Carey, with her self-isolating roomies (friends of hers that we love), are coming to our backyard for a grand "social distancing Easter day." Carey and her roomies are making a lot of the meal, and we will end our time with a fire in the fire pit and s'mores.

How good to be reminded of Jesus' resurrection and the sure hope that it gives us . . . me. In my imagination, I'll be joining Mary Magdalene, grateful that Jesus sees me, says my name, and calls me to Himself and to God the Father.

Blessings on your Easter Sunday! Thank you again for praying for me: I never grow tired of hearing people tell me they are praying for me. Your prayers are a gift.

Love,

Leslie

. . .

APRIL 15, 2020

Today I had a phone call with Dr. Brennan, so here are a few updates for you!

My knees are 85% not bad—they are just tight across the kneecaps. But no pain, and I can do regular life. I'm so grateful.

I will be on 20 mg steroids till Monday, and then for several days I'll go to 15 mg and taper down by 5 mg till I'm off.

No BRAF side effects yet. Dr. Brennan said the side effects will start to be unmasked as the steroids taper off. He was kind to say, when I shared that I was starting to have that dread feeling about what could happen, that nothing could happen. But I am trying to keep reminding myself that my team, and Jesus as my Good Shepherd, will help me through any side effects—because there will side effects, I'm sure.

I also now have a wacky thyroid and will be put on thyroid meds to get that evened out.

Lastly, I have had insomnia for more than a week. Last Friday I started feeling so tired I could barely keep my head up, so ... naps (though I'm still not able to nap well). The past two days have been the worst, so Dr. Brennan is giving me some meds for that. (I have tried things to help, but they don't get me through the night.)

Steroids have now caused me to have a much rounder face than usual (the doctor said it would get puffier), so that's a thing. I guess I always get to work on my vanity, no matter what stage of life I'm in. But I'm really not complaining, just rolling my eyes at myself, because in the summer I'll be having breast surgery and things will be hard then.

But other than that, lots of lovely life is happening here.

Easter was wonderful. Time with Maggie, Carey, and Carey's 3 roomies was amazing. We worked hard at social distancing. They brought lots of good food. Ned made "Pandemic Approved" Easter baskets (candy in plastic bags). We talked, laughed, had an egg hunt, and roasted marshmallows in the fire pit. They stayed for 8 hours. The weather held out, so we could be outside the whole time (the only way we could've made it work).

On Tuesday, four lovely and gardening-talented friends worked on my backyard and made it so beautiful. I am abundantly blessed by them—my dear backyard looks perfect and fresh.

I've been reading *Mr. Putter and Tabby* through Facebook Live to friends' children and I couldn't be happier. Reading to children is one of my top 10 favorite things to do, and the Mr. Putter and Tabby stories are the best early reader chapter books.

Please do pray for my mom. In her assisted living home, they have to restrict people from interacting with each other, which means no eating at tables with each other, no bingo or events, no walking in the halls, and dinner in your room. Even though we talk every day, I miss my mom very much. She is healthier and stronger than she has been in a year or so, and I cannot believe that she has to live like this, and that she cannot see us. I know we all are going through situations like this so, if you think of her, thank you for praying.

One of my favorite singers (and a dear friend) Joy Ike wrote a song called "All the Time in the World"—it's so great and encouraging for this time of self-isolation.

Thank you for your prayers and care and love! It is a blessing and I'm so grateful every day.

Warmly,

Leslie

...

APrIL 17, 2020

Just sharing: by the end of today I took all my various (6 types of) meds at all the right times and with all the empty stomachs when needed. I have done it correctly two days in a row—hooray for reminders and timers on the phone! Just feeling proud of my scatterbrained self. Kinda feels like a miracle.

Also, the spring issue of *Cultivating* magazine is out. It is the most wonderful work, and I'm so grateful to be part of the community and to be given the opportunity to write for them. I have two essays and three recipes in this issue, and Ned is interviewed in it.[156] The whole community, led by Lancia Smith, is wonderful, generous, kind, creative, and thoughtful. They have been such wonderful supporters of me, as you all have been. I think you will enjoy this issue—it is full of beauty, truth, and goodness, and the encouragement to receive life.

Thank you for praying for me.

...

APrIL 27, 2020

Dear family and friends,

Last week, fatigue hit me earlier in the day than usual. My theory—I was on the other side of all that lovely steroid energy and at the beginning of fatigue from the BRAF meds.

Sometime Saturday night/Sunday morning, I could tell I had a fever (you know—chills, and it's so hard to get warm, no matter what you do!). Sunday I had a fever and just lots of fatigue. More fever last night. I thought I would feel awful all day, but today my fever broke, and I just felt tired.

This afternoon, the doctor had me come in for blood work and a quick check up. The labs revealed that my white blood cell count is dangerously low. I am in high risk for infection and maybe already have one.

They took blood for blood cultures from my arm and my port—to see if I have an infection in my body or in my port. They are taking me off the BRAF meds for a week or so to see if the fever is because of the meds. The question is—fever from meds or fever from infection? I've been told to call them if I feel even a little bit sick. Apparently with such a low white blood cell count I could land in the hospital. All this to say, I came home pretty teary-eyed and weary. For some reason, it just hit me hard.

I'm grateful to say that my fever doesn't seem to have returned, and I didn't feel as wiped out today like I did last week. And I'm ending the day not as sad but grateful tomorrow is a new day. Two happy things from last week to share:

- The podcasts I worked on this summer (interviewing friends connected with Square Halo Books) are finally up at our website.[157] Since the play I was producing and the conference I was planning were cancelled, having the podcasts complete so people can hear them is such a gift! With the help of a Rabbit Room friend, they even sound professional! (we worked with Juli Strawbridge to compose the opening music.)
- Luci Shaw, the first (living) poet I fell in love with, posted a poem in the comments section of my essay "Wilderness of Waiting Filled with Life" in *Cultivating*. What a sweet surprise and such a happy happy thing for me. Here it is:

OUR PRAYERS BREAK ON GOD
Luci Shaw

Our prayers break on God like waves
and he an endless shore,
and when the seas evaporate
and oceans are no more
and cries are carried in the wind
God hears and answers every sound
As he has done before.
Our troubles eat at God like nails.
he feels the gnawing pain
on souls and bodies. He never fails
but reassures he'll heal again
again, again, again, again, and yet again.

And in this crazy, hard, rocky time, I hope you can find Ps. 37:23–24 to be true. I picture God like a loving father holding the hand of His child, as His child works on the art of walking: "A man's steps are established by the LORD, and He takes pleasure in his way. Though he falls, he will not be overwhelmed because the LORD holds his hand" (HCSB).

Recording the first Square Halo podcast with Tom Becker, author of *Good Posture*

Again and again, thank you for praying for me. I am always grateful.

Love,

Leslie

PS—My mom is hanging in there and is working hard at making her life at her assisted living home work within the social restrictions. It is good to see her being herself—determined.

PPS—My knees are doing so much better, even though the steroids are tapering off!

...

APRIL 29, 2020

Hello! I just wanted to share that I didn't have a fever yesterday afternoon, through the night, or this morning. Although I don't feel 100%, I do feel good, which means I forget that my white blood cell is so so low. I bet I will need a nap later, but that's okay. Yesterday I spent time in my study and comfy chair reading, which was nice. I went back to reading *The Letters of John Newton*, which in the past has done my heart and mind much good. Also, the hymn "I Need Thee Every Hour" (but the Jars of Clay version) has been running through my mind.

I am still waiting for the blood culture results to return.

Thank you for praying for me and for encouraging me with your love and interest and care. It means so much and it humbles me.

Leslie

...

MAY 4, 2020

Hello friends,

I had blood work today, as well as a check-up with Dr. Brennan, and an injection for the breast cancer.

When I have blood work done, they schedule my appointment with Dr. Brennan an hour later. So I took some books and a journal today, with the intention of going to the meditation room, which I did. What a lovely room. One wall has slightly curved windows which face into the courtyard. In front of the courtyard and the windows is a little pool with rocks. There was sunshine and a breeze, so you can imagine how the water moved and the light played on the water and the rocks. The mediation room had comfortable chairs and lap blankets. I was alone for 60 minutes in this sweet spot and actually read, journaled, and just looked at the pool.

Here is an update:

- My white blood cell count is up a little; it is still low but not dangerously low.
- I don't have an infection, so last week's issues were side effects to BRAF.
- I do have a swollen right ankle again and inconsistency with my knees.
- The doctor is keeping me on 15 mg of steroids and then down to 12.5 for a week or so, before going to 10, etc. etc. (what I have been saying for the past month!!).
- So now I get to add another med (!) to deal with bone density issues because of steroids. (This one makes me smile: I have to take it once a week, and I must sit up for 30 minutes after I take it. And the day I take that I don't take any vitamins. Phew.)
- I am off antibiotics and back on BRAF (I am glad to be back on meds that fight the melanoma. Despite my tension over side effects, I am glad to be taking the meds).
- My eyelids and cheeks are puffy because of the steroids. Hooray.
- Dr. Brennan said I could use some weights to work on muscle mass loss due to steroids. And to keep up the walking I started this weekend. So here's to me putting that into my schedule. I'm glad, because the other day I was really missing working out at the Y.

I asked the doctor about why sometimes my emotions seem so much more roller-coastery than usual. He reminded me that I have been put in chemically induced menopause due to the breast cancer, I'm on the other side of the happy effects of the steroids, and my thyroid is still out of whack. I literally laughed out loud at him when he said that those three things. Two types of cancer and that triple whammy?

But the good news (this is an unscientific observation the doctor made): both tumors seem smaller. (Scans next month.) Insert dancing emoji here.

I'm having a hard time reading long portions in books and keeping big ideas going on in my brain, but I am working at reading each day. I'm reading a C.S. Lewis daily reader (bite-size Lewis readings I can do), J.C. Ryle daily reader (bite-size bits of Scripture and theology I can do), plus working through, still, James K.A. Smith's *On the Road with Saint Augustine* (I make my own bite-size chunks—it's really good). Before bed, I'm re-reading *The Letters of John Newton*, because he is so pastoral and full of grace.

But what I can keep reading in more than bite-size chunks is the book *Letters from the Land of Cancer*, by Walter Wangerin. I just feel myself slipping into this comfortable place in my brain when I'm reading him—his way with words, his storytelling, and his wisdom are already familiar; his cancer story is a great encouragement to me.

I read this the other day (about his taking slow walks in the snow):

> So these are the things on my mind these days: that I must spend slow time moving through the drifts—not only for the exercise after all. I go for the beauty and silent intimacy of the going. I go without the morbidity whatsoever. Maybe this is my last opportunity to walk in a winter's snowfall. Not to make a memory of it, but to know it now.[158]

I was arrested by his saying "but to know it now," because that is what I've always wanted in my adult life, and that is what I want now—to pay attention clearly enough to know what I am in the midst of or who I am with at that moment. I loved that he echoed my heart's thoughts. His words will echo in my mind as I walk through my days, either in the house or walking around my block or at a park. "To know it now …"

I'm grateful for the blue skies, the sunshine, the wind in the tree outside my window today. I'm grateful that my friend Ashley is bringing us dinner and another friend Terilyn is getting groceries for us tonight. Friends keep supporting us, and it is a gift. As are your prayers and encouraging words.

Much love,

Leslie

. . .

MAY 11, 2020

Hello! Today I had blood work done, and my white blood cell count is back to normal. So grateful. My red blood cell count continues to be below normal, but I am taking iron for that.

Yesterday, Mother's Day, was a good day. The girls came (as well as Carey's roomies) and the laughter and conversation was as sweet and bright as the chocolate cake and sunshine we had. We took a good walk at Rock Ford Plantation at Lancaster County Park. It was the first time the weather and my wonky knees cooperated and allowed me to get out of the house and the neighborhood. So happy.

Sunday's sermon focused on Jesus revealing Himself to Cleopas and his companion in the breaking of the bread. I love that story so much, and I loved how Pastor Luke saw the breaking of the bread and the opening of their eyes as a reversal of what happened in the Garden when Adam and Eve ate of the tree and their eyes were opened, but in shame. Here Jesus offers the bread, they take it, and their eyes are opened—not in shame, but to the fact that Jesus is alive. Pastor Luke also reminded us that even though Jesus had opened the Scriptures to them earlier, they needed Him to offer them the bread and to eat it before they could finally see Him. Scripture and Supper are at the center of us knowing Him. Just good encouragement!

Warmly,

Leslie

. . .

JUNE 1, 2020

Dear friends,

Today I met with Dr. Brennan. Good news: all my blood work was normal. And I can go grocery shopping as long as I wear a mask and gloves. (Though I've been so grateful for all my friends who have shopped for us, I am looking forward to shopping myself, just to do something that I used to do.)

Other news: I have one more month of taking BRAF meds before I get scans to see what is happening with both tumors. Still good—the doctor couldn't feel the tumor on my intestine.

Other, other news: some time this summer, after the scans, we will talk to the surgeon about scheduling breast surgery. Dr. Brennan said that I will most likely have a mastectomy. A mastectomy would be the best way to fight breast cancer while also fighting the melanoma. He told me that if I have reconstructive surgery that will happen down the road. For some reason, this idea of waiting for reconstructive surgery made me really sad and tearful. Having a mastectomy is still the part of this cancer that makes me the most ... something, I don't know the word, but it isn't positive. (I'm still working on this part of my life ...)

Dr. Brennan also told me that I cannot start on immunotherapy until I can get down to 10 mg of steroids (I'm still at 15 mg). My knees are still tight and bulgy when I wake up in the morning, and it takes a while to get them loosened up. BRAF meds are good, as they are fast and furious on the melanoma, but they have not proven to be as durable in the long run as immunotherapy meds. The hope is to restart immunotherapy after breast surgery, if my knees do what we want them to. The doctor is going to talk to a rheumatoid arthritis doctor at the cancer center to figure out other things we can try besides steroids.

I'm learning in a new way to wait, to be in the "now," to pray for the future but not to sit looking at the past or worrying about the future; to lament what I miss and to pray to God and to encourage myself to see the good of this quiet time before surgery.

I could tell I was about to spiral because of the things that I miss doing— the good work in and out of my home that made up the substance of my days. But I felt God almost lay His hand on me and say, "Slow down; take a look and be at peace." So everything from blue skies, clouds, and birds chirping to the small projects I'm working on at home—I'm learning a new way to pay attention and wait.

I've had a really good time reading to friends and their children through Facebook Live. Writing for *Cultivating* and working on a couple other creative projects has also been a gift. Meeting with family and friends on our patio porch has been very life-giving for me, as it gives me a little bit of ordinary. Life has been quiet and my steroids no longer make me hyper, so I've felt mostly normal in my "skin," and I think it was this normal feeling that made me start to feel sad about all the ordinary things that are no longer part of my life. (But maybe you can relate, too, as we all have had to deal with this because of COVID.)

Today I read from *Two-Part Invention*, a book about Madeline L'Engle's marriage to Hugh Franklin (they had been married for 40 years and he had cancer): "I do not want ever to be indifferent to the joys and beauties of this life. For through these, as through pain, we are enabled to see purpose in randomness, pattern in chaos. We do not have to understand in order to believe that behind the mystery and fascination there is love."[159] I first read this book after Ned and I got married, and it enlarged my imagination and helped me think about being married and being a woman; now I am re-reading and thinking about having cancer, as the story is about that, too. I'm glad I bought a used copy of it at The Strand in NYC this past February!

Tomorrow Ned and I celebrate 30 years of being married—what a thing to say! I am glad that the guy who was my best friend when I was 20 years old is my husband at 52.

Thank you for paying attention to and praying for me. I am always grateful and humbled by everyone's care.

Warmly,
Leslie

June 22, 2020

Happy beginning of summer!

This Wednesday I have a CAT scan to see what the melanoma tumor on my intestine has done. It seems to have shrunk, as I can't feel it and the doctor can't feel it either. But this CAT scan will show us exactly what has happened to it since I have been taking BRAF meds for 3 months.

This Thursday I meet with Dr. Brennan and my nurse navigator. I am assuming that we'll talk about surgery regarding the tumor in my breast. Even though each day I find myself retuning to Jesus regarding the mastectomy, and not without tears, I don't quite feel brave about this all. Despite that, I want to get more information and get a date in place.

Please pray for these two appointments. Not sure what to have you pray other than that the tumor has shrunk and all looks good, and that we can get a schedule in place regarding taking care of the tumor in my breast. My knees are doing so much better. I have been on 12.5 mg of steroids for a few days, and they haven't gotten worse. Very glad for that.

Ned's birthday was yesterday. It was wonderful collaborating with Carey and having Ellie, Maggie, and Carey's roomies help us pull together good food and fun to celebrate Ned. I haven't actually put together a celebration in a while, and it was good to plan and shop, cook and bake. But by 6 p.m. I was on the couch napping while they all played Ned's museum card game in the kitchen. For some reason, I still get surprised by how tired I get. I feel almost normal, until I am hit by a huge wave of being weary of people and activities.

I have been reading *The Sound of Life's Unspeakable Beauty* by Martin Schleske. He is a world-respected luthier (violinmaker). Through the book he shares the process and secrets of handcrafting a violin while also sharing how each phase can point us "toward our calling, our true selves, and the overwhelming power and gentleness of God's love."[160]

It's pretty wonderful. I continue to return to his ideas in Chapter 5, "The Arching and the Wood's Grain." Here he focuses on how the master craftsman brings about the *violin's true sound* while carving the arch and working with the wood's grain:

> The development of a good sound, which is the goal of all my work as a master violinmaker, is a sensory revelation of beauty and life. It is the same with the *sound of our life*. We need to develop a feel for the alluring power of Wisdom at work in us; we need to be overcome by love and the pressing power of grace that wants to create something beautiful through our lives.[161]

The idea of the sound of one's life is so compelling to me. Also, every day I seem to hear the birds in my backyard and neighborhood singing louder than usual, or maybe it's just that I am easily distracted by them. They really make me happy. I hope that you too are finding places to root yourself in God's care for and work in you.

NeedtoBreathe, my favorite band, released a new song called "Survival," and I love listening to it, especially while driving in the car. Good sound and good words.

Thank you for praying for me. I hope the summer sunshine is good for you!!
Warmly,
Leslie

. . .

June 25, 2020

Dear friends,

The news today is that we can be guardedly optimistic: the tumor mass that was on my intestine is not there, according to the CAT scan. (I still have to have a PET scan to confirm this.)

This could mean one of two things (other than it being a miracle—which it could be!): 1) The meds worked and got rid of the tumor; or 2) what we thought was a tumor was actually my body reacting to the Zolodex pellet that is injected into my abdomen once a month to fight the breast cancer. But even if that mass wasn't a tumor, I did need the melanoma meds, because melanoma is still in the lymph nodes under my left armpit. (Also melanoma cells can hide in the body without showing up on tests, so my meds were fighting something.)

As for the breast cancer, the tumor still looks stable. If the PET scan is good, we will take a break from the melanoma treatment and start talking about breast cancer treatment/surgery with Dr. Bleznak, the surgeon.

But back to the good news: for now, the words are "guardedly optimistic."

I've been thinking about these verses that I discovered (re-discovered?) in Ps. 107:29–30: "He stilled the storm to a murmur, and the waves of the sea were hushed. They rejoiced when the waves grew quiet. Then He guided them to the harbor they longed for" (HCSB).

I love the image of a safe harbor—God is both the one who calms the storm and guides the boat to the harbor, and He is the longed-for harbor. I don't always know what it means, in my everyday life (with or without cancer), for Jesus to be the one who will actually fulfill the longings of my heart, but I know it is true. Nothing has ever really filled the holes in my longing heart, so as Peter said, "Lord, to whom will we go? You have the words of eternal life" (John 6:68 HCSB). So I ask Jesus to be that for me each day, and for me to either keep trusting Him even when I don't "feel" Him fulfilling this prayer or to give me eyes to see that He is.

Also, this verse came back to my mind this morning when I was driving to my appointment: "The name of the LORD is a strong tower; the righteous runs to it and are safe" (Prov. 18:10 NKJV). This verse has been a foundational verse for me for so long. I have loved the image of a strong tower and the promise that God wants me to run to Him—to cry out to Him and to know that I will be safe in Him.

Thank you for your prayers this week!

Warmly,

Leslie

Saint Brendan
Ned Bustard

JUNE 30, 2020

Hello friends,

My PET scan is scheduled for tomorrow morning at 8 a.m. Thank you for your prayers about this scan: please pray that the tumor that wasn't seen on the CAT scan isn't on the PET scan, and also that there isn't any more cancer (besides what we know of in the lymph node and my right breast).

This is happy—the new med that Dr. Brennan put me on for my rheumatoid arthritis is really helping my knees. I have almost all normal movement. I'm so grateful for this.

It was so good to be at church this week and see church family, even if we were all spread apart and the singing was a little muffled because of masks (man, those masks make my face hot and my glasses fog up! It gets me cranky). This week we sang "By Faith," by Keith and Kristyn Getty. I love this song, especially the chorus. This is a great driving, singalong kind of song:

> We will stand as children of the promise;
> We will fix our eyes on Him, our soul's reward.
> Till the race is finished and the work is done,
> We'll walk by faith and not by sight.[162]

Also this from our bulletin:

> The central things of Christian worship are not so much things we do as events where God has promised to act. There is no "temple" in the city (Rev. 21:22). God and the Lamb take its place. That is our praise, our worship, our action, our sacrifice, even our seeking, are not the heart of Christian worship. God's presence, God's gift, the very fruit of the tree of life, is. Bath, table, prayer, and the word are important to "every seeking soul" because God is there, wiping away tears, giving life. (Gordon Lathrop)

What a thing to keep meditating on during the day—God's presence wiping away tears and giving life.

Sometimes I get hung up on all the good and wonderful things I did last summer—I felt so very "me" in following God's call on my life. I was writing, interviewing people for podcasts, planning the play and a conference, having people in my home, and hosting gatherings at the Square Halo Gallery. But none of that is happening this summer, and I think, "Who am I now?" and "What should I be doing before surgery," now that I feel normal for most of the day (until I need to take nap). I get so easily hung up on "shoulds," as well as just pining for last summer or worrying about what will I be doing next summer. (Maybe you can relate to this, too, in the midst of the COVID craziness.)

But I love Isaiah 30:15 (if only I could remember it more often): "For thus said the LORD God, the Holy One of Israel, In returning and rest you shall be saved; in quietness and in trust shall be your strength." And Hebrews reminds me to "fix [my] thoughts on Jesus" (3:1 NIV). And Philippians: "Forgetting what lies behind and straining toward what lies ahead" (3:13).

This all is working together in my brain and heart so I can remember what is true right now and just enjoy the nowness of quiet days at home, paying attention to family and friends, my garden, the blue sky and birds, and whatever my hands find to do. Also, books and poetry. (And NeedtoBreathe has a new song out, "Who Am I," so that's happy.)

Thank you for your prayers! And for your kind words and attention.

Warmly,

Leslie

...

JULY 1, 2020

Hello friends,

This evening I received the results from today's PET Scan. I was almost afraid to look, but I'm glad I did. Here is the direct quote from my doctor:

PET looked very good.... All the changes in the abdomen are gone.

Happy happy happy to say that there isn't a melanoma tumor on or in my intestines or any part of my body!

There is still "stuff" in my left armpit lymph nodes, like before, and something in my right armpit lymph node. I have a message in to my doctor to have him explain what it is.

Thank you for praying!

Today I also had one of those injections in my abdomen for my breast cancer (I would tell you the name, but the name never stays in my brain). I was sitting in the chair with an ice pack where the pellet is injected (the needle is not thin at all. I always ask for ice to numb the spot. This helps me not feel it go in). I was waiting for the nurse to get everything together; happily, I was alone, the floor was quiet, and I had big, clean windows to look through. The sky was really blue and the clouds dramatically fluffy. I was trying to keep my mind and heart from wandering down unhelpful paths, so I asked the Lord what I should think about Simeon and Anna as they met baby Jesus, Mary, and Joseph at the Temple

(I just read their stories yesterday). And this very quickly came to my mind: "They waited and they trusted. They showed up to the Temple, the place of God's presence. They knew God's words and believed."

I'm going to believe that was the Holy Spirit's prompting and encouragement. Waiting and trusting, returning and resting. Grateful for God's care in all of this.

I don't meet with Dr. Brennan till next week, but I plan to call him tomorrow to have him explain it all to me. But this looks very good.

Warmly,

Leslie

. . .

JULY 10, 2020

Hello friends,

This week I learned a little more about carrying the sweet and good along with the anxiety and the dread. I have been grateful for the past week: time spent with family and friends, around my picnic table and kitchen table, in my living room, at local restaurants, out on the river in a kayak. How grateful I was for these hours of happy energy that allowed me to pay attention to and share in ordinary things; each time was preceded or followed by a good nap, of course.

However, this Wednesday night I got that pit-in-your-stomach feeling, as I was headed toward Thursday's afternoon meeting with Dr. Brennan to discuss the PET scan and what was next (breast surgery this summer?). Thursday was a hard day, but also a wonderful day, as we celebrated Elspeth's 19th birthday.

The sweet with the bitter, laughter and tears, and lots of hugs for it all. I'm grateful for Dr. Brennan and the other surgeons on my team. They have spent much time discussing with more specialists what is next for me. Here is the plan:

- I will stay on BRAF pills for the next three months. Reason: they are going on the assumption that what was on my intestine was a tumor. They want to keep fighting whatever melanoma cells might still be in my body and to keep the tumor from returning. In Dr. Brennan's words, "Melanoma is the life-threatening cancer," so if the tumor returned that would be very bad for me. So they don't want to take any time off the meds to fight the breast cancer by having surgery.

- This means no breast cancer surgery this summer (queue up subdued happy dance in my brain). My tumor is stable and has actually gotten a little smaller; compared to the melanoma, it is not as "life-threatening" right now—the doctor's words. We are still managing it, with the two meds which starve the hormones that feed it. Most likely surgery in mid-fall?

- After three months of BRAF meds, I will get scans. If all looks good, they will take me off BRAF meds and put me on immunotherapy to keep fighting the melanoma.
- There are, of course, variables that can change this course of action. They will put me back on the one immunotherapy med called nivolumab. This med is not the one that caused the arthritis in my knees in March. But because I have still been struggling with arthritis this spring and summer, my knees could flare up. If it does, and if we can't control it with arthritis meds, they will put me back on BRAF meds. (Steroids and immunotherapy don't mix.)
- If my first few weeks on immunotherapy go okay they will schedule me for breast surgery. On immunotherapy, I could have a lumpectomy and radiation.
- If I have to go back on BRAF, then I have to have a mastectomy. One cannot have radiation if one is on BRAF meds. And for long term remission, it is good to have radiation. I won't have to have radiation if I get a mastectomy. (And then maybe down the road, reconstructive surgery?)

My knees have been doing so much better. Today I started on 10 mg of steroids, which I will do for 2 weeks and then go to 7 mg for 2 weeks. I have started yoga (for beginners, of course); it has been really good for me physically and mentally. Hooray for "Yoga with Adrienne" on YouTube.

I am grateful that I can put breast surgery off for a little while longer. How wonderful to think this summer could be full of time with family and friends, time at church, my nose in books, and my feet in water. Even though I get weary easily, I hope to wander around downtown Lancaster this summer, as well as around some Lancaster County trails, to cook and bake, and to work on some creative projects. Let's hope that as my steroids are reduced, BRAF side effects—like fever, rash, loss of appetite and hair (!), and a bunch of other things—don't happen.

If, as you look over this long letter, something jumps out to you to pray for—well, thank you for praying!! I don't take your prayers for granted, as I know my family and I have been sustained by them.

Yesterday I listened to "Joy Invincible," by Switchfoot, while driving home from the doctors. I don't know why I decided to listen to it, as it really makes me cry. But it is so good—its words and sound.

Hallelujah nevertheless
was the song the pain couldn't destroy
Hallelujah nevertheless,

you're my joy invincible—
joy invincible, joy[163]

This week the lovely summer issue of *Cultivating* was published. I'm still
working on reading everyone's work. So far, all I can say is—it is full of lovely and
encouraging abundance. I have two essays in it and one recipe.[164]

Thank you for paying attention to me through this. I'm grateful each day for
how God gives and gives; I just have to keep my heart and eyes attentive to even a
little of it all, and I am encouraged.

Love,
Leslie

. . .

AUGUST 1, 2020

Hello friends,

Happy days: the arthritis meds must be helping my knees feel so normal,
because this Thursday, my steroids go down from 7 mg to 5 mg.

I think the only major BRAF side effect that has appeared (but not consis-
tently) as my steroids have gone down is that I'm extra tired. Last week I was very
tired and also cranky or extra emotional or having an identity crisis. But most of
this week, I haven't been as tired during the day. I'm really grateful. Please pray
that side effects continue to stay at bay.

This past Monday, I went to the cancer center for genetic testing. I feel like
I'm in a science fiction story. That people can test my blood to see if the breast
cancer and melanoma are hereditary and connected or not is crazy.

I've been asking the Lord to help me understand more what it means to find
refuge in the shelter of His wings—I know I need this reality in my life. Psalm
61:4 has been on my mind for the past couple weeks: "Let me take refuge under
the shelter of your wings!" Even though I believe and seek Him for it, I really don't
understand what this looks like in my everyday life.

One thing that came to mind when I started praying for understanding was
the line "Christ plays in ten thousand places" from a Gerard Manly Hopkins
poem.[165] So I have been keeping my eyes open for all the good, delightful,
unexpected, or ordinary things around me that make my heart skip with glad-
ness. It is one way to think on that which is true, beautiful, honorable, etc. Since
I already have been trying to pay attention to the "now" of each day, quoting this
short phrase—"Christ plays in ten-thousand places"—has helped me pay closer
attention and to find refuge in Jesus.

A few weeks ago, we went to the beach. I had to stay under the umbrella, with a big hat on. I wore a long-sleeved swim top to cover my arms, lots of sunscreen, and sometimes a towel over my legs. Because of the melanoma and the meds, keeping out of the sun is pretty important, especially between 10 and 3. I have always loved being at the beach, feet in sand, face to the sun, and that lovely feeling of sun-warmed skin has always been a favorite.

But I was grateful to Ned for making the effort of getting us to Cape May (especially since the Chesapeake Bay is his favorite). It was a good time with him, Maggie, and Ellie. One of the days we were there, as I was in that lovely half-sleep beach nap, I played around with what I had been seeing at the beach that fit with "Christ plays in ten thousand places." This kept me from feeling any sadness about not getting to be "all out" in the sunshine. This isn't a poem, just my favorite observations. Maybe they will inspire you to see where Christ plays in ten thousand places.

Christ plays in ten-thousand
   places…
Beach blue bike, morning ride
The greeting of a sun-glistened,
   shimmering ocean surface
Familiar pounding roar of
   the ocean
Baby dolphin's fin slapping
   the water
Laughing seagulls grabbing
   unoffered food
Birds skimming the surface
Beach reads and beach naps

The comfortable feeling of a hand
   covered in sun-warmed sand
Beach neighbors' impromptu
   dance party
Returning dolphins jumping
   through the wake of a boat
Ice cream in a pretzel cone,
   covered with colorful jimmies
Ocean waves splashing hard over
   a jetty of rocks
Pink and orange stealing out of
   a cloud-covered sunset

Thank you for your prayers and care and love—for paying attention, even when you have so much in your day, in your heart, and in your mind. I'm humbled and grateful.

Warmly,

Leslie

. . .

AUGUST 8, 2020

Dear friends,

This Thursday, after a mammogram and ultrasound, I found out that the tumor in my breast has grown, not shrunk like the doctor was thinking. I had found two small, hard spots under the tumor and called my doctor, which led to the tests.

This means that soon I will have a mastectomy. August 17th I'll meet with the surgeon and then we will go from there. A date isn't set but it will be soon.

This news has brought a lot of sadness and trepidation and tears. It is the part of this cancer shadow that has made my heart feel the heaviest and most fearful. I can't wrap my imagination around the surgery and the recovery and getting used to having a body part taken off. It is good to know it will help stop the cancer, but that is about it.

I won't go on about how I was looking forward to the next month of being with family and friends, and the projects I was working on, but that is something I mourn, too.

The Lord's Prayer and Psalm 23 are really sweet. They help me mourn and also help me to set myself in God. That place of mourning and trusting is where I am learning to be. Thank you for praying.

Sandra McCracken's "Sweet Comfort" plays in my mind throughout the day. I've been thinking about silence and my need for more of it. And then there is always "The peace of God, which transcends all understanding" (Phil. 7:4 NIV). Thank you for praying for me in this.

Love,

Leslie

PS—Also, to those who gave money to the GoFundMe that friends set up, the money went to paint and such for the house but also to fixing up our back, second story porch, which is off my study. It is lovely. I named it "Happy Place." Such a sweet spot to be. Thank you thank you thank you.

. . .

AUGUST 17, 2020

Good evening family and friends,

Today I had a visit with my surgeon, Dr. Bleznak. Thank you for praying; I felt pretty composed and steadfast as I waited for the appointment today and I hung in there (and only got teary once) while we talked. That felt like a miracle, because I was nervous for this meeting. He is a really nice man, friendly and comforting; but he also is very in charge, a knowledgeable and experienced doctor. I like him a lot.

Thursday, I meet with Dr. Brennan. So whatever I share with you today may actually change then, but here are some of the things we discussed. There are two goals to choose from when dealing with cancer—working toward a cure or managing symptoms. Since I have two cancers, the doctors are fighting the melanoma to get a cure (because that is the more aggressive one), while we deal with the "symptoms" of the breast cancer tumor. This is what we have been doing all along, but for some reason, it was made really clear to me today.

Because the breast cancer tumor has grown, surgery needs to happen now. But Dr. Bleznak thinks, due to the tumor's size, that he can do a lumpectomy instead of a mastectomy. This was decided because the recovery for a lumpectomy is quick (1–2 weeks) compared to a mastectomy, and this will get me back on the melanoma-fighting meds quickly. And fighting melanoma is the biggest priority. Not that fighting the breast cancer isn't important, but right now decisions are made around the melanoma.

Breast surgery for now is not curative—it is for "treating the symptoms." This was the part that was disconcerting and reminded me that there are no guarantees in any of this. I had thought that a mastectomy was curative. I keep waiting for the "magic bullet"—for some doctor to say "this is what will make it all go away." Breast cancer cells can also act crazy and could be hiding in places we don't know about. The meds I'm on to starve the breast cancer of the hormones it feeds on can still fight it, as far as I understand. But this all still feels full of future unknowns, and I have to keep learning to submit to that. These unknowns make my heart very heavy for my family.

Dr. Bleznak was very encouraging and said that we aren't done fighting the breast cancer; for now we are just trying to get me cured of the melanoma.

Today I'm trying to hold loosely what kind of surgery I get. I like the idea of a lumpectomy for now, but the doctors will keep discussing me until Thursday, and Dr. Brennan will confirm the plan. Please pray for them as they keep working it out.

I'm grateful for your prayers and all the kind words we have received since the last post. I do feel sustained. That doesn't mean I haven't struggled or pray-cried. Last Friday, my spirit felt very heavy, and I couldn't stay focused on things. But God does provide ways to keep going, and I'm really grateful. There were times with family and friends that made me feel loved and made me really smile and laugh. What good gifts I was blessed with.

Thank you for praying (hmm, how many times have I written that this year? But I still do mean it). My doctor told me today that he was taken by how composed and strong I seemed, and by how well I am bearing all of this. I told him it was God (and your prayers), or maybe it was because I'm naive and really don't know enough to be upset all the time. But I think it really is how God has been sustaining me.

Warmly,

Leslie

. . .

AUGUST 20, 2020

Dear everyone!

Today the doctors, Ned, and I decided on the lumpectomy.

There are many pros and cons to taking this path, all depending on variables connected to what happens with the lumpectomy (can the doctor get all the tumor or will he leave some cancer cells behind?, etc). Thinking about these pros, cons, and what ifs can get little loud in my head, but today, I was able to hang in there with them and just focus on what is happening now.

I feel relieved that this is what we are doing right now.

Ned and I were reminded that this is long haul thing. But we are grateful for our doctors and for Julie, our nurse navigator. One of the best answers to your prayers is that Julie found us at lunchtime and we talked for 30 minutes and it was very helpful and life-giving. We went into our meeting with Dr. Brennan feeling a little more hopeful.

Thank you for your prayers. Today had hard things in it but also good things, because we came to a decision and have some type of plan.

Will keep you in the loop about the next big thing—surgery.

Today, on the way to the doctor, Ned and I listened to "From This Valley," by the Civil Wars. And here are some good words from *Every Moment Holy*:

We pray for good outcomes from
this procedure, O Lord.
We ask for good outcomes,
pleading that you would be
mindful of our mortal frailties,
but we know that regardless of the
tidings to come, you are tender
and present and sovereign over
all circumstance,
and what is more, you love us
fiercely and eternally.
Therefore I would trust you to lead
me well along the paths of any
wild and perilous country.
You are my shepherd.
This day will hold no surprises
for you. Let me rest in that.
Amen.[166]

...

AUGUST 25, 2020

Hello!

This Thursday is the day for my lumpectomy. Dr. Bleznak will be doing the surgery, as well as a sentinel node biopsy in my right lymph nodes. Dr. Brennan, my oncologist, wants to make certain that there isn't any breast cancer there.

Please pray that Dr. Bleznak gets all of the tumor and doesn't leave behind any cancer cells. (Apparently he has a very high success rate at getting all the tumor.) This is one of those variables that can have future ramifications. If he does not, he could go back and get whatever he missed, but Dr. Brennan only wants me off melanoma meds 2 weeks. So having extra surgeries gets complicated due to the melanoma meds.

Please also pray for a smooth and quick recovery so I can get back on my meds. I'm so glad to be having a lumpectomy right now. And I'm so grateful for a plan to be moving forward. But even with this, new issues could come up. But I'm focusing on *the now* and trusting God in it, as well as the unknown future.

I just finish re-reading Wallace Stegner's *Crossing to Safety* (so good!). Near the end of the book, as the main characters face the impending death of one of their loved ones, Stegner writes: "It was not a rescue according to any Pritchard formula, but a desperate improvisation like much that has followed. *And every detail of that long improvisation has tightened the bonds that hold us together.*"[167]

I love how the author makes certain that we see that *the details of improvisation* was what kept them all together; it didn't separate them. That sentence got underlined in my book because sometimes this all seems like a long improvisation. And in some ways it is a long improvisation—the doctors try something, that doesn't go according to plan, so they try something else. But I do know that "underneath are the everlasting arms" (Deut. 33:27). So to the Lord, the Good Shepherd, it's not a long improvisation.

Somehow it's all working together, and in that "somehow" His goodness and mercy—His steadfast love—are in it all and before it all and underneath it all. As Keith Winder, one of my pastors, recently preached on John 6:16–21, Jesus has gotten into my boat in the storm, and He's getting me to the other side.

Something I will be praying this week and Thursday, from *Every Moment Holy*:

> Today, as I submit myself to
> this procedure, I ask, O Lord, that by
> all means your care toward me would
> be manifest, for I am utterly dependent
> upon you. Give to my body immunity and
> vitality that I might recover quickly. Give me
> strength and health to resist complications.
> Give to my medical providers wisdom,
> skill, and insight. And by your Spirit,
> transcend even what body and medicine
> at their best might do. Where it is needed,
> bring the healing of your own touch
> to bear in my mortal frame.
> Be merciful, O God.
> Show your goodness to me, and to those
> who share my concern. Be now my physician,
> my mender, my healer. Even in the midst of this
> procedure, let me rest in you. . . .
> O God unshaken by any circumstance,
> be now my rock and my refuge.[168]

A couple of songs have meant a lot to me recently: Andrew Peterson's "You Are Always Good" is perfect (and a little hard to sing along to without crying). And then there is his song "His Heart Beats," which gives great and good hope.

Thank you for praying for me this week and this Thursday and in the days to come. I continue to find all your care such a wonder and a gift.

Peace and all good to you,

Leslie

...

AUGUST 27, 2020

Ned here.

Leslie is still recovering from the anesthesia, so she asked me to update you all (sadly, that means you get no poetry, music, or deep thoughts).

The surgery to remove her breast tumor went smoothly. Afterwards, when I spoke with Dr. Bleznak I asked him if the surgery went well. He replied, "If it didn't go well, I would still be in there right now making it right." He's a great guy and his team really respects him. They liked Leslie, too.

The doctor said he took out a 6 cm tumor (triple the original size), with room to spare. He said something along the lines of "of course the microscope always has the final say" but assured me that he took out all the cancer he could find. And our nurse navigator told us that his averages for doing that were much higher than the rest of the country.

He also took out some nodes to have tested for other possible traces of cancer. Leslie is expected to heal within the week, so she can get back on the meds for her *other* cancer.

Thank you for all the prayers.

Please keep praying.

...

AUGUST 28, 2020

Dear friends,

Thank you for your good words and attentiveness in my direction. Ned and I were just saying this morning that all of you have your own burdens to bear, so it really is a wonder and a gift that you take time with me/us.

Yesterday went well. So much to be thankful for.

All the staff were so kind and gentle. I know it's their job, but they really made each step go well. They were part of God's care to me.

As Ned shared, my surgeon is wonderful. He is such an expert, so in control and very kind. As the nurses were getting me ready for surgery they all said they would have him as their surgeon. That's a good thing to hear as you are about to go under.

Surgical rooms are very bright and chilly. And the table is very narrow, but the arm rests are pulled out, so my arms could be stretched out for whatever they were hooking me up to.

The surgical nurses were also wonderful (and their hair coverings were colorful and interesting to look at). After they made me all warm and cozy and ready for surgery, right before they put me under, and while I was praying in my head, one of the nurses was talking about how fast her mother typed. It was so funny to me—here I am about to have surgery, I'm praying, but the last thing that I have going in my head is a nurse's mother's typing speed.

I had the most wonderful post-op nurse. She was an older Mennonite woman with a white head covering. I know I talked a lot as I started to wake up, and I got teary. Whatever I said made her say to me that before I really started to be awake there was something about me that made her think I was a Christian. (I wonder what that could be because I was just sleeping—Jesus shining through?) But she was an angel to me. She was also a Christian and said so many words that just blessed me in my teary state! She also recited Psalm 1 over me for some reason—the King James Version (which is really lovely and comforting). I'm so grateful she took care of me.

We got home around 6. Ellie and I hung out on the couch. Later we watched *Captain America*. Ellie has decided that we will watch all the Marvel movies in chronological order—so that will be what I'll be watching for who knows how long during the fall. This is good, because I have such a hard time deciding what to watch these days. Sometimes I prefer just looking at the screen saver photos that roll through; they are so pretty to look at.

Today, she and I will watch the 6-hour *Pride and Prejudice*, as well as a Marvel movie. Won't that be fun? Later a NeedtoBreathe live stream concert will be on, and I'll watch that. So that's all happy. Ellie will help me remember to take my meds and to switch out the cold compresses every 20 minutes.

The sun is out and the cicadas are loud—it feels like a good summer day.

How glad I am that today I am home recovering from a lumpectomy, and not still in the hospital recovering from a mastectomy. What a wonderful answer to prayer for right now. Thank you for being in on this.

With much gratitude to the Lord for this day and for my family and for you all.

Under the Mercy,

Leslie

. . .

AUGUST 31, 2020

I just wanted to let you know how I was doing and to thank you for praying. This weekend went well. I kept pretty quiet—we did watch 6 hours of *Pride and Prejudice* (the 1995 BBC version, of course) and several Marvel movies. Ellie was really good at making sure I was taking meds and replacing my ice packs. (My sleep isn't that great, but it rarely is anymore.)

Sunday I took a walk and enjoyed the extravagant loveliness of the blue skies and the clouds upon clouds. We went to friends' house for dinner and spent time with some folks that we love a lot.

Today feels good. Another walk. Still trying to keep quiet.

But feeling good and grateful. Peace and all good right now.

This Thursday I meet Dr. Brennan and will most likely learn of the pathology report and what, if any, cancer was left behind, and if I have any in the lymph nodes. For now, I keep my mind and heart from worrying and am just glad for a good recovery. Thank you for praying!!

Under the Mercy,

Leslie

. . .

SEPTEMBER 3, 2020

Today I saw my oncologist. He said the lymph nodes are clear of breast cancer. But the surgeon was not able to get all the cancer cells with the lumpectomy.

The plan right now is to put me on immunotherapy (just one of the meds that goes with immunotherapy, not the two I was given in March) to fight the melanoma and to also make it possible, in 4–6 months, for me to get a mastectomy.

This is hard news, and I feel really sad. It makes this cancer stuff—having two cancers in me—feel so much harder and more real than it has recently.

This week felt really good and hopeful. I know God is a God of hope and of tears, but right now my heart is weary of this roller coaster.

Thank you for praying for me. Please keep praying, as well as for Ned and my girls. Yesterday I was walking and praying and these verses came to my mind:

You will seek me and find me,
when you seek me with your whole heart. (Jer. 29:13)

The LORD is near to the brokenhearted. (Ps. 34:18)

So I know that I can seek God with my broken heart and that He will be near to me—He promises that He will be found by me, and He will have my broken heart. I'm glad He knows that I will be seeking Him with a broken heart. I trust He can make it whole.

I've been listening to "Love Will Bring You Home," by Sandra McCracken, a lot. I'm grateful that I've had this song in me these past two days.

Under the Mercy,

Leslie

. . .

september 8, 2020

Dear friends,

I met with the surgeon today. I have to say again, I'm so glad for Dr. Bleznak and his kindness, strength, and expertise. He and Dr. Brennan met with the tumor board today, and they all came up with a new idea that Dr. Brennan is considering.

This week I should start on immunotherapy (nivolumab). The big prayer and hope is that I will not have the rheumatoid arthritis like I did this past March.

The second part of the plan, and this is the new part, is to add Herceptin (a miracle drug for those who have breast cancer and are HR2 positive, which I am). Usually this is added to chemotherapy, but I can't have chemo because of the immunotherapy. They are considering this as another way to keep the breast cancer in check while they treat the melanoma.

Dr. Bleznak said that there are many cases of women with breast cancer and melanoma. But my case is pretty rare. He said there isn't a guidebook for me, so they are going to keep trying things.

Please pray for the doctors as they finalize this plan—whether to try the Herceptin or not.

Adding it to the immunotherapy would be a pretty new thing to try (it hasn't been done often before). Please pray that my body would respond to restarting the immunotherapy well, and that I won't get rheumatoid arthritis (or that it would be manageable). All these plans rest on immunotherapy. I learned that the breast cancer cells he couldn't get out are very close to the skin. There would be complications regarding my skin that kept him from getting everything.

I love the new NeedtoBreathe song, "Mercy's Shore." Sometimes I can really relate to what they are singing about, but I like the hope near the end of the song. This feels like a lamenting song. There are a lot of lamenting songs in Psalms, but it is good to remember that the last several psalms are all praise songs. I'm learning to trust God that when we sow our tears in prayer, we will someday reap joy.

> My arms are tired and weary
> These wounds are on full display
> I've tried every door in the hallway
> There's just nowhere that I feel safe
> I see the light but never find the surface
> I don't know if I can swim no more
> White knuckles and wild horses
> One day we'll wash up on mercy's shore ...
> We can rest in the arms of trust
> There's no way that we can say
> We've earned our way into light
> All we have to do to is stay[169]

This weekend was full of time with family and friends; time with Elspeth and my lovely mother-in-law on Friday. I was grateful to have Maggie home for a quick visit. We drove around Lancaster County and listened to music, and went to Cherry Hill Orchards for apples and Frey's Greenhouse for the first installment of fall flowers. Also, sweet time with church friends Saturday and Sunday. So good. Monday I felt pretty low, but today, after a long walk and time readingbooks and writing letters on my porch, my heart feels steadier.

Thank you for praying and for all the ways you have been part of how God is loving me and my family through this shadow and valley.

Under the Mercy,

Leslie

. . .

SEPTEMBER 11, 2020

Hello friends,

Today is the day I get my first cycle of immunotherapy. Dr. Brennan has decided that instead of one large dose once a month, I will receive a smaller dose every two weeks. I think this is in the hopes of avoiding that awful rheumatoid arthritis again. Please pray that I don't have major side effects or complications.

I am still waiting on his plan concerning the Herceptin meds for keeping the breast cancer in check. Please pray for wisdom for him and the other doctors in regards to this decision. I would really like to have this medication—if that is the best thing for me, of course.

Yesterday I read in Revelation 1:12–16 about when John is on the island of Patmos and meets Jesus:

> Then I turned to see whose voice it was that spoke to me. When I turned I saw seven golden lamp stands, and among the lamp stands was one like the Son of Man, dressed in a robe and with a golden sash wrapped around his chest. The hair of his head was white as wool—white as snow—and his eyes like a fiery flame. His feet were like fine bronze as it is fired in a furnace, and his voice like the sound of cascading waters. He had seven stars in his right hand; a sharp double-edged sword came from his mouth, and his face was shining like the sun at full strength. (CSB)

I loved thinking about all these metaphors describing Jesus. I don't understand them all. But the two that got my imagination the most and made me so grateful were "his voice like the sound of cascading waters" and "his face was shining like the sun at full strength." Two of my most favorite things in nature are the sound of running water and the sun shining brightly.

Thinking through these two descriptions, I remember that Jesus offers us living water (John 4:14) and that He says He is the light of world. Also, one of my favorite verses in the Bible is Proverbs 4:18: "The path of the righteous is like the light of dawn, which shines brighter and brighter until full day." I love how this is all connected to and wrapped up in Jesus. And that my favorite things in nature are two of the ways John describes Jesus. I also like thinking about how Jesus is the Word of God made flesh, and how His voice is so beautiful and life-giving—like the delicious sound of cascading, moving water. Poetically it all moves around in my heart and mind and gives me a place to rest in Him.

(As an aside, I was thinking about how to picture hair as white as snow and a white robe, and all I could picture was Gandalf the White from *The Two Towers*. More reasons to love J.R.R. Tolkien.)

Then John 1:17–18 says, "When I saw him, I fell at his feet like a dead man. He laid his right hand on me and said, 'Don't be afraid. I am the First and the Last, and the Living One. I was dead, but look—I am alive forever and ever, and I hold the keys of death and Hades'" (CSB).

He keeps reminding me, even though I get so weary of this shadow of cancer and COVID and how it all affects my family, that He says He is with me and that I don't have to be afraid. He is the Living One.

Please also pray for my girls, as life is full of its own burdens and they also have this shadow in their lives, too.

Thank you for praying for me, dear friends.

Love,

Leslie

...

SEPTEMBER 15, 2020

Hello friends,

Here to ask for prayer for my knees (doesn't that sound awfully familiar?).

Nivo infusion was Friday. By Friday night I could feel some tightness, but I was happily distracted by an out-of-town friend, Annie, who came for an overnight stay (we went kayaking Friday night, which was lovely).

Saturday I woke up to tight knees and I felt rather sad. But Annie was here so, again, I was happily distracted. We walked for an hour-and-a-half to loosen them up, and then later I took her around Lancaster City—so a lot more walking. It helped my knees, so that was good.

I woke up Sunday morning with tight knees and tight elbows—and feeling worse than Saturday. I was so very depressed. So I walked for an hour, after taking my arthritis meds. (To be honest, I also did some crying out of fear that I was heading into the same issue I had in March. I prayed about how I wanted to stick to immunotherapy and how having these knee issues scared me. It was nice I was wearing a baseball hat and could hide all my tears.)

I came home and read the information sheet for Arimidex, my new breast cancer med. This new med can also cause joint and muscle pain. And for that, I read, I can take Advil. So I tried Advil, and within 30 minutes, my knees and elbows were feeling better. I could feel a difference. It was not perfect, but it wasn't as much pain or tightness. It felt like a wonderful, quick answer to prayer.

Since Sunday I have been walking for an hour in the morning, taking my RA meds, as well as taking Advil 4 times a day. And my knees and elbows have been very manageable.

Dr. Brennan took me off of Arimidex for a week to see if the joint and muscle pain was from that. He told me he was encouraged that things got a bit better over the weekend, but that we have to be very attentive to any changes. And I thought, yes, it's hard not to pay attention to any changes to my knees; it's like a fog looming in my brain.

Please pray that this joint pain is because of the breast cancer meds, and that if it isn't, the rheumatoid arthritis is manageable, so that I can stay on immuno-therapy. And that we can start Herceptin for the breast cancer soon (Dr. Brennan said we'll start this once we figure out the side effects of the other meds). And pray also for my endurance (and Ned's and the girls', too). This all just feels hard.

This week I read in *The Sound of Life's Unspeakable Beauty* this lovely sentence: "I want to co-operate with holy grace in every moment of my existence."[170] I love that, especially connected to Psalm 90:

> Teach us to number our days aright, that we may gain a heart of wisdom.... Satisfy us in the morning with your unfailing love, that we may sing for joy and be glad all our days. Make us glad for as many days as you have afflicted us, for as many years as we have seen trouble. May your deeds be shown to your servants, your splendor to their children. May the favor of the Lord our God rest upon us; establish the work of our hands for us—yes, establish the work of our hands. (vv. 12, 14–17 NIV)

I've always loved that last part about God's favor resting upon us. Somewhere I read it as "May the beauty of the Lord rest upon us." I really love that!

Thank you for praying for me, my family, my knees, and, of course, this shadow of cancer.

Under the Mercy,
Leslie

. . .

September 20, 2020

Dear family and friends,

Just a quick update to say that my knees are still tight, but not swollen—they are manageable. Yesterday I went to the Y (happy dance!) and used the bike for almost 20 minutes. This really helped my knees, so I'm thinking of adding that into my day (plus I just love being at the Y). I meet with Dr. Brennan on Thursday. Hopefully he will keep me on the immunotherapy and then add Herceptin.

My emotions are hanging in there—I miss teaching and theater and all those lovely people at Veritas Academy, but I'm starting to settle into some daily life-giving rhythms. Life is quiet, and that finally feels good.

I'm reading *The Fellowship of the Ring* right now. I reread it each year, and I'm amazed each time that there are new beautiful things to discover. Here is one passage I must have loved last year but just rediscovered this week:

> Frodo stripped the blankets from Pippin and rolled him over, and then walked off to the edge of the wood. Away eastward the sun was rising red out of the mists that lay thick on the world. Touched with gold and red the autumn trees seemed to be sailing rootless in the shadowy sea. A little below him to the left the road ran down steeply into a hollow and disappeared.[171]

How does he do that? It's so gorgeous! I'm going to miss showing these things to this year's 8th grade class, but I'm glad to have this picture in my mind.

Recently I took a walk around Buchanan Park and climbed a rock that was at the edge of the park. I took my shoes off to feel the hardness and the warmth underneath. And I thought to myself, "The ground is still hard." And "Jesus is the rock that is higher than I am." These are good things to keep remembering.

Thank you for praying for me. It really is sustaining!

Under the Mercy,

Leslie

...

September 25, 2020

Dear family and friends,

Thursday I met with Dr. Brennan and also had my second immunotherapy infusion!

I'm very grateful that so far my knees haven't gotten worse since my second infusion—stairs are not fun, sitting too long makes them very tight, but daily life is manageable. Friends gave me a muscle and joint rub (wow! And thank you!) and that has helped, too—especially my cranky elbow joints. I must confess I never thanked God for working elbows, but now I realize how useful they are!

Herceptin will be added into my life once the insurance folks approve. Dr. Brennan said the insurance company will be confused by approving immuno-therapy and Herceptin for one person. He told me that it's unusual to combine these two drugs—we are in mostly uncharted territory. What an adventure. After I told him he'll learn so much more for future patients, he said he would have been glad for me if he wasn't. He's so kind. But this is the road we are called to—learning to see how nivolumab and Herceptin can be in one person, fighting two different cancers.

Dr. Brennan told me I can go to the YMCA to ride a bike (yay!) but not swimming (no mask with swimming. I didn't tell him I didn't wear a mask when I was biking—there wasn't anyone around me!!). I asked if I could go to the movies and, without batting an eye, he said, "No." (Ugh!) Hopefully something will change by the time *Wonder Woman* comes out so I can see it in the theater. He did say I could go to museums, as long as PA COVID numbers don't increase.

Ned and Leslie in Ocean City, MD

Ned and I went to the beach and stayed with our dear friends and Square Halo partners, Diana and Alan. They are great cooks and very generous. I love the beach; it was good being there.

Thank you for praying—I'm always grateful.

Warmly,

Leslie

. . .

OCTOBER 7, 2020

Hello family and friends,

Tomorrow I start Herceptin and the second month of nivolumab. According to today's plan, I will get Herceptin for a year. I will have 2 more months of immunotherapy and then a PET scan in December.

Right now, my knee joints and leg muscles are the biggest thing I need prayer for (other than my roller-coastery energy levels). I wake up every morning with this feeling of "Okay, get the knees working." Sleeping well at night is almost impossible because my knees get worse from being still; I can feel that as the night goes on. I wake up with what feels like rocks on the tops of my knees. But during the day, I am grateful I can manage, even if I hobble more than I would like.

Tomorrow, I have PT for my knees. I'll be getting that twice a week. Please pray that they can give me more ways to manage my knees.

I am grateful to say that the issues with my elbow joints have cleared up. I have no idea what caused them or why they cleared up. But, phew, not being able to get your hands to your face to brush your teeth, wash your face, or put your contacts in is no fun. Dr. Brennan and I think the breast cancer meds, not the immunotherapy, caused it. I'm wondering if this problem will come and go.

I've been talking with God about the idea of a childlike faith. It started when listening to "Child Again" by NeedtoBreathe:

> In the cosmic light
> In the by and by
> I wanna see your heart
> Through my younger eyes
> I wanna hear your voice
> In the rain and wind
> I wanna know it's safe to be
> A child again . . .

I don't want to go back to how I viewed God when I was child or to how I thought He viewed me. Even though I believed in Jesus as a Savior, I didn't really feel a sense of love or wonder or freedom or grace. God was pretty far away and scary, and Jesus said crazy things. But throughout my life as a Christian, God has done the work of moving toward me, bringing me near, and making His love real to me. I know He has been holding on to me. But the idea of a child-like faith was pricking at my mind and heart. The song ends with these lines:

> Let my past mean nothin'
> Make it powerless
> I am free like a river
> You're my hope unbroken
> You're my innocence
> I am free like a river
> I'm a child again[172]

This Saturday, I was listening to Paul Miller (author of *The Praying Life* and *The Loving Life*—two life-changing books for me). He was discussing how Jesus was so in communion with God that everything He did was in obedience to God the Father. He didn't say or do anything outside of what God the Father wanted. In Him was pure love, trust, and obedience. In that way, He was the perfect child. Paul Miller then went on to say that when Jesus invites us to have the faith of a child, He is offering us another way to image Him, to be like Him! I had never heard this idea before, and it came during the week I'd been talking to God about this idea of a childlike faith and what that meant.

I've also been listening to Tim Keller's preaching on 1 Peter, and he focuses on how suffering and trials can form us to be more like Jesus.[173] The "dross" is separated from the "good stuff." Just as metal is ready to be taken out of the refiner's fire when the person working with the metal shines it up and it shows his reflection, our sufferings can work in us to make us like Jesus. I have found deep gladness in meditating on the idea that a childlike faith and trust in God the Father is a way for me to be more like Jesus. This cancer journey can also form me to be like Jesus. In the end, being more like Jesus also means I'm becoming more the me that God made me to be.

This Eric Peters song brings it all together:

Like a child without reality
Alive within the mirth and mire
I want to lose my sense of gravity
And see with recovering eyes
Children hide themselves behind their hands
And peek through to be found once again
This is the world turning upside down
When the light that was lost is found
Come see the dawn with the darkness refused
Today is yesterday made new[174]

Isn't that beautiful? "Today is yesterday made new ..."

Those years of struggling to believe and to rest in the grace of God's love for me can be redeemed through His faithful work in me. It's one of the places God has said, "You don't have to look back to those years and feel stuck in regret; I'm restoring you." He does that in such specific and good ways.

May you see how He is doing that for you, in the places of your brokenness, discouragement, and sadness. He promises to be found by those who seek Him. We can offer Him our hearts, broken in so many ways, and He will draw us near and renew and restore those broken pieces. He may take His time and He will do it "over the long haul," but His promises of steadfast love never fail. He who began a good work in us will keep working towards its completion.

Thank you for your prayers!
Under the Mercy,
Leslie

. . .

OCTOBER 8, 2020

Dear friends and family,

Thank you to those who were praying for me today. Lots of Herceptin and nivolumab coursing in my body; the new adventure has started. I'm like a little meds trial—one doctor friend said medical papers will be written about me.

Overall things went well; I always get such excellent care and kindness. One of my aides is a Christian; I asked her to pray with me from *Every Moment Holy* (the prayer for a medical procedure). That was a blessing.

During the last 6 minutes of the Herceptin infusion I developed the shivers, though I didn't feel very cold. The nurse said it was a side effect some first-timers experience with the infusion. My room filled with nurses all trying to work through what to do; they kept taking my vitals. In the end they gave me Benadryl, which settled the shivers down and put me to sleep. I somehow got home—all is foggy (I had driven myself so Ned had to get there and drive me home)—and I've slept a ton the rest of the evening.

Earlier today, PT was great! She used a rolling pin with deep ridges and rolled it over all my knee and calf muscles. That loosened them up. She also gave me some strengthening and stretching exercises. Feeling grateful for today and trying not to worry about the upcoming days and how my knees will respond.

I've been listening to Josh Garrels a lot this week, especially "Beyond the Blue" and "Sweet River Roll."

> Sweet river roll over me
> Let my body find peace
>   and let my mind be free
> Oh my soul sings to Thee[175]

Much gratefulness for you!
Leslie

. . .

OCTOBER 22, 2020

Just a quick update:

Today was the second half my second dose of nivolumab, plus more Herceptin. Because of my reaction to Herceptin last time, they gave me Benadryl beforehand; thus I had a lovely nap through all my infusions. Dr. Brennan agreed that we can keep going with the immunotherapy, even though he is concerned about my achy joints and muscles.

This week I also had an appointment with a doctor in rheumatology. She is prescribing a couple of meds that will help with the swelling and pain in my knees, elbows, wrists, and thumbs. I'm so grateful. Physical therapy has been a big help.

Sleep is hard, as my joints and muscles get stiff and painful during the night. Some mornings I'm into doing all the exercising and moving around to get loosened up. Other mornings I cannot muster any willpower to do anything because I feel mentally and physically tired. And no matter how my morning goes, I'm still ready for a nap by 2 p.m. Some days I don't have the brain energy to do anything, even read. Other days, I'm able to get good things done—like finishing a book, walking in the woods, folding laundry, or making applesauce.

The best thing that has happened recently is the work I have been able to put into crafting some poems. I love poetry but have not really felt I could write any. But last Friday, early morning, I was wide awake in bed and playing with images and phrases that were rolling around in my mind. So I went with it and wrote 4 poems. And over the weekend, with some thoughtful help from a poet friend and a few others, I have been editing and crafting them. This feels like a gift from God, and they make me so glad.

Thank you for praying!

Warmly,

Leslie

...

NOVEMBER 16, 2020

Dear friends,

I talked to the doctor this morning and heard GOOD NEWS. There are NO melanoma tumors in me right now—NO old tumors and NO new tumors. The melanoma in my left lymph nodes is stable. I am so thankful for the right now.

I will still be doing immunotherapy infusions for 3 more months. After that, scans and a biopsy of my left lymph nodes. Then depending on how the scans go, we will move onto dealing with the breast cancer.

Right now I am keeping life quiet, as I get tired easily. Although I'm grateful for my community of friends and family, I haven't had much head space for a lot of people time.

Two lovely creative activities have kept me busy—writing for the Christmas and winter editions of *Cultivating*[176] and pulling together an Advent video (with paintings and poetry about the Annunciation) for The Black Barn Collective.[177] When I first started writing for both groups, I didn't think I had anything to give, but I ended up getting good work done. What a blessing!

Thank you for your care and for being in on this with us. You all are a gift and blessing to us.

Love,

Leslie

···

NOVEMBER 20, 2020

Ned here.

Over the years, after I would recount the various things I was making, people we were meeting, or places we were going, my dad would say, "Well, your life certainly isn't boring."

Yet now I feel like I am in a roller-coaster season of life that makes the past couple decades look boring.

People often ask me how I'm doing, and I honestly can say that life is amazing—never better. Really. I am making the best art I've ever made, I've got new book deals and podcast interviews, and complete strangers are buying my art (and even reaching out to request commissions). My three daughters are blossoming in amazing ways—I'm so proud of them—and each time we talk together I love them more. On top of all that, Leslie and I have never been closer, *and* she is blazing with creative output: poetry, podcasts, online lectures, book development, and more. I've always said my wife is awesome, but now I wonder if that is too small a word for her.

But if you are reading this, then you know that there is more to the story. To offset the incredible highs in our life right now, we have equal lows. Of late, each morning I have to lift my dear wife out of bed and help her to stand, only to have her collapse against me, weeping into my chest because her joints are so swollen. She is overwhelmed by the pain, and often can't imagine even getting halfway down the hallway. We have a liturgy that is nearly an hour of getting dressed, drugs, rubbing lotion on every joint, and *Every Moment Holy* prayers when we can pull it together. Once she is up and going, she is usually so tired she takes a nap again (unless she has a doctor's visit scheduled).

I then try to sneak in some billable hours, only to find myself so tired and in a fog that I find it hard to focus. All my work now is wonderful, creative stuff that requires me to be at the top of my game mentally, resulting in To Do lists that flail around helplessly in my studio, desperate for me to attend them.

But I need to take care of Leslie. I want to take care of Leslie. And I'm so grateful I am able to care for Leslie— just think, each time I need to help her out of a chair, I get to hug her and kiss her and tell her how much I love her! What could be better? (Curiously, our dog finds all this affection VERY upsetting.) By the middle of the day, she is shuffling

A Liturgy for a Husband and Wife
Ned Bustard

around the house pretty well and writing her poetry and giving me that bright-as-yellow smile, and I forget all about how the day began.

So, how are we doing? It would be great if I could say life was a bit more boring than it is.

I'd love for life to be a bit less wonderful and a bit less horrible. And I wish the Living Will the doctor wants us to update wouldn't just squat in the hallway, staring at us forebodingly.

But God continues to provide abundantly for us. This week we were able to have Slesser Renovations fix our front steps and replace our front door (thanks to the generosity of my dad and those who have donated to Leslie's GoFundMe campaign). Also this week, friends came over and winterized our backyard. I'm pretty useless with house maintenance stuff, and it makes Leslie so happy to see stuff get done, so when things like this can happen, I am incredibly grateful. And the letters and cards and gifts don't stop.

Hopefully this post fills in the gaps and helps add depth to my answer when you see me next and ask how I'm doing and I answer with a short quip like: "My cup overflows." And it does. It is overflowing with all of the above and more.

Please keep praying for healing, hope, perseverance, and our daily bread.

DECEMBER 10, 2020

Hello family and friends,

Just a short update to keep you in the loop since Ned's last entry.

The rheumatoid arthritis meds (I take 3 different kinds each day) have started to work, and my knees feel so much better. Yesterday I "tested" out of physical therapy, as the PT work has strengthened my knees considerably. The inflammation is down a lot (I can even wear my favorite black boots). I can almost walk up and down steps normally—one foot after another, instead of dragging myself up or carefully making my way down. Sleep this week is almost better. I can mostly take care of myself now. I still can't get up from the couch without help; also, my hands, wrists, and shoulders get really stiff and weak at night and into the morning. But next week I meet with a hand PT/OT person, so hopefully I will get some help with that weakness. I'm slowly starting to do ordinary things more often: it's great to have a spark of interest and to actually be able to do them—things like plan dinners and go shopping. This week I'm going to make my friend Margie Haack's Cuban rice and beans, enchiladas, and scones.[178]

Last week I had some mysterious virus that laid me low for 5 days. Grateful it wasn't COVID. But it certainly drained me of a lot of energy! I thought I might never want food again.

Next week I start a three-month series of infusions twice a month. After that, we will most likely figure out the next step for the breast cancer—radiation? Surgery?

Also, the end of next week marks the day I discovered the lump in my right breast and this whole thing started. Not sure what to say to that. There is so much to be grateful for: God has been faithful and taken care of me and my family and He has sustained us. I'm grateful I'm still here, and for all the doctors, nurses, and aides who have taken care of me and made sure I'm still here. I'm overwhelmed by how God has brought so much love into my life through family and friends (you!). But right now, I think I'm pretty soul weary . . . a little empty. I love the Advent season, but right now it feels a little flat. I'm just living in that and not striving to figure out how to make things better.

Prayers are simple, and sometimes it's hard to focus on Scripture (although I admit, the English murder mystery I am reading right now is really good—no problem reading that). I thought I would read Athanasius's *On the Incarnation* during Advent, but I can't seem to stay focused. I'll keep trying, as I did love it the first time I read it. Ned and I are watching a lot of *Madam Secretary*. I know Jesus holds it all together, and I'm thinking about that. I hope you can read "Bethlehem,

Year Zero," by poet Andrew Roycroft.[179] It is so poignant and beautiful and true.

Thank you for your sustained interest and care! You are a gift to me and my family. All the prayers all year have been so much of what has kept us—God has been answering not just my prayers, but yours.

Warmly, and with much love,

Leslie

. . .

December 11, 2020

Ned here again.

As Leslie wrote, we lost most of last week to fever and fatigue. We thought she was better but then today she spent the whole day sleeping. I couldn't even get her interested in going downtown Christmas shopping. She woke up for a few hours and asked for pizza—bacon and tomato from Dominion—but then didn't eat even one whole piece. We watched *The Mandalorian* and then began watching Sandra McCracken's concert but she couldn't make it through—chills and fever are back, and all-over body pain.

Please pray for my Love—that she will recover and can enjoy Advent.

. . .

December 16, 2020

hi friends,

just sharing that i'm still pretty sick, which is very discouraging. i finally had a decent sleep last night as i had a painkiller for my back and sleeping pill. i just have no energy or appetite, and because my lower back has been hurting, i can't get comfortable at all, and sometimes i have a fever. i reached out to my nurses but am not sure what else to do (they have helped some by prescribing the two meds, but they only gave me painkillers for 3 days and it wasn't until Tuesday morning that they really kicked in).

i had this 2 weeks ago and it started to go away after 6 days. ugh. grateful for a friend's chicken noodle soup and for saltines, but it is so frustrating to feel hungry but most food sounds horrible.

i don't have covid so that is nice, but whatever this is, it's really bad. and i am really tired.

thank you for praying,

Leslie

. . .

December 19, 2020

Dear family and friends,

Just a short update: I had more blood work done on Thursday and Friday, as well as a CT scan for back pain. It turns out I have an inflamed liver, a side effect to the immunotherapy. So most likely the doctor will increase my steroids to 40 mg. (I hope this works, because that amount of steroids will most likely make it harder to sleep. Sad.) I am also low on potassium because I am not eating much. But Ned's uncle, a pharmacist, recommended that I ask the doctor for a specific painkiller, and it has been helping a lot—so that is a relief. I still feel like I have no energy, and I cannot imagine ever liking food again or sleeping through the night. But maybe there is a light at the end of the tunnel.

Please also pray for Ned, as he is working so hard to keep us going, get ready for Christmas, take care of me, and get work done. He's been great.

Thank you for praying and for everyone's kind, encouraging words and gifts. You are such a blessing.

Love,

Leslie

...

December 30, 2020

Dear family and friends,

Thank you for praying for me recently. What a hard month December was. But the week of Christmas, after getting off one of my RA meds, I started doing better. This week's blood work showed that things are getting back to normal. Tomorrow I have the first of the next 6 infusions of nivolumab, plus Herceptin. What a thing to do on the last day of the year. But I'm really grateful to do another round of immunotherapy.

I'm off the arthritis med that caused my liver to inflame (it was really close to being dangerous), but that med is what helped get rid of the inflammation in my muscles and joints and manage the pain that went with it all. So it seems I'm once again asking for prayer—that by some miracle, I may not struggle with so much inflammation and pain.

This week last year our family entered the door to cancer after it was confirmed that the lump in my right breast looked like cancer. And where am I right now? Grateful that we are still on the fighting side of this. Grateful that the cancers haven't spread. Grateful that the melanoma tumors are gone. Grateful that most of the breast cancer is gone. Grateful for all the hard work of my doctors, nurses, and aides. Grateful for nivolumab, Herceptin, Zoladex, and all the other meds I can't pronounce. I wonder what this year will bring; I am glad God knows.

I remember last year saying that this would be the way I would learn the reality of Psalm 23. And it's so true:

The Lord is my shepherd, I shall not be in want. I have been learning to trust Jesus as the one who goes before me and holds all this in His hand. All year I have never been in want or need of anything. Ned has been with me every step of the way and has loved me so well. My girls and family have loved me. I've had an overabundance of your prayers, care, love, gifts, friendship, other people's tears.

He leads me beside quiet waters. He restores my soul. I have been very glad for reading in my study, sitting on the porch off my study, kayaking, going to the beach, and taking walks in the woods and in my neighborhood. And all the poetry, artwork, stories, British murder mysteries, sunshine in the trees, clouds and blue skies, and bird songs have kept me going.

He leads me in the paths of righteousness for his name's sake. This year, the Holy Spirit has been helping me work through heart and sin issues; He has been kind and has helped me to keep trusting that Jesus covers my regrets and shame and teaches me more of His ways. It's all grace and kindness, and it is amazing.

Even though I walk through the valley of the shadow of death, I will fear no evil for Thou art with me. Your rod and your staff they comfort me. Knowing I have cancer but not knowing the outcome, and waiting for the results of so many tests, feels like walking through the valley of the shadow of death. And I'm grateful that Jesus has helped me/us walk through it.

You prepare a table before me in the presence of my enemies; you anoint my head with oil, my cup overflows. When I was thinking of this verse, I remembered all the different types of breads friends gave me during the first two months, when I couldn't really eat many foods. Thick toast, cinnamon rolls, scones, bagels—it was all so yummy and good. And then those wonderful gifts from Rabbit Room friends—what a wonder! All the meals, cookies, flowers, and cash gifts. It's been so much goodness. Thank you.

Surely goodness and mercy will follow me all the days of my life and I will dwell in the house of the Lord forever. This has been one of my all-time favorite verses. I don't remember a day I didn't love this verse and its promises and what it taught me about who God is. And this year I have learned that even when this unthinkable thing has happened to me and my family, God has shown me His goodness and His mercy. And I'm glad and grateful we all have the hope of eternity in the presence of God our good Father.

When all this started, a dear friend said to me, "You will have to give yourself more grace than you will ever know—give yourself all the grace." I have also been learning, as another friend encourages me often, to rest in Jesus holding on to me. I don't have to work for His love; He has given it to me, and I can have that peace. This has been a year of learning this. Thank you for being in on it all with me. You are a gift.

Love always,

Leslie

. . .

January 16, 2021

Hello!

This week I had blood work done ("labs look good"), met with Dr. Brennan, and had infusions (with yummy snacks like Lorna Doone cookies).

The immunotherapy med is still giving me issues—which Dr. Brennan and I talked about. Other than the normal cranky knees, my shoulders, upper arms, wrists, hands, and fingers are not doing great. Like before, things just get more stiff and swollen during the night. Mornings are once again "not fun" and I need Ned to help me get going, which he does with much kindness and humor.

Other than that, life is fine, and it's been so nice to have the girls all here. We are all keeping our days pretty low key (and watching a lot of *West Wing*

Vanessa Joy Films

at night). I've been working on some poems based on several Andrew Wyeth
paintings.

With much gratitude for you all—for your kind words, emails, texts, cards,
and gifts. They are all a blessing to me!

Thank you for your continued care and attention.

Love,

Leslie

...

January 24, 2021

Just a quick note to share that my recent mammogram, breast ultrasound,
and body PET scan show no new tumors or cancer growth. The radiologist is
concerned about something in my arm, but Dr. Brennan thinks it's where my
injection for the PET scan was. I will see him on Wednesday.

The hard thing for right now is an ongoing headache—my eyes feel strained,
and my stomach feels sick, like I have motion sickness. If I stay still, don't look
at screens, and keep the room quiet and dim, I can do okay. I just had a massage
from a dear friend and that helped. It may be from how tense my neck is. But
I'll talk with my doctor on Monday. (The ironic thing is—the more I keep still
the more stiff my joints and muscles get.) This has been a slow build-up since
Thursday, but it hit me hard yesterday, all day, and is lingering today.

So please pray. Thank you.

Love,

Leslie

...

January 26, 2021

Just a quick update. Feeling much better today—no headache since yesterday,
able to do more normal life, and even my joints and muscles don't feel as bad.
Grateful for today. Thank you for praying!!

I meet with Dr. Brennan tomorrow; I know we will review the PET scan, and
I imagine we will talk about breast surgery. And then on Thursday I have my
infusions.

This afternoon I hope to work on some writing projects. That makes me glad;
to have the ability and the desire to do something thoughtful and creative feels
like freedom right now.

Last week I was thinking a lot about trusting God in the midst of cancer,
and I could tell I was beginning to spiral about the possibilities of not doing

immunotherapy if my joints and muscles kept being stiff and inflamed. I felt God encouraging me to remember that He is trustworthy—there is nothing more certain in all eternity or creation than His trustworthiness, even when what He calls us to is hard. I know He finds me and welcomes me in when I flail and fall because of worry and stress; I am grateful for this gift of His grace. But I do want more Spirit-infused brave steps on the firm path of God's trustworthiness and steadfast love—for me and my family. (I guess I'll start meditating on writing a poem about this . . .)

I recently discovered the Dwell app (Scripture read in cool accents, soothing music in the background) and the Pray as You Go app, a guided prayer/meditation rooted in Scripture. Each day has a classic or contemporary song (quiet and worshipful, sung by wonderful voices), Scripture, and thoughts about the Scripture. Both are wonderful ways to start the day or to be renewed in the middle of the day or early evening.

Much love to you all!

Leslie

. . .

January 28, 2021

Hello friends,

Yesterday in my meeting with Dr. Brennan, I learned that the spot on my left upper arm isn't related to the PET scan injection. You can feel something hard there, though the skin doesn't look like anything is wrong. Tomorrow I have an ultrasound, and if that shows it is cancer, I will have a biopsy to find out what kind. And then we will go from there. Dr. Brennan said that things other than cancer show up on PET scans.

I have an appointment with my surgeon, Dr. Bleznak, on Monday. How this meeting goes depends on what is in my upper left arm. He can take out the lymph nodes under my left arm. Once I have recovered from that, it looks like I will go back on the BRAF pills for the melanoma and have scans in 3 months. Dr. Brennan is waiting on the mastectomy for now until we know about my arm. Melanoma is always the top priority, as the breast cancer still seems stable.

They are also scheduling a brain MRI because of my headaches last weekend (although I have been fine since Monday). I asked for something to keep me calm. The last time I had a brain MRI I almost had a panic attack because the thing they put on my head is so close to my face, and I can't see anything except through a little mirror. There is cool air that comes on my face and that helps me keep breathing deeply. It's the most closed in and vulnerable I've ever felt. Dr.

Brennan prescribed something to take an hour before the MRI that should help me stay calm. I am so grateful for that.

Thank you for praying. I hope we hear something about the spot in my arm tomorrow.

I think I'm in a bit of denial that there is the possibility of something else—so prayers for me and my family will be such a help. I want to abide deeply in Jesus and trust God, as I know He is trustworthy. That peace that surpasses understanding is such a good thing. I know that God is working out His plan, and that the ending will be right somehow, but the unknowns are not easy. This reminder that there are no guarantees hits me hard, especially when I think of Ned and my daughters. Most of the time I keep away from the cliff of "what ifs," but sometimes I make my way to the edge and peer into the gorge of "this may not work out well." Then I back away slowly because it is too painful. I try to fix my eyes on Jesus so I don't fall in.

Thank you for being in this with me.

Leslie

...

FEBRUARY 1, 2021

Dear friends,

The ultrasound report on my left upper arm says that the spot we saw on the PET scan has a concern for cancer (maybe melanoma?). The blood vessel growth to it indicates cancer.

Dr. Brennan has asked Dr. Bleznak to remove it as well, and at the same time to remove the lymph nodes that have melanoma (in my left underarm). Then this spot can be biopsied, and we can learn what it is. As of now breast surgery is put on hold. Dr. Brennan is talking about going back to BRAF meds after surgery, but that could always change.

I feel sad and in denial that we are dealing with another cancer concern. I'm grateful I am at home and have Ned around to talk to during the day. I'm grateful that Elspeth is at home, too. But I miss Carey and Maggie. My heart is heavy that my family (including my mom, the rest of the Symons family, and the other Bustards, too) have to carry this burden.

I am still learning to trust and rest in the Lord—He knows what's ahead and has it in hand. I don't have to know why we are called to this. I know the good things God has done this year to show me His love and his presence; that grace is a good gift.

But I do wonder about what is next or what the other side of this shadowed valley will look like. In the meantime, how do I live well in it?

Thank you for praying—for your prayers in the past and for your continued prayers.

Love,

Leslie

. . .

FEBRUARY 9, 2021

Dear friends,

I feel like I need to write a poem about being on a roller coaster. I get motion sickness easily, so I'm not a huge fan. You should ask Maggie about our Hershey Park trip we took together two summers ago . . .

Today, I met with Dr. Bleznak, my surgeon. He did an ultrasound of the spot in my arm and is sending me to get a vascular ultrasound to confirm his suspicion that it is not cancer. Based on the shape of it (and the location), he doesn't think it is melanoma or cancer. (If I understand correctly, cancer cells, when you look at them on a ultrasound, look like they have a raggedy side. This was smooth all around.) He thinks it is a blood clot in an inconsequential blood vessel—meaning that since it is not in major veins or arteries, it isn't dangerous.

We also talked about lymph node surgery. Dr. Bleznak used to be an expert surgeon in lymph node surgery before he became an expert in breast surgery. (I'm so grateful for him!)

There is a risk in this surgery. When melanoma patients have this surgery, more of the arm area (I forget all the correct words) has to be removed, making the risk for lymphedema higher. Breast surgery is still on hold for now. But the idea of getting everything that has melanoma out of my body sounds great.

I am struggling with headaches again. I started taking sulfasalazine again for my stiff joints and swelling hands. I hadn't taken it in a couple of weeks, and I wanted to see what would happen. Would it cause a headache again, like it did two weeks ago? And it seems to have done it again. Ugh. Hoping it won't be as bad as last time. The doctor said it is okay to stop taking it.

Thank you for praying and for bearing this with me. Please pray for my family, as this is feeling roller-coastery for them, too.

Love,

Leslie

. . .

FEBRUARY 11, 2021

Hi, it's me!

The news about the spot they thought might be cancer or might be a blood clot: last night I had a vascular ultrasound (isn't it amazing that there are things like ultrasounds for blood vessels?). Today Dr. Brennan told me it is not a blood clot. They are not sure if it is cancerous; it may be, but they won't know till they can biopsy it. Dr. Brennan and Dr. Bleznak are figuring things out. I think I feel a little denial that we are back again to this uncertainty.

Today I had infusions—second to last one for the immunotherapy. After thinking I might not to get to the end of the cycle because of all the crazy side effects, I'm grateful to have pushed through (with Ned's help and everyone's prayers). The last immunotherapy infusion, as of now, is February 24. I will still be getting infusions of Herceptin for the breast cancer. That will go on till the fall. I love going to the cancer center. The nurses and aides and everyone are kind. It is such a nice place to be cared for. Also, new favorite—Lorna Doone cookies.

I wrote a poem yesterday called "That Sense of Hope," as I was thinking about what hope might feel like, and what it might feel like to know you have a sure hope, though you can't feel it in the moment. I was also thinking about friends who have had a rough year (maybe a different kind of rough than mine, but still filled with hard, sad things), and I dedicated this poem to two friends who are also writers and who have been encouragement to me.

Thank you for your prayers (always!) and kind words. And for reading my news again and again.

Love,

Leslie

. . .

February 19, 2021

I stole Ned's sweater because it is cozy, and today I needed cozy and comfy.

Lots of tests and appointments next week. I have a CT scan set up for Tuesday, my regular infusions and meeting with Dr. Brennan on Wednesday, then an MRI on Thursday, and a meeting with Dr. Bleznak the surgeon and Dr. Bast the plastic surgeon on Friday.

The MRI will help determine if they can operate on the hard spot in my arm. The CT scan is just to make sure everything is still okay. These findings will help the doctors figure out the next surgery and treatment steps.

Yesterday I felt the desire to either have a temper tantrum or to feel sorry for myself, especially because every day I have to ask for Ned's help again and again and then again for things like putting on shoes and socks, opening a milk carton or tying my headband and more. My hands are usually weak and cranky. Ned doesn't complain and is always kind, ready to help, and sometimes even wonders why I don't ask him quicker. This physical helplessness and dependence is a picture of how God is teaching me His deep love and grace. He wants me to admit that I really need Him and that in every way, whether I feel it or not, He has moved close and is taking care of me.

So today I am sitting in my favorite corner of the couch by the window, with a YouTube fire going, working on creative projects. I've talked to a friend on the phone and made birthday lunch plans with my mother-in-love and sisters-in-law and friends. These are good things. The need for a temper tantrum has passed. And *WandaVision* is tonight, so there is that, too.

Also, in case you missed it, Ned will have two books coming out with IVPKids. In October, *Saint Nicholas the Giftgiver* will come out, which he wrote and illustrated.[180] And then in the spring, *The O in Hope*. This is a poem written by Luci Shaw and illustrated by Ned. It's been pretty wonderful watching this unfold—that Ned is the illustrator of a Luci Shaw poem is such a gift! So despite the hard things, there have been some pretty great things happening, too. Much to be thankful for.

Love,

Leslie

FEBRUARY 26, 2021

Dear family and friends,

Today Ned and I met with Dr. Bleznak and Dr. Bast about my arm and what is next. The plan is for me to have surgery to remove the lymph nodes in my left side (the ones that have the melanoma). During this operation, Dr. Bast will remove the lesion in my left upper arm.

This surgery will happen in the next couple weeks. The way I understand this all—the goal is to get rid of macro cancer (like in the lymph nodes and the lesion) so that the melanoma treatment will fight micro cancer cells. This surgery is not curative but will do a lot to fight the cancer. The doctors were encouraged to see that the CT scans revealed no more cancer tumors in my chest and abdomen. They didn't show any obvious growth of breast cancer. But the doctors are acting on the idea that the thing in my arm is cancer, as it has grown and has a lot of blood flow around it. The lesion is on or very close to a bundle of nerves.

The surgery will result in drainage, and recovery will take about 2–4 weeks. I also will have increased risk of lymphedema, but they can get help for me in this if I have it. I am glad to know that the doctors think that having surgery will do good, despite the risks of surgery near nerve bundles and lymphedema. They are still not sure about the mastectomy yet—whether to do it sooner, while I am on break from immunotherapy, or later.

Ned is helping me see the good steps that are going on. But it does leave me sad, quiet, and overwhelmed. I have been having more issues with my hands, knees, shoulders, and upper arms this week, so adding recovery and side effects to surgery feel like a lot. Not knowing what is ahead feels like a lot to process. I'll keep living in the moment (even if that includes lamenting in the midst of the good things).

For a week I've been writing poems in a tanka form. It's been a good challenge; it keeps my mind busy. Tanka poems have 31 syllables and 5 lines (5-7-5-7-7 syllables for each line), all in one sentence. The first half describes something and the second half responds to it. I am going through the alphabet, and I have done letters A through P so far. As I write them, I try to capture how the ordinary and the spiritual are all part of life.

Also, my friends invited me to be on their podcast to talk about the creativity they have seen in me during this time with cancer. I feel like a rambled a lot, but they seemed glad to have me conversing with them.[181]

Today I sit in this space of waiting and lamenting—I feel quiet and weary, though I know that even when the end results feel like a mystery and a little too far off, there is still good life and hope this side of heaven. I'm not really excited about surgery, recovery, and side effects, or about the idea that the thing in my arm is probably cancer, but I am glad for a plan and for good doctors and nurses and aides.

Thank you for your prayers!

Love,

Leslie

. . .

MARCH 4, 2021

Dear friends,

I just wanted to let you know that surgery on my left arm—to take out the tumor and lymph nodes—is scheduled for March 23. (Once the tumor is out, they will biopsy it. They are assuming it is cancer as it keeps growing. If it is cancer—what kind? Probably melanoma.)

I'm still learning about recovering from this surgery, although I do understand there will be a drain in the place where the lymph nodes will be removed (ugh). And I will have high risk for lymphedema.

We talked about the mastectomy happening at the same time, since I will not be on BRAF meds yet, but for now that is not going to happen. The cancer cells in my breast seem to be stable—no new growth that they can tell.

So many complications. And right now it feels rather heavy and hard. Lots more tears—coming quicker than before.

Carey and family (and Carey's roomies) threw me a surprise birthday party, which was so very happy. I love family time, parties, books, cupcakes, balloons, and flowers so much. Carey has taken over the role of party planner, and she is great at it!

Carey's spring break is at the same time as my surgery and my recovery, so she plans to come here and help. What a blessing.

I'm grateful for many little and big things during the week—seeing Ned's artwork ready for the printer; conversations with writing friends about poetry and essays; Ellie bringing chai teas from Starbucks for me; Maggie calling me on the way to the subway to talk; purchasing a new Rifle Paper journal and Dana Gioia's memoir for myself; an artist friend who wanted to use one of my poems for her artwork. And it's always nice to be remembered on one's birthday—cards, gifts, flowers, and messages do the heart good!

But my hands, wrists, shoulders, and knees are super stiff now, and that is discouraging.

Thank you for praying for me. I'm learning a little more about lamenting and wrestling and asking more of God.

This week some wonderful words came my way from "Now in This Hush," by the innocence mission:

> For we give our hearts to fear
> For so we give our minds to worry
> If I could brush this sorrow dust
> From off of our faces
> And see our joy again, may I? May I?
> O let us make a joyful noise resound
> O let us make a noise and hear it[182]

Love,
Leslie

...

MARCH 18, 2021

Dear friends,

This coming Tuesday is my surgery. I wish I understood all the details, but here is how it has been worded on the MyLGHealth site:

> DISSECTION/BIOPSY/MASS—AXILLARY NODE with Dr. Bleznak and EXCISION MELANOMA UPPER EXTREMITY with Dr. Bast.

I go in the morning and then come home later that day! Thank you for praying for me, for the surgeons and nurses, and for my family—and then, of course, for my recovery. And even for a sweet miracle that the thing in my arm isn't actually cancer.

Whether I'm feeling the side effects of the tumor or just the heaviness of the situation and the nearness of surgery, I have been roller-coastery with emotions and energy. I'm not surprised by this, nor am I giving myself a hard time for it. When I am so sad that praying and reading Scripture doesn't seem doable, God shows me He is the one holding onto me. Through faraway friends texting truthful words, close-by friends checking in, and others sharing Scripture that has been encouraging them, the breath and breeze of the Holy Spirit refreshes me and strengthens my heart. I am so glad for this. And I can then keep going forward, knowing that God does have it in hand, and He is faithful and good— His strength is made perfect in my weakness and dependence on Him. This really is my story right now.

The only thing I have head space and energy for is poetry and the psalms. The poets Malcolm Guite, Billy Collins, and Moya Cannon have been good companions this week. I get these great plans for reading more (the book piles in my study!!!), but by the time I get in my cozy chair, I've lost most of my energy. Naps are a wonderful thing again. (Nighttime sleep is up and down due to stiff joints!)

So many kind people are keeping us going—longtime friends painting our bedroom and my study; Sunday lunch chats with church family; a meal train set up for after surgery; offers of help for after Carey goes back to NYC. One friend made the most perfect oatmeal bread, I'm afraid I may overeat it.

Maggie is home now for spring break. Carey comes home on Saturday for her spring break. She will be with us for a week, and then will stay with her roomies as they come to Lancaster and stay close by for another week. These are such good things.

Ned continues to keep me (and Elspeth) going, even as he keeps up with his own work. Please pray for him to hang in there and stay healthy. He helps me get out of chairs, opens things for me, and even makes dinner when I lose all energy (and more things, but I don't need to share all the details!).

I have gained much encouragement through Malcolm Guite's new book *David's Crown*; his meditation on Psalm 3 has been a balm.

> Lie down and rest.
>   Let him look after you,
> And in the morning when
>   you rise again
> Then let him lift your head
>   and change your view.[183]

I also want to thank those who have given us money through the GoFundMe website. Words don't feel adequate to really express our gratitude.

We bought a new bed (ours was much too old). We also bought a few other nice things, like a new bedspread and curtains for our newly painted bedroom, a hallway runner, and spring throw pillows for our couch. There are other ways the money has been used through the past year. And every time we use it we are humbled by everyone's generosity. Thank you!

Your prayers for and goodness to us is really God's hand in our lives. It truly helps us keep going in this time of unknowns. Thank you, again and again.

Love,

Leslie

...

MARCH 25, 2021

Dear family and friends,

I am grateful and have felt sustained by all the prayers, encouraging words, attention, and gifts that people have given me and my family this week. I wish I could respond to everybody personally, but that would take a long time, and I only have so much head space at the moment.

The surgery went well. The tumor in my arm, which had grown significantly in the last two weeks, was completely taken out, with large margins all around.

The doctors also went ahead and removed the cancerous lymph nodes on my left side. Because they took so many nodes out, I will most likely be struggling with lymphedema on and off for the rest of my life, which is discouraging. But it is a small price to pay for getting macro cancer cells out of my body. Everybody at the hospital was wonderful.

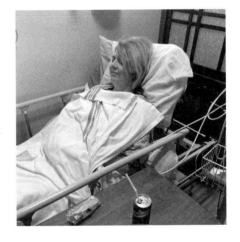

Whatever meds they gave me have helped loosen up my tight, cracky joints and muscles. It was wonderful to experience almost normal movement. They are returning to how they were presurgery, but it was nice to have a moment of relief.

Carey is at home with us, doing an amazing job of keeping us going (she even cleaned out my refrigerator!!!). She has also been pretty heroic in dealing with the drain that is coming out of my left side. This drain is to help clean out the lymph nodes. It is not as gross as we were expecting, but it's still not great. The places where the incisions are healing look bruised and battered, but so far they seem to be healing nicely. I have to keep my arm elevated above my heart, so everything feels comfortable at the moment on the pillow.

We are enjoying watching TV and talking and taking things easy these last few days. So blessed by the abundance of gifts you all have given us—flowers, chocolates, gummy bears, ice cream, English muffins and jam, tea, and yummy dinners are just a few examples of how overwhelmingly generous friends have been! It has been a blessing to me to see and hear the ways people have been reaching out to Carey to support her as she supports us (if you live close by, she drinks a Starbucks venti unsweetened iced coffee, black). So thank you, again!

Although I am not ever happy with this cancer stuff, this time with Carey has been incredibly sweet for me. Carey and I watched a new Audrey Hepburn documentary on Netflix, which was delightful since we used to watch her movies together when Carey was a teenager. I was struck by the fact that even though Audrey Hepburn's early life was so hard, and she suffered much loss and heartache, she still opened herself up to love fully and delight in the beauty of the world. She gave herself to others, even in her darkest moments, in ways that have inspired and encouraged me in this second chapter of my cancer journey.

Much love,

Leslie

...

APRIL 5, 2021

Hello family and friends,

Today is a warm sunny day; I'm sitting in my study with the porch door open. There is a slight breeze; the tree in my view is waving back and forth a little. Blue sky peeks between all the bare branches, and I can hear some birds twittering. What a friendly greeting as we enter into the week, still thinking about Christ's resurrection and how this reality offers true hope. Thank you for praying for me and my family these past two weeks. Having Carey with us, taking care of me, was a gift. She worked hard, and it felt good to just let her be in charge. (She is back in NYC now.)

Physical recovery has been going well. Having a drain coming out of one's side with bodily fluids emptying into a cup is a weird thing. Carey and Ned were troopers in taking care of it. The place where the tumor was removed—upper left under arm— is healing. But it is bumpy, and the space is swollen. I said to Ned that the sutures make me look like Frankenstein, but he said I was more like the Bride of Frankenstein, which made me laugh. Although I am healing, much still feels uncomfortable.

Here is a rundown of what has happened/what we have learned:

- The tumor in my arm was metastatic melanoma. It is all out!
- Dr. Bast did have to cut some nerves. Over time, they will grow back, but for now my left arm has odd sensations, yet at the same time doesn't really feel anything.
- Dr. Bleznak took out 22 lymph nodes. After the biopsy we learned that only 4 had cancer, and less than 10% of the melanoma was active. So despite the growth of a tumor, the immunotherapy was working well in the lymph nodes.
- I'll be meeting with physical therapists who can help me learn how to deal with lymphedema. The reality of lymphedema does haunt me— I find myself checking my arms and hands often, comparing them to see if my left arm is swelling too much. When watching TV, or reading, or sleeping, I try to keep my arm up. I do need to do more reading on this stuff (I am just now starting to have head space for reading and thinking). I am grateful to have a dear friend who does massage work for lymphedema.
- I met with my new oncologist, Dr. Brennan's partner, Dr. Sivendran. She is wonderful, and I'm grateful to have her. One metaphor she shared with me, as we talked about what it means to have stage IV melanoma, is that living with it will be like playing "whack-a-mole" with a chronic disease—there will be times of quiet and then something will come up, and we will work at whacking it down.
- Right now, all the known cancer is out of my body. There could be (and most likely are) small cancer cells that we cannot see. But it is good to know that all the "big stuff" is gone.
- Once I'm healed up, I'll get a PET scan and start taking BRAF meds (again). Dr. Sivendran has been using a new type that doesn't cause as many fevers (which I struggled with before). BRAF meds are fast acting and powerful. Dr. Brennan is planning on keeping me on them as long as they keep fighting the melanoma.
- My rheumatologist, Dr. Adusumilli, is anxious to help me get back to a "quality of life" where I don't struggle so much with tight and cranky joints and muscles. She increased my steroids to 15 mg, which has made a huge difference. My knees are working much better, my shoulders don't hurt as much, and the fog is lifting from my brain. My hands are getting better. She is going to have me get occupational therapy to work on my hands.
- I am starting to feel much more me, but I find that one day I might do a bunch of things and spend time with people and then the next day need

to sleep and lay low. I get ideas for things I want to do, and then realize, a few hours later, that I had planned too much. I feel slightly anxious to get back to caring for my family and my home, so I'm trying to take baby steps towards something that may be a good normal. But when I get tired, there are many tears. I really should go to bed by 9 p.m. to keep from getting overwhelmed.

I've been thinking and praying a lot about what it means to keep my eyes on Jesus in this new season and to rest in His love for me. The reality of the unknown is sharper now. So many words come to mind, and I talk to God about them—peace, lament, rest, hope, grace, trust, refuge, weariness... my life is hid in Christ's. Ned and I both feel weary. We are grateful for so much, but I think things are starting to pile up a little in us—the reality that cancer is part of life for now and the future. Even if I don't have any tumors right now, we're aware that the shadow of stage IV cancer can rear its ugly head someday.

I listened to Russell Moore and Tim Keller on Saturday on Russell Moore's podcast—what an encouragement. Tim Keller also has cancer, and the things he spoke of hit home. It was good to hear about the things he has struggled with and how the resurrection of Jesus means everything will be okay one day.

Poetry—reading it and writing it—continue to be a means of grace. And I've discovered some new-to-me poets, which has been a delight. I continue to return to some of the Lent poems of Maurice Manning.

> O teach me to untangle hope
> from hope that's false,
> and lead me farther down the winding path
> and whatever else
> you think I need, because the angle
> of the woven slope
> of love and grief is steep. Unless the bind
> is by design.[184]

Thank you again for your care and all your good words. It is hard to keep up with all the gifts, food, cards, and love! I do hope your Easter was a delight!

Love,

Leslie

. . .

APRIL 14, 2021

Dear friends and family,

Well . . . yesterday I had a PET Scan and it showed two new tumors. I have a 1.5 cm tumor by my right rib cage and a 5 mm one on the back of my right shoulder. The silver lining is that they are not embedded in any organs. I start BRAF meds on Friday. They are powerful and fast acting. Starting on them was already the plan, even before these two showed up. The doctor is also considering surgery to remove the new tumors.

I realized life would be like playing whack-a-mole, but I was hoping for some time between tumors. I do really love my doctors and feel good about their work. The theory is that these happened because I was off immunotherapy while recovering from surgery, and the melanoma is active and aggressive. And so in this short window of time, tumors started.

Physical therapy for lymphedema has been good, and I love my therapist. Her work and know-how gives me relief.

I'm not sure what to ask for in prayer—other than what I have asked for in the past. Please pray for Ned and my girls; my mom, Anne; mother-in-law, Brenda, and father-in-law, Dave; and for all my extended family. I really do hate the shadows these are for them. Pray for Maggie as she is wrapping up her senior year in college; she has a lot to do. And I'm so ready to just celebrate her and her hard work.

In attempts to keep moving forward in life, this week I worked on a poem about a Cézanne painting. After reading the poet Rilke's words about Cézanne, I've been trying to capture some of what I feel when I see his work.

Sandra McCracken's song "On High Places" has meant a lot to me this year, as have other songs from her recording *Patient Kingdom*. And today I discovered "Holy Water," by We the Kingdom—a singable song that makes me happy.

I can honestly say I'm pretty weary and tired. I'm physically tired, though recovery is going well (sometimes I overdo it. I yawn a lot these days). But my head and heart are weary. I'm hearing "Be still, and know that I am God" (Ps. 46:10) and so, after saying lots of words to God about life, I've just been trying to be peaceful and quiet. But sometimes just doing regular housework is pretty great—I love ordinary things. Carey comes home for the weekend, so I'm looking forward to hanging out, shopping, and watching a movie with her.

Thank you for your prayers. Your care continues to be a balm to my heart—a sweet gift of God's love to me.

Leslie

APRIL 28, 2021

Hello friends,

I just wanted to share a few things:

- I started the BRAF meds a few weeks ago.
- The tumor by my rib cage—the one I could feel—seems to have shrunk a lot. I can't feel it anymore.
- The BRAF meds make me so tired. I seem to be able to do one or two things in the morning, and by afternoon, I am so tired and ready for a nap. I plan to ask my nurse navigator if I will feel this for the rest of my time on these meds or just while my body gets used to them.
- This week the muscles and joints in my legs and arms have been tight and cranky again. This has been frustrating. I hate it when getting off chairs or up stairs is hard.

I haven't had any words for poetry or essays. It feels sad to feel so blank and empty. I hope it's just because I'm tired. But I did discover two lovely poems recently: "Biscuits" by Willa Schneberg, and "Praying" by Mary Oliver.

Some lovely activities: my mother-in-law came to visit last weekend, and we bought plants and went to dinner; lunch with my artist friend Hannah Weston (who is collaborating with me on a poetry and art show at Ned's gallery); and a sweet visit with a friend and her young children. This Saturday Lynette, my dearest friend since 8th grade, is coming to visit. Next weekend, Maggie graduates from The Kings College, so Ned, Elspeth, and I will join her, her roomies, and Carey for the weekend in NYC. I told Maggie I will keep myself quiet all week so that I may have more energy for our happy celebration in NYC.

Thank you for reading and for praying. I'm still in this cancer shadow, but grateful that this most recent tumor has shrunk and that I can't feel it.

Love,

Leslie

. . .

JUNE 21, 2021

Last update for a while?? I met with Dr. Brennan today. He's going to reduce my BRAF meds a little (they'll be strong enough to be effective, but not so strong that they affect my liver like before). My echogram showed a little bit of change in my heart—not a lot, but enough that he wants to stop the Herceptin infusions till things are figured out. I'll be getting another echogram in two weeks. Going to weekly labs to keep a close check on things.

I'll have a PET scan in August and then maybe restart Herceptin for the breast cancer. He was really glad to see that my joints and muscles are better.

So there you go. My hope is that I'll keep this lovely feeling of a regular, moving body so that I can back to exercising and yoga. And I'm hoping I won't be as tired as I have been these past 2 weeks, so that I can start doing summer-y things with family and friends.

Leslie with Georges de La Tour's *The Penitent Magdalen* during a private tour of the The Met

This weekend I felt so normal—I had forgotten what that felt like. I think the last time I felt this "all me" was November 2019. I didn't hurt and I wasn't tired. Lovely.

NeedtoBreathe has a new song that I love called "Sunshine" (also, I'm seeing them live in October!!). "Tell them you are feeling alright, we're living in the sunshine..."[185]

Thank you for your care and love and prayers!

Leslie

...

JULY 26, 2021

Hello! Today I had blood work (as I have had once a week for a while), and it was good to hear that my labs look good—my liver numbers are back to normal. Also my echocardiogram showed that my heart is doing fine.

Tomorrow I meet with a cardiologist who specializes in oncology patients. This appointment will help Dr. Brennan know what to do in August about putting me back on Herceptin for the breast cancer. Herceptin can cause irreversible heart damage. BRAF meds—the ones I take to fight melanoma—can cause reversible heart damage. The echocardiogram I had earlier this summer showed a little change that concerned Dr. Brennan, thus the reason I am not on Herceptin for now.

I am also reducing my steroids. I hope my joints and muscles will continue to be okay.

I have a PET scan on August 9 to see if there are any tumors (!!!!!). On August

11, I meet with Dr. Brennan to discuss next steps. Hopefully I will start back on Herceptin.

This summer has felt like a miracle and a gift from God. I have felt very good. No tight joints, no inflamed muscles, no brain fog. I have felt just like my regular self, pre-cancer. I never thought I would feel this way again. Once my liver numbers started to improve, the side effects to the meds evaporated (except for occasional tightness in my hands and knees). I even have more energy, and I don't have that heavy feeling of fatigue that can show up anytime during the day (except this energy hasn't manifested itself into regular creativity in cooking dinner or baking or working on the garden). So, to say this summer has been busy would be an understatement.

I've enjoyed time with our daughters, worked on creative projects, spent time with friends, hosted newcomers to church, attended our church anniversary celebration, and traveled to Laity Lodge in Texas and to Utah for a wedding. Next week we go to Virginia with our girls, Ned's mom, and extended family (very excited). Then friends are taking us to Ireland for 2 weeks in September (!!!!!!!!).

My most recent creative project is to put all my published writings and podcasts in one place—my own website called *Poetic Underpinnings*. I have included, and will keep posting, new writings and meandering thoughts, as well as my poetry, and the creative work of friends or favorite art makers. The website is up, even though I am still tweaking it. I hope you check it out—it's been a good work for me to do, with the hope that it will be an encouragement to others, too.[186]

Please pray for tomorrow's meeting with the cardiologist. (If anything is bad I will let you know.) Also, please pray for my PET Scan—that no tumors have made themselves comfortable in me. And if so, pray that I'll have the grace and strength to face whatever it is, as well as faith to keep trusting God in all things.

Grateful that you are praying and caring for me and my family. It continues to humble me, sustain me, and give me much for which to be grateful.

Love,

Leslie

...

AUGUST 9, 2021

Hello family and friends,

This morning I had my PET scans. (Thank you to those who reached out to say you were praying for me. I was grateful that you remembered!)

Dr. Brennan said the scans looked reassuring. The tumors from the spring are gone and there are no new tumors. The only thing they were not sure about is

Leslie with her mother, Anne Symons, and kayaking with her mother-in-love, Brenda Bustard

an "unspecified change in the pelvic area." (So maybe an MRI to check it.)

So I'm feeling grateful—it feels a little surreal to be able to say that I have no tumors right now. This doesn't mean remission. I have to stay on meds to keep the melanoma away.

We just got back from vacation with Ned's family. It was wonderful watching all the cousins laughing and playing together. The house was fantastic—it looked out over the water and the sunshine on the water. Also, the sunsets. One lovely thing I did was sit on one of the paddle boards and paddle over to where the sunlight was glittering on the water.

The happiest thing is that I'm still feeling normal and with normal energy. After we came back from vacation this past Friday, I had energy all day on Saturday to get the house back in order, go grocery shopping (even to Cherry Hill Orchards for local fruit and veggies), and then make a new pasta dish and dessert for the family. Yesterday we had church and then a nap; the girls and I made a wonderful corn chowder for our friend Joy, who came over for dinner. Joy's sister and her family came over for dessert, and we just hung out and enjoyed each other (especially Joy's little niece who stole all our hearts!). It's been so nice to feel "just like me" for so long.

Ned and I are getting ready to go to Ireland with our friends Doug and Lise; we leave September 5 and will be away for two weeks. Wow—there are no words to describe how excited and overwhelmed I am by this gift.

Please pray for my joints as I am reducing my amount of steroids and am hoping that I'll feel fine with this!

Love,
Leslie

AUGUST 16, 2021

Hello! Today I had a mammogram, and happily the results showed that there is no new activity. What a nice thing to report. Right now I don't have any melanoma or breast cancer tumors taking up space or growing in me.

Dr. Brennan said we will keep doing BRAF meds till my body stops responding to them (no exact time as to how long the BRAF meds will keep working). And after that we could try immunotherapy again or maybe something new will be out and we can try that. I have one more Herceptin infusion to go. The Herceptin, plus a couple other meds, is keeping the breast cancer stable. The Herceptin has made me tired again (which has caused me to feel melancholy). But since I only have one more infusion, I am hoping that sometime later in the fall that weariness will go away (like it did this summer when I took a two month break from it). Dr. Brennan said that even when I'm not having infusions the Herceptin keeps fighting the cancer.

Since Dr. Brennan would like to get me off steroids, I am down to 7.5 mg. Unfortunately my knees, elbows, and hands are tight and achy—mostly in the morning. This has added to my melancholy. I think once I'm used to it, I'll be fine. I am thankful that I had 5 or more weeks of totally feeling fine—like pre-cancer me. It was a good break.

Carey and Maggie are back in New York. It was lovely to have such a long time with them this summer.

If you live in or close to Lancaster,

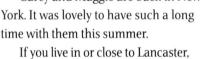

Leslie and Hannah with their show

please join me September 3 at the Square Halo Gallery for the opening of *Hannah Weston: The Alphabet Poetry of Leslie Bustard*. My very talented friend Hannah illustrated 26 of my tanka poems with calligraphy and paintings. She is amazing, and her work has really made my words shine.[187]

Ned and I are starting to plan our two-week trip to Ireland with our friends Doug and Lise (happy dancing!). After that trip, I will take a short trip to Colorado to attend an Anselm Society conference ("imagination redeemed"—what a wonderful topic!), where I'll spend time with some Cultivating friends. I'm grateful for all of September's plans. Ireland seems very surreal and dreamy!

Thank you for praying for me and for your encouraging words!

Much love,

Leslie

OCTOBER 4, 2021

Hello friends!

It's been a while since I posted … Life has been pretty sweet. Our trip to Ireland and my visit to Colorado Springs made September a full but delightful month. I am glad to be home and am trying not to race through my to do list, which includes catching up on housework, trying new recipes, reading, studying poetry, working on the Square Halo conference, and spending time with family and friends. I am so glad it is fall!

Leslie at the Giant's Causeway

I have also been working on the new book *Wild Things and Castles in the Sky: A Guide to Choosing the Best Books for Children*. Carey, Théa, and I, with Ned's help as graphic designer, are on the homestretch—all the essays are in, the book lists are almost all compiled, and the book is about to have its final proofing. The final printed book will feature forty-five essays written by forty wonderful folks who love children and who also love good books. Carey, Ned, and I made the cover images by hand: we had lots of fun planning our little people and cutting them and the clouds and castles out with paper and painting the background. (The background pages are words from *Winnie the Pooh, The Lion, the Witch, and the Wardrobe*, and *Alice in Wonderland*.)[188]

The past couple of days I have been writing a poem about a scar from my lumpectomy last summer. It's a little more transparent than I am used to being, but it is true about some of my recent thoughts. Also, I've been enjoying Katy Bowser Hutson's poems from *Now I Lay Me Down to Fight,* a book of poems she wrote during her cancer fight. Her honesty about her body and emotions and the vulnerability that she shared on her CaringBridge and in her poems have helped me a lot. I really love these two:

TREATMENT IS A GAUNTLET
Katy Bowser Hutson

Treatment is a gauntlet,
battering at each attempt.
To the victor goes the spoils:

The life you've been living,
That you never quite knew you wanted so badly.
Let them stick you, amputate parts of you,
Pump you with medicines and chemicals,
Let them explore you, help you.
You alone are the vision-keeper of what your life is.
You, and your Maker and your dear ones.

After Mastectomy

Katy Bowser Hutson

I blipped into waking
A skipping record
Singing Holy, Holy, Holy

Pricks and sticks and snips and
Twinges and twitches and tenderness
I did nothing but sleep

My breasts are gone
they did their job
They were occupied territory so they had to go
Will I get them back when everything's all right again?[189]

Last week I met with Dr. Brennan. My blood work looked good—except one
thyroid test, which just means a meds readjustment. I had a Herceptin infusion
with one of my favorite nurses (who is moving to another hospital . . . sad). My
steroids are down to 8 mg a day. I'm hanging in there, and my joints only get tight
in the morning and later in the day when I need to take some more Advil.

Just like during the second half of the summer, I am still feeling very much
myself, which is a lovely answer to my prayer "Lord, will I ever feel like I did
before I found out about cancer?" I am grateful to say I still haven't had issues
with lymphedema.

Although I feel good and my labs look good, I still have to remain on meds to
keep all the tumors away. I have a PET scan in 6 weeks. Won't it be wonderful if I
still don't have tumors and the BRAF meds are still doing their job?

Our trip to Ireland really was dreamy (even though Doug and Lise weren't
able to join us, because Doug had COVID! They are such special friends—we
missed them and had looked forward to this time with them). Ned and I loved

being together and experiencing all the beautiful places we visited—the museums we explored, streets we walked, and people we spent time with. It is hard to say which place was our favorite or my own favorite.

To Doug and Lise, who organized and planned this trip for weeks as a way to make one of my traveling dreams come true and to refresh us after many months of dealing with my cancer, and to all those loved ones in The Rabbit Room community and beyond who gave us money for this trip—I don't have enough words for this. Your generosity made us speechless. Several times I asked Ned, "Who am I that people are so kind and generous to me and to us?" I don't know the answer to that, but thank you for seeing me and for caring for me and my family during this time of cancer. Your generosity and how unworthy I feel of it is a real, real picture for me of God's abundant grace and love found in Jesus.

Since the beginning of this cancer journey the story of the friends of the paralyzed man and their work taking him to Jesus through the roof has been an encouragement to me—my life is an outworking of this story. All my friends through their love, gifts, and prayers (especially prayers) have upheld me and taken me to Jesus. This trip became another aspect of this story.[190]

Thank you for your prayers and for your kind and generous care for me and my family!

Much love,

Leslie

...

NOVEMBER 11, 2021

Dear friends,

Monday I had my PET scan and am happy to say that I don't have any tumors right now—nothing old and nothing new. Feeling very glad! Yet I have been feeling fatigued and have a hard time staying on top of things or being motivated or focused. The doctor is having me do another round of blood work next week. My liver numbers were slightly up, so he wants to see if the increase in this fatigue is due to a liver/meds issue. He is also calling for an MRI, as melanoma can go to the brain, but this is just a precaution, to cover all the bases.

I keep taking stumbling steps toward getting my days into some type of rhythm, but nothing is really sticking. Today I started reading *A Small Cup of Light* by Ben Palpant (phew, his writing is poetic). He shares a hard story about an illness and how he lost control of how to spend his days, which hit at his idol of being productive and busy and "winning." He writes about how he just wanted normal back so badly he was missing the ways God was reaching out to him. That has caused me to ponder what it is that makes me want my normal self (and the way I used to be able to do things) back. I thought I could come home from Ireland—where I felt good almost all the time—and just return to my regular ability to live my life, as well as my regular enthusiasm for caregiving, exercising, reading, ideas, etc. But all these things come and go.

Even before cancer God was showing me that I could quit striving (out of fear/inadequacy/not-enoughness), and that He really is "in my boat." But I am back to that question of what should I be doing (which isn't a bad question, I know, but it does have some that striving feeling in it). Yet before I could work out that question even a little, I hit this wall of fatigue. Gratefully, the work of putting the *Wild Things* book together (thank you Carey, Théa, and Ned) and the Square Halo conference[191] overall has gone well, as has the last week writing for *Cultivating* magazine. But even when working on these three projects (which I love), I feel easily distracted or weary of working. Today I had a lovely morning of home life—yoga, reading, making applesauce, pumpkin bread and lunch, and few other things. But by 2 p.m. I was ready for a nap.

All this is to say that maybe I'm still called to stretches of quiet—that my brain and body are recovering from the roller coaster of these past two years of cancer—while also walking in faith/courage/trust for the future. Being tumor-free and having moving joints hasn't guaranteed a return to "me before cancer" the way I hoped it would.

But I am grateful for much: taking a quick trip to NYC to see Carey and Maggie, reading Seamus Heaney poems, seeing a couple of movies with friends, going to coffee shops to work, enjoying afternoon fires in the backyard and walks in the sunshine, receiving helpful feedback from various friends on a couple of poems, the release of Ned's two new books (*The Giftgiver* and *The O in Hope*), prayer time, yoga (I can finally do poses that I couldn't do a while ago), and weather chilly enough for me to wear my new sweater from Ireland (as many times as I can!).

Thank you for reading and praying! Praise God for no tumors! Pray for a clear mind and that I would learn how to *be* me and *do* life while resting in Jesus and what He has for me now.

Gratefully and with love,

Leslie

. . .

DECEMBER 4, 2021

Dear friends and family,

I meant to write this post earlier—but when things are feeling almost normal,

I get caught up in the ordinary of everyday (which is super sweet!). But several folks have checked in, remembering that I had tests going on (thank you). So, there are no tumors taking up room anywhere in my body, and my brain is just fine, too. Dr. Brennan wanted me to have a brain MRI because I shared that I was not only feeling sluggish and easily distracted but I also just felt brain fog. Since melanoma can go to the brain, he had to get that checked out. MRI went well—I think I actually fell into that half-sleep that is always so pleasant.

I also met with my rheumatologist this week. She was glad I was doing better, but our conversation went like this:

ME: "I walked all over the place in Ireland and climbed on rocks and had more energy than usual."
DOCTOR: "I'm glad—but your hands are still swollen."
ME: "I know, but really I'm so much better. My knees and elbows are hardly ever stiff." (I go on to explain when the stiffness happens.)
DOCTOR: "I know you are glad you're feeling better than you have for a long while, but my goal is to make *all* the inflammation and stiffness go away."

Hooray for excellent doctors! She is looking into changing my meds to really deal with the remaining issues. My steroids are down to 5 mg, so I am feeling a little more stiffness than usual. But I'm so glad to be heading toward getting off the steroids.

I'm grateful for this time right now. This time last year I was so sick—the sickest I have ever been, and it lasted all day and all night for more than two weeks. It pretty much wrecked December. I think we only celebrated Christmas because Ned was such a superhero. This December is the first time in most of my adult life I have ever been free of responsibilities beyond what I want to do. What a delight. I have been slowly decorating with fresh greens and making cookies. Last night we celebrated Ned's book release party, so I helped a lot with that. What a good time. I sat on the floor and read the books to kids and had such a delightful time talking to and enjoying them!

Thank you for praying for me. It's nice to be in this period of peace. I hope it lasts a long time, but I know God knows this story, and so I am working at doing life with gladness and gratefulness and trust for right now and for whatever is up ahead.

However you mark these days leading up to December 25, I hope there is grace and peace and joy.

Much love,
Leslie

FEBRUARY 18, 2022

It is true in many ways that no news is good news. I had a mammogram a couple weeks ago and all was clear. Hooray!

I told my daughters and Ned, and then totally forgot to share it with other family members and here on the CaringBridge. (I do apologize!) I'll have another mammogram in the summer. I don't feel any tumors (not that that really means anything). Bloodwork continues to be fine.

So the *now of life* is good. I get tired still, but I also feel pretty much like myself. I've been getting together with church friends and being a little more active. My biggest issue is that I want to spend time with so many people, but I also wants lots of alone time to read and write. And I don't like cooking like I used to . . .

This past weekend was Square Halo conference. We sold out (with a wait list of 50+). I have heard lots of wonderful feedback from those who attended. My hope that it would be a gift to people—a delightful, refreshing time, with good talks and immersive experiences—came true with the help of the most fantastic people. It felt good to work towards this conference and see it happen. It was a gift for me to accomplish something that meant so much to me and then to have the energy to enjoy it.

Welcoming guests to the 2022 Square Halo Books conference

Since working towards the conference took up so much time and energy, I haven't done any writing and I've done very little reading. I'm hoping to get back to all that, but this week I keep crashing into naps or binge-watching ice dancing YouTube videos or Olympic skating re-runs (like Dorothy Hamill in 1976). But that's okay.

I am bothered by a continuous weight gain. It is one thing to gain weight and accept why it happened (did I tell you my oncologist said, "We have chemically altered your body—so it will be really hard to lose"?), but it is another to realize how much I have put on in such a short time (only 5 months). So I think I'll once again talk to the doctor about it. My steroid intake is down to 5 mg a day—so that's a good thing. I'm grateful for a husband who does love me all the time and is a refuge for me from the crazy thoughts in my head!

I'll be back sharing with you after the results of March's PET scan.

We are into the third year of this cancer-land. I'm grateful for the *right now*. For feeling normal and having the head and heart space to care for other people in my community. For interesting projects to work on. For a slow life that doesn't include all the side effects and issues of the past two years.

Much love to you. Thank you for caring these past 2+ years.

Leslie

. . .

MARCH 1, 2022

Hello friends,

This is just to share—happily—that today's PET scan was clear and clean. It's quite a relief to say this and to have the BRAF inhibitors still working. I've been on these meds for almost a year to keep the melanoma from growing. This time two years ago it was confirmed that I had stage IV melanoma and stage II breast cancer. This time last year, I had a growing tumor in my arm and then surgery to take it out. Before surgery I was struggling with so many side effects to the meds. Getting ready for the day, walking up stairs, and doing other daily things was hard, and I needed Ned's help so much. There was much to feel weary over.

What a year this has been. Yesterday was my birthday. I'm grateful to look back and see all the blessings and the gifts: Herceptin infusions to fight the breast cancer, no tumors in my body for 9 months, trips with Ned to several wonderful places, time with close and extended family, lunch dates with my mom, visits and talks with friends, wonderful teaching, worship, and communion each Sunday at Wheatland, reading, studying and writing, an art show with my friend Hannah, *Wild Things and Castles in the Sky* with Carey and Théa, and the Square Halo conference. Praise the Lord for this abundance.

I'm singing Sara Groves's wonderful version of "Praise to the Lord" and thinking about these words from *Every Moment Holy*:

I once again entrust all things to you, Jesus.
For you are the Captain
    of my passage through this storm.
You are the King
    who leads me home from lonely exile.
You are the Lover
    who embraces me in the midst of my grief.
You are the Redeemer

of all lost and broken things
    now yearning to be made new.
Your mercies are everlasting
and your promises are true.
You are the very author of life,
and the conqueror of death,
who has promised
to remake this world,
this sky, these gardens
and cities and stars,
    and also, yes, my own
    failing flesh,
raising it new and
    imperishable.

So seal my heart
    unto that day, O Christ.
So inhabit these holy spaces,
    these hardships and sorrows,
    this precious hope of glory.
So cradle me in my present frailties.
So commune with me in my grief.
So shepherd my passing.
So command my resurrection.
Amen.[192]

My Lighthouse from "A Liturgy for Dying Well"
Ned Bustard

Thank you for being in on this journey. You have been much of the goodness of God to me!

Love,

Leslie

. . .

MARCH 23, 2022

Hello friends!

A year ago today, I had surgery to remove a tumor and some lymph nodes from my left upper arm—and now here I am a year later. So much goodness between then and now: no tumors; blood work has been okay. I still need naps, and some days I get more things done than others. But overall, I am so glad for how life is right now.

Thank you for all the ways you have helped sustain me and my family over these past couple of years. Right now all the meds are doing their jobs. I don't know how long the BRAF inhibitors will keep working—maybe a couple more years, maybe five more years? Maybe longer? Once they stop the melanoma tumors from growing, Dr. Brennan said he will try immunotherapy again or maybe there will be other new melanoma meds that will work. And there are still no breast cancer tumors growing. I'm grateful for that.

Dr. Brennan is making the time between visits and blood work longer than it has been before. I guess I'm learning how to live life a little more normally—without so many doctor appointments.

I keep writing, which makes me so glad and grateful. *Wild Things and Castles in the Sky* will be coming out in April. What an extraordinary adventure I have had with Carey and my friend Théa and all the writers who have been part of this project. Also I submitted some poems in a few online journals and some were accepted. How fun is that? Calla Press published one called "Ordinary Goodness."[193] I am still having fun working on my *Poetic Underpinnings* website, focusing on good books, meditations on Lent, and my little hobby of taking photos with my phone.

Wild Things and Castles in the Sky

Thank you and thank you for all the grace and prayers and care you have given me. I am always grateful.

Leslie

. . .

MAY 23, 2022

Dear friends,

A short update about me will be at the end of this note. Today I am asking you for prayer for my mom, Anne Symons.

Recently we learned that she has two spots of cancer on her right lung. She also has a blocked artery in her neck and in her legs (which causes numbness in her legs). She was on a good trajectory to get these vascular issues dealt with, but then we found out about the cancer. We are waiting for the biopsy to be scheduled and then, from there, treatment.

Please pray for her heart and mind—for peace that surpasses imagination. For the biopsy and the treatment plan. For excellent, caring doctors (I have been blessed with such great care and loving nurses, aides, and doctors, and I want this for her, too). For me and my brother, David, as we advocate for her and help her through this. For her to be healed of the cancer in good time so they can then deal with the vascular issues (and that these vascular issues won't cause problems between now and then).

Thank you for praying!

I am doing okay. I won't see Dr. Brennan till June 10. The time between my visits with him is longer than it has been before. I guess this is what happens when you are tumor free for a year! I will have a PET scan and mammograms this summer. So for now I am still doing life assuming I don't have tumors and the meds are working.

There is much to be grateful for. For a while in May I felt really melancholy and lethargic and did not feel up to doing even things I loved. Naps were my favorite activity. But after some time gardening with my hands in dirt, and walking in the sun, and being with some friends at different times, I'm feeling more myself and doing some things I love. Again, thank you for praying for me and also for my mom!

Love,

Leslie

. . .

June 27, 2022

Hi friends, this is Ned.

I had been meaning to send out a joking email to say that y'all need to keep praying even if we don't have any bad news to report. But I can't do that now, since there is bad news . . . .

This morning while driving home from a PET scan appointment, Leslie started to lose feeling in one side of her body so she pulled over and she seized in the car. Someone found her and was able to help her and she was taken to the hospital. They are doing an MRI this afternoon to determine more about the size and location of the tumor.

Please pray for Leslie.

. . .

JUNE 28, 2022

Ned here again.

Leslie was encouraged this morning by this meditation and asked for me to share it with you all. Here are the lyrics to the song featured in the reflection:

> When you pass through the waters I will be with you
> And the depths of the rivers shall not overwhelm
> When you walk through the fire you will not be burned
> I am the Lord
>
> And there is nothing to fear
> For I am with you always
>
> In the depths of your sorrow I wept beside you
> When you walked through the shadow I drew you near
> Yesterday, today, tomorrow—always the same
> I am the Lord[194]

This image (*right*) is from *Every Moment Holy*, but it was originally created to be a reminder to Leslie that she is in the boat with Jesus while the storm rages. In her mind she paired this image with the meditation. I listened to the song above while typing this entry, and I agree that it is rather providential for us this day.

I don't know much at this moment. Leslie spent the night at the hospital. We can go in at 10 a.m. I heard this morning that a neurosurgeon is going to be meeting with her because they might do

The Church
Ned Bustard

surgery. TODAY. This has all escalated very quickly.

Leslie is concerned that she hasn't been able to get her hair colored. But that might be a moot point if they do surgery. She is also bothered that the kitchen needs to be repainted. On the plus side, all the girls are in town. That is a comfort to Leslie.

Thanks for your prayers. Our good God is outside of Time and Space hearing them—and they matter.

...

Ned again.

Leslie has a tumor that is about 2 cm long (the doctor said that is a small tumor) on the left side of her brain. It is deemed in a "safe" space to operate since it is on the surface and not down in the brain. She will be having a craniotomy tomorrow (the surgery will be about two hours). She will undergo a couple doses of localized radiation post-surgery (with a "cyberknife"). Probably come home Friday. Recovery should be a few weeks.

Leslie expressed her gratitude for the medical care but also told the doctor about how she sees God's hand through it all.

They have shaved some of her hair to do the surgery but you wouldn't know from looking at her. Currently we are sitting in the hospital room debating if she should cut it all short and go gray. But I think her girls are gonna lose that argument—Leslie simply enjoys being a blonde too much!

...

June 29, 2022

I just got off the phone with Leslie as she was heading into surgery.

She asked me to share a song and a poem with you this morning: the song is by Eliza King and is a lovely reworking of Psalm 23 called "I Shall Not Want." The poem is by Luci Shaw, of course, from her new collection *Angels Everywhere*, and is titled "Plentitude."

The girls and I gathered this morning to pray together and we prayed "A Liturgy Before a Medical Treatment," but then I saw that there is "A Liturgy for the Morning of a Medical Procedure" which is certainly very useful for today. Now I'm not sure which one Leslie prayed as she went in. But if you have time, maybe you can pray them both over her.

Here is an excerpt from that prayer:

We pray for good outcomes from
this procedure, O Lord.
We ask for good outcomes, pleading that you
would be mindful of our mortal frailties,
but we know that regardless of the
tidings to come, you are tender
and present and sovereign over
all circumstance,

and what is more, you love us
fiercely and eternally.
Therefore I would trust you to lead
me well along the paths of any
wild and perilous country.
You are my shepherd.
This day will hold no surprises for you.
Let me rest in that.
Amen.[195]

And since you are praying anyway, please pray for my girls. This is a lot for them to carry and process. Pray for the Holy Spirit to comfort them and give them hope in this dark season.

And of course, pray for Daily Bread for me—I didn't work last week while we were on vacation, I'm not working this week in the midst of this medical crisis, and I am not sure what work will look like in the coming weeks . . .

. . .

We just spoke with the doctor. The surgery went well, the tumor is out. He doesn't know what type of tumor it was. She will be in ICU overnight and home in a few days. Follow-up radiation will happen in a few weeks.

. . .

June 30, 2022

How much does love cost?
About $3.85, plus gas.
I went to see Leslie today and she immediately sent me back home so she could keep sleeping. So I had to pay for parking and stuff and only got to say "I love you" before coming back home.
The nurse said she was doing well, even if she was tired (they keep waking her up to check that she is okay, so no surprise that she is fatigued). She will get an MRI later today and might get moved downstairs later tonight. She is being kept in ICU right now because the rest of the hospital is so full. One perk of being in ICU is that she gets more attention from the ICU nurses than she would from the busier nurses on the other floors.

. . .

JULY 2, 2022

Hello dear family and friends,

I'm home!!!

Thank you for all the prayers and help and care.

I'm feeling okay. Slow, but more with-it than I expected. Recovering from brain surgery isn't as complicated as recovering from other surgeries. Something to do with all the blood up there. I'm told that I can do regular things, just to be aware of my energy, etc. (Not hard to do.)

We found out today that the tumor was a melanoma tumor. I will see Dr. Brennan this week to learn more about the next steps. Something about radiation.

People at the hospital are wonderful. I was well cared for by everyone. Today's breakfast and lunch actually tasted good. I am looking forward to lots of sleep, as I haven't had good sleep at all.

My head and heart feel weary and tired. I'm not surprised that I have a hard time thinking of what is next or if I will actually care enough to try to do anything or talk about anything. Also, since there is still some swelling in my head, I sometimes bump into things or have a hard time writing in a straight line or typing the right letters on my phone. But the inflammation will go down with steroids, and so that should clear up. Because I had a seizure, no driving for six months.

Once again, I'm on a slow road to somewhere new in this body and spirit. But I'm grateful I am here. I am grateful for Ned and my daughters and my family and friends and all of you who have paid attention and taken care of us through good words and prayers.

I read poems from Luci Shaw's new book *Angels Everywhere* yesterday. I don't think I have read a book full of poems that speak so much of things I love. She sees what I love to see and writes about it the way I would want to write about it. So much about trees and light and water. It has been the best comfort. Thank you to Luci for this book and to Phyllis for sending it to me a couple of weeks ago.

And "I Shall Not Want," by Eliza King, was on repeat all week and was just perfect for me. I'm grateful for this song. Psalm 23 has been so important to me these years, and this song makes it new and has been a balm. Aren't these lovely words?

I shall not want
For where He leads me to lie
There's always green pastures, blue sky
And where He leads me to rest
The water's quiet there

The whole world is quiet there
I shall not want
For He invites me to know
The abundance of His table
And I am seated in view
Of every valley that we've walked through
And He restores my soul
And awakens buried hope
In the chaos and the noise
You're the still, small voice.[196]

Again, thank you for your prayers and kindness. My family—I feel heavy-hearted that they have to keep dealing with this too. So our friends who come and go and give food and love are helping us carry our burdens.
Much love,
Leslie

...

JULY 4, 2022

Hello friends,

Just popping in to again say thank you for all the encouragement. I am healing well. I don't even have bandages anymore. I was up at 3 a.m. this morning and was just basically wide awake all day (except for a short nap). Also it's amazing what things I have gotten done since coming home—thanks to Ned and Elspeth's help, as well as the steroids and anti-anxiety meds. Lots of purging and reorganizing many corners of BookEnd. My study and porch are looking par-

ticularly sweet, and the Square Halo closet of books has been organized, as has my kitchen pantry. After dinner, I told Ned I would just water plants and he found me weeding (I think he was standing there for a while too, because he was kind of laughing at me). I hope I can slow down tomorrow. I'll be on these new steroids to help with the swelling in my head for about two weeks. Please pray for Ned, because I really am on a steroid high.

I'll see the oncologist this Thursday and learn more about the next steps—most likely some type of radiation. The only real issue is me running into things (like walls, which I hate!) and missing bottom steps (which I also hate). Ned really has to be with me if I am coming up or going down stairs so I don't miss and fall. Also words are hard to find—speaking or writing. Grateful for friends who came over today to help with cleaning, to give us yummy 4th of July food and to hang out with us at dinner.

This is all bizarre. I think the bigger reality of having a seizure and brain tumor and surgery and everything that has gone with it will hit soon. For now . . . it's all surreal.

With so much gratefulness for you and your prayers,
Leslie

. . .

JULY 7, 2022

Ned here.

It is the seventh day of the seventh month. Today is the day people around the world celebrate one of our favorite bands: The 77's! One of their songs we especially enjoy is "Nowhere Else." The chorus goes like this:

> There is nowhere else
> I'd rather be than in your heart.
> There is nowhere else I wanna be
> but in your eyes, in your arms[197]

And that is always how I feel about Leslie. Today "nowhere else" included going to see the doctor. Here is all the news from that visit:

We love Dr. Brennan, but he started us out with pictures of Leslie's brain. Not my favorite thing. But it was good to see how the tumor was there and now it is gone, and that the swelling is going down. There will be some radiation treatment soon to sweep up any microscopic cancer cells the surgery might have missed. But I told you about that in an earlier post I think. There was also a small blemish on the recent PET scan that we think is a bruise from hiking in Deep Creek that the doctor will have them treat as well—just in case.

I am happy to report that we are going to start back on the big cancer pills this Saturday. Leslie had to stop taking them for the surgery. Both Leslie and I are glad to get back on them since they are so fast and effective. Of course, they will eventually stop working, but there was some hopeful news on next steps: the first thing was a brand-new immunotherapy treatment has just been approved and that promises to be nicer on Leslie's joints, should we give that a try. It is called Opdu-alag. The other possible path was suggested to us by Kathy Keller, the wife of Tim Keller, founding pastor of the church in NYC that our older girls attend. Last week I sent Tim a surprise book we've been working on for a number of years honoring his ministry,[198] and after he thanked us in an email, Kathy sent a follow up email telling us about a new cancer treatment through the NIH. It has a 50% cure rate for melanoma. So Dr. Brennan is reaching out to them on our behalf.

We are so grateful for all the support and care we have received this week. Please don't stop praying for us—it is still a rough road ahead of us. The nurse commented on what a positive attitude Leslie and I had in all of this. We gave credit to the Lord's care exhibited through all the people praying for us, feeding us, helping with house projects, and more.

That, and the new puppy Leslie just got.

Did you hear? Due to some generous folks among our readership here, we got a cavapoo this week. Leslie is THRILLED. I haven't seen her this happy outside of a NeedtoBreathe concert. I always say, "Whatever makes Leslie happy" but—a puppy??? Now we need you to add to your "praying for Leslie's fight against cancer" prayers *for ME* as we add a puppy to the mix!

In non-puppy news, we are glad to have the NYC Bustard Chicks home this weekend to help celebrate Elspeth's 21st birthday. Please pray for them, too, as you pray for Leslie—it is no fun to have your mama sick with cancer.

...

JULY 14, 2022

Hello family and friends,

Just a quick update. I saw my surgeon's PA today—she checked to see how the incision (on the back of my head) was healing. Everything looks good and is healing well.

It was encouraging to hear that it's normal for me to need to sleep so much. Since my brain and my head are still healing, my brain is resting. I usually take a 2–3 hour nap every day. The steroid high is over. I have little bursts of energy but also very little desire to do much. I've enjoyed my new puppy Milly-Molly-Mandy, and I've enjoyed wandering around my backyard. I was trying to read because I have so many interesting books on my shelves. But I don't last long with a book—the PA said that is normal. Even being with people feels overwhelming after a while. But as the summer goes on, I'll keep improving and being able to care about more things and doing more things. Ned's "one thing a day" rule is still in place and probably will be for a while.

I'm grateful for all the help folks have given and offered.

Tomorrow I have a diagnostic mammogram. Pray that there is still nothing happening there!

Monday I have the cyberknife radiation—radiation that will be very directed to the spot where the tumor was. I'll also have an MRI on Monday to see how things are going in my head.

The Anselm Society just released a conversation I had with Brian Brown about "making the most of our time" and gratitude (and *Wild Things*).[199] I'm humbled and honored that they invited me to be part of their "Why We Create" series this year. I really enjoy the vision and work of Anselm Society.

I worked on a poem called "Invitation" while on our family trip to Deep Creek Lake. I loved sitting on the dock, watching the swallows fly around, as well as the light on the water. Sometimes words are not enough for how lovely the sunshine on the water's surface is as it winks and glitters. Thank you for your prayers and kind words. You all are such a gift to me and my family.

Leslie

...

JULY 15, 2022

Hello friends,

Today I had a mammogram, which turned into two mammograms and then an ultrasound. The findings are the following: "RIGHT breast masses at 2 o'clock are suspicious for malignancy; therefore, ultrasound-guided core needle biopsy of one of the masses is recommended." (There are two very small spots that look like cancer.)

I have a biopsy scheduled for this Tuesday morning.

So prayers for Monday, as I have radiation where the tumor was removed in my head, and then for Tuesday's biopsy. And pray that it isn't cancer—that would be so nice!

Much love,

Leslie

...

JULY 19, 2022

Dear friends,

I am so very grateful for you all. Your prayers and encouraging words continue to be such a gift to me. I am still amazed by you all.

I thought I was going to have radiation yesterday, but my appointment was actually to get me ready for radiation—meeting the doctor, getting a mask made that will keep my head in place, a CT scan, and an MRI. I will probably have 3–5 radiation appointments, every other day.

Today I had the biopsy for the two spots in my right breast. I will find out the results on Thursday. There is a possibility that it is melanoma.

Keeping quiet today as my biopsy incision needs to heal. Working on a puzzle and enjoying my puppy, Milly-Molly-Mandy.

Last night I watched *Respect*—the movie about Aretha Franklin starring Jennifer Hudson (both women are so incredible). I think today I'll watch her gospel concert *Amazing Grace*. Wow—I love her version of "Amazing Grace." (I admit: even though I love John Newton, I usually find "Amazing Grace" boring. But not this version!)

When I know more, I'll let you know.

Much love,

Leslie

...

JULY 23, 2022

Hello friends,

I want to give you some more details of the cancer spots found in my right breast. I've copied and pasted various points from Dr. Bleznak's notes because it's hard to keep up with all the details and names of things:

> She has another tumor, likely recurrence but given change in phenotype possibly a new primary, in the RIGHT breast. . . . The patient, her family, our nurse navigator, and I had an extensive discussion today and at this point we are all agreed that we will not proceed with any breast surgery. [The] phenotype of this tumor will not respond at all to her current ovarian suppression and antiestrogen therapy and Dr. Brennan may wish to consider another form of anti-HER2 treatment. Based upon today's discussion, I have made a referral to Palliative Care Medicine to initiate conversations about goals of treatment.

So there you go—maybe a third cancer because this tumor seems different from the first breast cancer.

Thank you for praying so much!! I will see Dr. Brennan the beginning of August. I'm not sure when radiation starts. I am really feeling the lowest I have felt these past two-and-a-half years and I feel an incredible lack of desire to do anything. I'm taking very long naps. My puppy does make me smile so much.

Please also pray for my mom, Anne, as she is also dealing with possible cancer as well as clogged arteries and vascular issues. I haven't seen her in ages because of my health stuff. She is struggling with her oncologist and with what is and is not going on. Please pray also for my brother, David, as he is the primary person helping her. I'm so thankful for family friends who are helping mom by driving her to tests, etc., and for the people at her assisted living home as they take good care of her too. Pray for a good plan of care for my mom and also for peace of mind and heart!

Much love,

Leslie

. . .

AUGUST 2, 2022

Hello friends,

I received my first radiation treatment today. I didn't feel a thing—but I had to wear a mask made specially to fit over my face and to hold my head still. I kept my eyes closed the whole time, as it did feel a little dystopian movie-ish to have all these huge, sleek, shiny machines around me while I was lying on a table with a mask over my whole face. I'll be back on Thursday, and then more radiation next week. I came home and slept for a few hours.

Last week, Ned and I met with a palliative care doctor. We had good conversations but also hard ones. We talked about issues wrapped up with cancer and life. I'm glad to have this doctor available to help me with our questions and struggles. I meet with Dr. Brennan this Friday and my brain surgeon next week.

This past weekend Carey's dear roommates came to visit. It was such a good thing to have them here (even though I still napped often). Good food, laughter, puzzles, and game time. I love them a lot and having them here helped me feel better Monday morning. I'm starting to feel better emotionally (it helps that I am taking anti-anxiety meds). There have been things I'm grateful for: Carey was here and we watched a cute, romantic K-drama and did puzzles together; friends brought meals and lots of flowers; my friend Lynette visited. But it's been a heavy time.

Also wonderful is that Maggie is home for the week—what a surprise for me. She can work remotely this week and so is doing it here, so this week I'll have Carey, Maggie, and Ellie around. Even though I'll be napping more than usual (side effect of radiation) and the girls all have their own responsibilities, it is sweet to have them close by.

I wrote a blog post for the Square Halo blog about some good novels and picture books.[200] Phew—so glad to be able to write something. This also makes me happy: Story Warren just published my series of two posts called "Poetry for the Lazy Hazy Days of Summer."[201]

Please pray for my mom—Wednesday morning is her biopsy. We are all anxious to know what is going on, so we can learn more about what is next.

Thank you for your care and kind words. I read them all and feel humbled and very cared for.

Leslie

. . .

AUGUST 7, 2022

Hello!

Praise God my dear mom does not have cancer! They don't know what the spots on her lungs are—maybe leftovers from COVID? She sees the oncologist on Tuesday to wrap up this part of her health journey. And then she will be able to get back to taking care of her vascular issues. This is a relief for her and for me and for David.

I have three radiation appointments this week and then radiation will be finished. I also will meet with Dr. Hernandez, the surgeon who removed my brain tumor this week. Friday was an appointment with Dr. Brennan. A lot of information to keep track of and decisions to make concerning treatment and meds. The brain tumor and the new cancer cells add complications and questions. Although I'm not as sad and down as I was a week or so ago, I still feel the heaviness of these new things in my life.

I'm still taking long naps—sometimes twice a day.

Milly-Molly makes me smile—her eyes are so sweet. I'm trying to teach her to be okay on a leash—today she looked miserable! My favorite thing about her, other than how she will cuddle with me and take naps with me, is her love of running toward the couch and making a long jump onto it.

I'm reading *Forward Me Back to You* by Mitali Perkins—so good. And it feels good to be reading.

Carey will be home for another week, which is such a gift. We've been watching Korean dramas, which has been very enjoyable (*Romance is a Bonus Book* and *Extraordinary Attorney Woo*).

Thank you for praying and for your kind words and care!! I am always humbled and grateful for them—and for you.

Carey shared this song with me and it's amazing and perfect—"Fear is Not My Future," by Maverick City Music. It's long but do keep listening, especially when Kirk Franklin starts talking. We love Kirk Franklin and this is such a good song.

Warmly,

Leslie

. . .

AUGUST 9, 2022

Well, hello again,

I just talked to my mom and it turns out that she *does* have cancer. She met with her doctors today and the report had been misunderstood when it was read to her last week.

But I'm thankful to say she was in good spirits. She really likes her doctors and her nurse navigator. They plan to do another test on the spots where the cancer is and then, most likely, she will have five days of cyberknife radiation. It's a little roller-coastery—this having cancer then not having it and then having it. But I'm thankful that mom is being brave and hanging in there! And also for my brother and for the friends who are helping her. Also, the people at her assisted living home take such care of her and love her. What a blessing.

My radiation was put on short hold because on Monday the machine stopped working when I was lying on the table. And they were unable to get it fixed for today. So I hope it happens tomorrow. It would feel like a relief to know that the radiation has hit any extra remaining cancer cells. We won't know the results for a while as I won't have an MRI right away. Apparently, the inside of my head will look like a mess with some swelling due to the radiation. So we need to wait a few weeks before doing an MRI to see how things went.

As I have said before, thank you for your prayers and your encouraging words. You are a blessing!

Leslie

. . .

AUGUST 15, 2022

Hello once again,

Today I finished radiation. Getting radiation wasn't hard, but I am glad it is done. I am grateful to say that each day I feel a little lighter inside my mind and heart, even as the past few weeks have been tiring physically and emotionally. I am so glad for anti-anxiety meds.

Please pray that the radiation destroyed all the cancer cells. I'll have an MRI in a few months to check on how successful the surgery and radiation was. But one thing I understand is, now that the melanoma has metastasized into my brain, it is quite possible that a tumor will return to my brain within the year (worst case would be three months). And depending on where it is it could prove to be one of those "snowball effects" that leads to the point where surgery is impossible. The BRAF meds are working well on the rest of my body, but they don't create a barrier to the brain, which is why a tumor is very likely.

Dr. Brennan looked into a new immunotherapy for me but told us that, because of the way my body responded to immunotherapy the last two times, the side effect risks are much higher than the curative possibility. So we'll have to make decisions about whether we'll want that immunotherapy when the BRAF meds stop working. BRAF meds give fast results but have a 2–5 year durability, and I'm well into the 2nd year. Dr. Brennan said he expects 1–3 years for me (although he also said he could be very wrong).

These facts have weighed heavily on me these past couple of weeks—almost as if I'm in a whole new chapter of living with cancer, thinking about the length of my days, and loving my family. Feeling a little more light these past two days has been a gift. I like slow days and quiet, but also every now and then time with friends and time at church. Caring for Milly-Molly-Mandy makes me smile.

I'm grateful that Jesus is always listening and that He hears my sorrow and my lament and my questions. And I'm very aware that my length of days could be longer than the doctor expects. Certainly, I would like it to last longer.

Please pray for the following (though there are probably other things to pray for, too):

- That the melanoma would stay away from my brain (for longer than a year!).
- That the new breast cancer would be silent until the doctor decides what he wants to do. (It is hard to do a lot to fight the breast cancer because of the melanoma.)
- That the BRAF meds keep fighting the melanoma (for longer than the doctors expect).

- That I can accept that I require more quiet than I ever have before and therefore can't accomplish all I would like to do. (I want to number my days aright to gain a heart of wisdom. I want God to show me what He would have me do with my days. I don't want to be sad so much.)
- That I would be courageous and would love my family and my community well as they love me and care for me.
- That my family can be courageous and would know Christ's sustaining faithfulness, love, and strength in their everyday lives.
- For my mom, as she will be undergoing one more test for the spots of cancer in her lung and then radiation for the cancer. Then she will need surgery for her clogged arteries in her legs and neck.

Thank you all for your care and prayers. You continue to be a gift.
Love,
Leslie

. . .

SEPTEMBER 21, 2022

Dear friends,

I'm writing to share several things and to ask for lots of prayer.

First—I've been feeling stronger emotionally in many ways. Not as melancholy, although weary deep down. Naps are still very important (for some reason I needed two today). But things like meals, laundry, and writing projects get done more often now (although today I just kind of meandered around the house).

I have a PET scan on Monday. Please pray that there are no tumors!

Second—my mom has had a rough summer. She has been in and out of the hospital, but now that she's home, she is slowly gaining strength and cheer—she is trying to join in the buildings activities and trying eat. Ned and I took her to lunch this past weekend. I was so glad to be with her and to find some food she likes to eat (most foods don't interest her and what she will eat, she can't eat a lot of). My mom is trying her best to be okay each day, though emotionally this has been a hard time for her.

Next week she has a CT biopsy to get a final reading on the cancer before they move on to treatment. Please pray for her spirits to keep improving and for her to rest in the knowledge that Jesus loves her—and for her appetite to improve.

Third—Ned's mom, Brenda, had been sick for a while and was also dealing with a lack of appetite. This landed her in the hospital. Then this past Sunday, while still in the hospital, she had a stroke. She is paralyzed on her left side (arm and leg). Yesterday she passed her swallowing test—which was encouraging. If I understand the details correctly, she was moved to a Step Down unit today and they are making plans to get her to a rehab place.

This has all made us sad, as we know that something like a stroke and being paralyzed from it is overwhelming, and she is feeling the burden of this emotionally. Please pray that the medicines they have given her and the therapy she will begin will help her regain ability in those areas that are paralyzed. Pray that she can turn her heart and mind to trusting Jesus in this, and that He would be real to her.

Please pray for Ned, as he also feels the burden of all of this (me, his mom, and my mom, as well as just wanting to care for and love his daughters well—plus his work and other responsibilities).

Please pray for my brother, David, as he is the main point person for my mom.

Please pray for Melissa, Ned's sister, as she is the main point person and caregiver for Brenda (as well as for their dad, Dave), and for Michelle, our sister-in-law, who has also helped care for Brenda at different times.

And just for the Bustard family and the Symons family (my side)—grandparents, parents, all our children. So much—it really makes me more aware of how fragile we are and how much we need God's intervening grace and mercy, strength, and comfort. I think we all are weary and need to know how real and close Jesus is to each of us—miracles and light in the darkness, too.

Thank you for sharing in this with me.

Love,

Leslie

. . .

September 27, 2022

Hello friends!!

Today I found out that my PET scan showed that I don't have any new tumors. What a wonderful thing to share. I still do have the new cancer spots in my right breast; they are keeping a watch on this. I'll have a highly specialized brain MRI at the beginning of November. My next prayer request is that no tumors are in my brain.

Please pray for my mom as she has her biopsy tomorrow morning. She is nervous about it and ready to have this part done. Results should be in this week.

And please keep praying for Brenda, Ned's mom. She has been moved to a rehabilitation home. She is getting good care, as well as physical and occupational therapy. Please pray for healing and for her spirits—that she will gain strength in her heart and body to do the work to get better. Also pray for my sisters-in-law as they spend time with her.

Thank you for your prayers for me and my family (my whole family). Even though we are sustained by the prayers and care of friends, it's all a lot.

Love,

Leslie

. . .

OCTOBER 4, 2022

Ned here.

Not because Leslie is doing poorly and *can't* write, but because she is doing well and *won't* write this post. She is always reluctant to do anything that looks remotely like she is promoting herself! But I am ALWAYS happy to hype her.

This weekend Leslie and I visited our moms (who both seemed to be doing a *bit* better, but who still need lots and lots of prayer for the long journeys they must travel) and at one point, while Leslie was out walking her dog, Leslie's mom asked me how Leslie was doing. I told her I thought she was doing well, because on the trip down she was pitching essay ideas to me. After the brain surgery Leslie was very low and did not have the mental or emotional energy to be creative.

And that made me reflect once again on how much Leslie has blossomed during this fight with cancer.

When people ask me how I am, I will say it is the best of times and the worst of times, but I usually focus on the "best" part—how Leslie has blossomed. I wear the "artist" hat in our family but I have to say, the creative output Leslie has generated over the last few years has kept me breathless trying to keep up. Her observations about cancer and God's creation have been transformed into lovely poetry, figuratively and literally.

During our recent trip to Nashville to sell Square Halo books at the Sing! conference, our friend Diana declared that we should publish a book of Leslie's poetry because it had spoken to her so deeply. I shot the idea down immediately, since poetry books sell so poorly. But then the next week our friend Katy asked Leslie when she was going

Signing copies of *Wild Things and Castles in the Sky* at Landmark Booksellers

to release her poems as a book. Diana and Katy are two very different women, but both are wise, godly, and insightful. I would be a fool to ignore them both. BUT poetry books *do* sell poorly. So what should we do?

The solution seemed to be to remove the burden of the books having to sell well by covering the investment required for their production. Therefore, I set up my first ever Kickstarter campaign. If this campaign is successful, it will pay for the printing and shipping costs for a book collecting the poetry Leslie has written over the past few years (plus an early one from years ago that she loves too much to leave out).

Do you love Leslie's poetry? *Then order the book.* If you say to yourself, "Oh, I want to support and encourage Leslie so I must buy this book," *please DONT order the book.* The best way to support Leslie is to lift her up in prayer, asking God to heal her body, care for her family, and somehow get me to clean out our basement.

Speaking of prayer, please pray for me and the girls when you are praying for Leslie. We have all contracted VSDF—that is, Valley-of-the-Shadow-of-Death-Fatigue. Leslie needs healing from cancer, but me and the girls need healing from VSDF. For example, I have three art exhibits this fall, three lecture/workshop trips, and a new kids' book in production—all WONDERFUL things, and I have a hard time *feeling* any of it. I can't imagine how the girls are really doing. Pray that God shows up to us, that we all see Him in undeniable ways, and that He gives us the hope and care that our hearts need. Oh, and pray for our Daily Bread, of course—I always need work!

But I digress. The point of this post is to tell you the exciting news that Leslie has a new book coming out: *The Goodness of the Lord in the Land of the Living: Selected Poems by Leslie Anne Bustard.*[202]

. . .

NOVEMBER 2, 2022

Hello friends,

Prayer requests for our family:

- Please pray for my mom, Anne, as she has been going to radiation. Since she was able to let go of her anxiety over it, she has been doing well. She is still struggling with a lot of pain in her leg and foot from her vascular issues that will hopefully be taken care of after radiation. Her doctor has been helping with this—but there are still issues.

- Please keep praying for my mother-in-love, Brenda. She is working hard in therapy and putting on a good face, but she is also dealing honestly with sadness and sorrow over what her life may look like with parts of her body paralyzed. My mother-in-law has loved her independence. She is a fabulous friend and loves being creative in her home and for others, so this is such a huge and sudden change. My sisters-in-law are superheroes—making sure she is getting the right care, is in the right place, and all sorts of other things. I'm grateful for them. What an example they have been of what family does for each other. Please pray for Mom, my sisters-in-law (Melissa and Michelle), and our family as we seek to support Mom in all of this.
- I have my brain MRI tomorrow. I've been happily doing my days as if all is okay (except, of course, for the obvious things)—we are not in emergency mode. And overall, I've been feeling really good. Tomorrow's MRI will either show that the surgery got rid of the tumor and then the radiation eradicated anything else, or it will show either remaining cancer cells or another tumor. Of course I am asking for prayer that there is no tumor in my brain.

Last week I started back on Herceptin to deal with the new small breast cancer that revealed itself this summer (it's a mutation of the first one, not a new kind of cancer as we originally thought). I'm really glad to be back on Herceptin and will be getting those infusions every three weeks. Please also keeping praying for Ned and the girls (and our parents and family) as they carry this burden/walk in this shadow.

Taylor Leonhardt's song, "Poetry," has meant a lot to me recently:

Isn't it so hard for most of us
To find the kind of patience that will trust
The slow steady work
Of God beneath the surface
Every moment working for our good[203]

Also—to those who backed my Kickstarter for *The Goodness of the Lord in the Land of Living*—thank you! It ends today, and I received double the amount Ned and I wanted. *Phew*—how exciting and humbling! I can't wait to share this book. I am grateful that one of my favorite writers, Hannah Anderson, wrote the foreword.

With love and much gratitude,
Leslie

. . .

NOVEMBER 3, 2022

Dear, dear friends and family, just one lovely thing to share—my most recent MRI showed no cancer in my brain. As my doctor said, "The MRI looks good!"

So, thank you for praying and praying. I am humbled again and again by your care and attention and kindness and by your many prayers to God. Once again, I am grateful to not be in emergency mode.

Thank you, also, for praying for my mom and my mother-in-love and our families.

Love,

Leslie

. . .

DECEMBER 13, 2022

Dear friends,

Just as I can imagine life has been for you, the past month (plus) since I last shared has had much muchness in it for us. Some of it has been wonderful (like a week visit for me to Northern Ireland), and some of it has been hard.

Last week I had a breast ultrasound to see how the two tiny cancer spots in my right breast were doing. The test showed that there has been growth in both, but the growth is still very slow, which makes the tumors really tiny. Dr. Brennan said, "Very slow changes. I am pleased with the results."

I'll have a PET scan at the beginning of January and then a brain MRI at the beginning of February. Still prayers that there will be no tumors anywhere.

My hair is starting to come in on the back of my head—now instead of a huge bald spot, I have a little bit of bald around the incision scar. The hair coming in is really, really short and gray.

Please continue to pray for Ned's mom, Brenda, and for my mom, Anne. I have said to some friends that it is easier to deal with my own cancer than it is to see these two lovely and wonderful women going through such hard physical things. Thank you for praying for them. I am grateful and they are, too.

I pray you are having a blessed Advent season and that your Christmastide is joyful.

Love,

Leslie

. . .

DECEMBER 18, 2022

Dear friends,

I just wanted you to know about my mom. We went to the appointment with the specialist to talk about the next steps for the clogged veins in her legs and the bypass surgery to deal with it, and to discuss the CAT scan she had had two days before the appointment. We found out from the CAT scan that most likely she has multifocal metastatic cancer in her liver and also in her abdomen wall. We don't know anything else right now. I've talked with her nurse navigator and I'm waiting to hear what the next steps are.

She is sad but she is also just waiting to see what is next.

We spent time with Ned's mom on Saturday. Brenda looks lovely—but she is still, of course, wrestling with what it means to not have any function in her left arm and leg. Her caregiver Maria is a gift. But do pray for Brenda—for healing and also for help as she learns to have her caregiver living with her. My mother-in-law has been living on her own for 35 years! So many adjustments.

I discovered the song "O Christ, Draw Near," by Paul Zach, this week—it's just perfect.

Thank you for your prayers!

Leslie

...

JANUARY 3, 2023

Hi—this is Ned again.

Yesterday I was thinking I would make a light-hearted post to encourage y'all to PRAY HARDER because it is so easy to forget to pray for people and I want everyone in the world to be praying for Leslie and this grueling battle with these two cancers.

Then last night we found ourselves in the ER with Leslie having symptoms very similar to those which lead directly to her brain surgery this past summer. Leslie and the girls had had a wonderful day together shopping, and then during dinner Leslie missed the door to the fridge, spilled water all over the table, and then couldn't get a glass of water to her mouth. We were devastated, thinking for sure the brain tumor was back. We called our doctor and he sent us straight to the hospital. When we got there, Leslie's symptoms were worse, and her blood pressure was unusually high.

Two CAT scans later (ordered by the ER doc, Dr. Katz—poetic, huh?) Leslie, Carey, and I were sitting in our room waiting for an MRI. Our pastor stopped by with some chicken cheese steaks from Dominion Pizza and he shared some Scripture with us and prayed (I'm so grateful for the support of our church family! In addition to the cheese steaks, another member of our care group came and installed a new rug in our home to encourage Leslie).

I kicked Carey out around midnight (no reason for us all to suffer on the horrible ER chairs).

Leslie soon got the MRI. I read *33* to myself while she was gone.[204] When Leslie got back from the test, the nurse brought in another cot for me, and Leslie and I tried to get some sleep. Suffice to say that the accommodations were *not* the most romantic or comfortable my wife and I have shared over the past three decades.

Our cancer doctor came in this morning around 10:30 and asked why we were still there. Hadn't we been told yet about the test results? No, we hadn't.

He told us that he had seen the MRI around 2 a.m. and that although it showed a tiny tumor (6 mm) in a new spot, and some inflammation where the old tumor was, Leslie wasn't in immediate danger. He couldn't say why Leslie had the seizure for sure and was apologetic for how noncommittal and unhelpful his diagnosis was, but he was going to talk to Leslie's brain surgeon doctor today. He also told us that on his way out he was going to get the paperwork going to get us discharged. Of course, it was at that point a nurse came in to tell us they finally had a room ready for us upstairs. We told her we were being discharged and she went to find a doctor to do that for us.

While we were waiting, our cancer doctor called us back and said he had talked to our brain surgeon and he had reviewed the MRI and wasn't concerned—he had seen the small tumor shown in last night's test a while ago. Then the Lanc General neurologist who checked Leslie out last night stopped in. He told us that anytime you tinker with the brain you set up the conditions for a seizure and believed that this new crisis was likely attributed to that. He said we could just go home and keep a watch on it or perhaps take some low-level anti-seizure meds. We chose to add in the meds to the battery of pills Leslie is already taking, just in case. So, the big takeaway is: don't try to sleep in an ER and PRAY HARDER—because, as Tim Keller has said, "Prayer is how God gives us so many of the unimaginable things he has for us."[205]

. . .

January 4, 2023

Dearest friends,

I just wanted to let you know that today I felt pretty good. I had a good night's sleep and then also a late morning nap. This afternoon Ned, the girls, and I talked with a palliative care doctor; we needed to talk about different end of life issues. What a surreal conversation. But I'm grateful for this doctor and for her wisdom and ability to guide us and care for us.

I don't know what is going to happen next, but I feel like I experienced a miracle this week. I prayed a lot during the night, as I was just so sad about the seizure and afraid I had another brain tumor, and I wondered what could possibly be happening. I prayed to God could I please be like that king you told was going to die and who set his face to the wall and asked to live, and then he lived longer. I knew God heard me say I wasn't ready to die yet or be really really sick or have another operation. I still want more time with my family and friends, more time to read and be creative, more time in my home and with my church.

Even though it is weird that they don't know why I had this seizure-like experience and what is happening in my brain, I am so glad I felt close to normal today. Now, not to overdo my days.

Christmas had a lot of sweet things—time with my daughters and Ned has been amazing. Even though we carry a heaviness about Ned's mom and my mom, I'm grateful that the five of us have been able to be together, reading, watching TV, laughing, playing games, talking. It has been a gift—words can't describe how glad I have been.

Thank you again for praying for me and my family. Your care has been so amazing! Please continue to pray for my mom and Ned's mom.

Much love,

Leslie

...

January 12, 2023

Hello dear friends,

I wanted to share a few things:

- I had a PET scan this week and learned that I don't have new tumors. What a relief. I am grateful for your prayers and for how God is answering them with a "yes, no cancer emergencies for Leslie right now." I've felt fine, even since last week's seizure. Wow. It's been three years this month since I discovered I had cancer. These two cancers aren't going away—but I am grateful that right now I don't have any melanoma tumors; I'm grateful my meds are still working.

- Please pray for my mother-in-love, Brenda. She continues to have physical therapy but it really looks like her paralyzed left arm will stay paralyzed and her paralyzed left leg moves a little. This is so discouraging to her. She has a good in-home caregiver and friends coming over and taking her out. But she has been an independent woman for a long time—one who relished in creating beauty around her and hosting gatherings and caring for her garden. She can't do what she has done for so long. This is hard. Pray for her, as she has to get used to this new life; pray that she may find, by God's grace, new ways to be creative or to live that can encourage her. Also that she would know that, even though she can't "do" like she used to, she is still loved deeply by us and by God.

- Pray for my mom, Anne. My brother, David, along with his partner, Sharon, and Ned, met with my mom's PCP and also a palliative care doctor. It was a good meeting in that they are wonderful and really care for my mom—but it was so hard. The doctors have come up with a plan to deal with her pain. Not only do her legs hurt from vascular disease, but her back has developed a lot of pain and rather quickly. Also, she has a mass that can be felt in her abdomen wall—and it seems like it is growing. We are hoping that we can get a biopsy of this mass and also a PET scan—just so we can see where everything has spread. According to the doctors, she is looking at having metastatic cancer that has spread in and from her liver. We are frustrated with the lack of guidance from the oncologist. Please pray that we can find a new one. But also please pray for us as we figure out how to keep Mom comfortable and as we work through not knowing how much longer she has. We feel certain there is no opportunity for a cure, so we just want to make her days comfortable.

I am heavy-hearted and numb and weary. My heart is sad for Brenda and for my mom, as I know that I can't do much for them except love them and serve them. I am glad I feel okay. I'm grateful for all the people, like my sisters-in-law, my mom's two doctors, and my brother and Sharon, who are caring for these beloved women.

Thank you for praying and for paying attention to and caring for our stories.

I recently discovered (and just love) the song "The Borderlands of Heaven," by Jon Lowry. It encourages my heart.

Leslie

January 30, 2023

Dear friends,

Thank you for carrying our burdens with us. This morning, our beloved, brave, and loyal mom and mum-mum, Anne Symons, while in a deep sleep, woke up in eternity and the radiant light and love of Jesus.

We had been starting to grasp the reality that she didn't have many more months to live, but we didn't think her death was around the corner. She was moved to hospice this past Thursday night. Ned and I visited her Friday and I was rather overwhelmed by the change, but since she was talking and laughing at times (and also being a little bossy with me), I thought she was getting to a stable place. David saw her Saturday and thought the same thing. But she took a turn yesterday morning. And it happened so fast that the nurses did not have a chance to inform us. When Ned and I arrived yesterday, we were met by her nurse and told what was happening—her body was starting to transition toward the end.

I am grateful that we had nurses to guide us and help us understand what was happening as they gave my mom such good and kind care.

David and my daughters also came.

How grateful I am for the hours I got to spend by her side, holding her hand, playing music she liked, and speaking of walking into the enfolding grace of Jesus. It was really hard to see her still dealing with pain and also so out of it. I know she knew we were there. But she couldn't talk and she was often agitated from her pain, despite the different pain meds.

Around 11:30 p.m. it was decided to give her more morphine through an IV drip. David stayed with her through the night. We had all said good night, and I told her I would see her in the morning. I knew she might die when I was gone, so I thought it could be more like "I will see you in the morning with Jesus one day." The morphine drip put her into a deep sleep, where she was not agitated anymore because of her pain. David says around 6 a.m. her breathing went really shallow and then, while he was with her, she died.

I'm grateful for the hope of heaven and for the hope of resurrection and of new creation. That because of Jesus and His life, death, and resurrection, and also because God always keeps His promises, all sad things will come untrue. I'm grateful she is whole and healed and experiencing life in ways I cannot understand yet.

So much more to say about my mom and her love and care and faithfulness.

And much to say to thank God for David and all who have helped us care for her this year—like her PCP Nicole, friends Ellen Swafford, Jim Wadsworth, and the Lengkeeks, as well as the fine people at Ingleside Assisted Living.

Thank you for your prayers and care. My mom loved Michael W. Smith. We both loved "Agnus Dei," which I played for her.

This Keith and Kristyn Getty song, "Christ Our Hope in Life and Death," was a comfort to me last night (and I hope Mom, too).

And she loved Enya's "Watermark," as it was what my bridesmaids walked down the aisle to when Ned and I got married. (She was pretty proud of herself for getting Ned and me together.)

May the resurrected and resurrecting hands of Jesus uphold and comfort and encourage us all our days.

May the Lord teach us to number our days aright, that we may gain hearts of wisdom.

Even so, Jesus, come quickly.

Love,

Leslie

. . .

February 1, 2023

Dear friends,

I just wanted thank you for all your kind words and prayers for my family and me at Mom's death. All your messages have meant a lot to me. At some point, if I have the headspace, I would like to really respond to each one.

Just as I have been seeing God's care during these past few years with cancer and with Mom's various health issues, I can see how Jesus is a Good Shepherd in this particular valley. His steadfast kindness and mercies do follow us day in and day out. And you are all part of that.

Monday I sat on our bed with my daughters and looked at lots of photos of Mom through the years—mostly pictures of the girls as littles hanging out with her. What a delight to remember those good days. Right now, although I know sorrow will look different in the days to come, I feel this sense of grace and peace that she is whole, and that David and I don't have to worry about her in all her pain or about how to help her and where to take her. God has her where all sad things come untrue. What a hope—this treasure of eternity and new creation. And this treasure felt so close as we all gave Mom our love Sunday night.

Much love,

Leslie

. . .

February 22, 2023

Hello family and friends,

Last Tuesday I had a brain MRI. The radiologist saw two very, very small new tumors in my brain and then a larger one in the same place where my tumor from last summer was (just not as big). When we met with Dr. Brennan, he also shared some really hard news: most likely I only had a few months to live—the tumors have grown so fast from last month (they didn't appear on my last MRI from mid-January).

My brain surgeon saw the MRI scans that night and expressed on Thursday that the spot which looked like cancer may actually be scars and dead brain tissue from the radiation. This gave us a little more hope over the weekend (and gave me the head and heart space I needed to be the hostess for the Ordinary Saints conference on Friday and Saturday).[206]

Ned and I saw my brain surgeon yesterday, and we talked through everything. Is this a tumor? It is hard to tell—but because there is more blood flow to that spot, it does look like one. When you compare the recent MRI with January and October's MRIs, you can see an empty spot, indicating dead brain tissue, and also a small, mushroom shape that lights up, indicating a lot of blood flow (which is a possible sign of cancer).

After our conversation concerning surgery or immunotherapy, and after the brain surgeon talked to my oncologist, it's been decided that I'll have brain surgery to remove whatever it is. I'll have radiation first on the two small ones, then I'll have surgery to remove whatever is in the space of my first tumor. That way they can get rid of it and also biopsy it to confirm what it is.

This is an aggressive approach, and it is risky. But none of the options seemed really good. I did want to have the surgery, so I am glad the doctors have decided on this direction. I'll probably still have another brain tumor in the future, but maybe the surgery will go well, and I'll get a little more than a few months. (The good thing is this spot with this possible tumor isn't connected to vital brain/body/emotion functions.)

Leslie signing copies of her book, *The Goodness of the Lord in the Land of the Living* to send out to those who supported the campaign

We told the girls; it has been hard on them. But they are glad for this new plan. And Carey and Maggie will be home this weekend for my birthday.

Thank you for your prayers. I so want this surgery to go well. I want more life. And for Ned and my girls to find comfort for this time, and to know God's presence in their lives.

Today is the first day of Lent. I am grateful to have this time to intentionally set my heart and mind on the coming death and resurrection of Jesus. I plan to keep off Facebook—it is too easy to escape into scrolling through all the reels and stories—and I want quiet deep down in my spirit. But I may do some writing and posting on my *Poetic Underpinnings* website. At least post about my new poetry book and write about the conference—which was so good. My hope for Lent is to keep doing the Bible readings my church has offered, and to read Esau McCaulley's book *Lent* (also something my church recommended). Hopefully I'll write some poetry and read some poetry and work on my collage books.

Blessings on your time of Lent. May you find space to reflect on God's grace, to lament the sin and brokenness the Spirit leads you to attend to and repent of, and to anticipate in fresh ways the love of Christ and the treasure of hope He offers His body, the Church.

And thank you for praying and hoping and sorrowing with me and my family.

Love,

Leslie

...

February 28, 2023

Ned here.

Just reaching out to tell you that today is Leslie's birthday!

Now, before you rush out and buy her flowers, please know that we *already have* three or four arrangements of flowers in our house at the moment from folks sending their condolences after the death of my mother-in-love. One is on the kitchen table, two are on the dishwashing machine, and one is in her study. There might be one in the living room, too—I forget. And while Leslie loves flowers, our house can only handle so many at a time. Of course, maybe you are thinking you will wait a few days for them to wilt and then send a fresh bouquet over in time for her radiation treatments or maybe in time for when she comes home the brain surgery. But then you think: Wait! What? Surgery? I wonder if there is a meal train? Ned and the girls need casseroles!

Let's step back a bit. First, I want you all to know that we have been over-whelmed (in the best way) by all the love we have received during this war with cancer. We have been amazed by how much thoughtful care has come from our church, family, friends, and strangers. But as we look ahead at the difficult days/weeks/months before us, I asked Leslie to make a list of things that she would *want* to receive if folks were desiring to do something to provide for her hope and sustenance. Here is what we came up with:

FOOD

We find our food needs/desires are pretty erratic and normal Meal Train dinners come to us with portions that are too large for the 2–3 of us and often with mushrooms in them, so instead:

—DoorDash or Hungryroot

ACTS OF SERVICE

—Things need to be cleaned around the house periodically

—Leslie likes to have the dogs walked

—We have tons of things that are bagged up and ready to get out of our basement and over to the Salvation Army

—We need our flower beds cleaned out and made ready for summer

HOME IMPROVEMENTS

Leslie loves me, but sometimes she wishes I could keep fix up our house a bit better than I can. For example, I needed to call my buddy Tom Becker this past weekend to hang a curtain. I'm not exaggerating. A *curtain*. Granted, these are larger things to do and require both money and skill, but if you feel like blessing Leslie in big ways, we need (or would like):

—A side fence (Leslie's dog has figured out how to break out)

—New paint on the stairs

—A new ceiling fan

—New paint in the guest room

—Repairs and paint for the eaves over third floor in the front

FUN STUFF

Egads, all that house stuff above makes me depressed. How about more interesting things:

—Dots. As in the candy. She likes them.

—Spring loafers in navy blue. (We are hoping the treatments go well and if they do, Leslie wants new shoes.)

—A book. We'd like to do a new book of Leslie's writings for her (did you buy her poetry book yet? It is wonderful). If you are interested in supporting that, please send money to Square Halo Books.[207]

—A tree (or two). Leslie loves trees and would like folks to donate nice yellow ones for our church to plant during the upcoming expansion. If you are interested in supporting that, please send money to Wheatland Church.

PRAYER

Honestly, all the above really doesn't matter. What IS crucial is that you all *pray like Hezekiah prayed in Isaiah 38* and get Leslie 15 more years. The Lord knows what is best, but I would really like to have more time to cherish my bride. Thanks.

. . .

MARCH 2, 2023

Dear friends,

Thank you all for your kind birthday wishes and for your encouragement. Several friends have given DoorDash—which is a fun thing to look forward to. And someone is my anonymous shoe fairy—also very fun for me.

Two important dates to pray for:

- This Tuesday, March 7, I have cyberknife radiation. This is to hopefully eradicate the two tiny spots found on the MRI.
- Wednesday, March 8, is my brain surgery with Dr. Hernandez. I don't know all the details yet but I will be talking to a pre-op nurse tomorrow about it all.

I am hoping and praying for what I think are the best things—that the spot that could be cancer is not cancer! That brain tumors stay away for much longer. That nothing emergency-like happens on the surgical table or afterwards (like hemorrhaging). That I make it through to a good recovery.

Dr. Brennan, Ned, and I decided the other day that after surgery I will stay on BRAF meds for the melanoma. In two months I'll have an MRI and a PET scan to check on any new tumors. If things still look good, I'll stay on BRAF meds. When they stop keeping melanoma from growing in my body, I'll go on the new immunotherapy. It's a tricky thing. BRAF meds don't make a guard against melanoma going to the brain, but it has been doing a great job so far for the rest of my body. Immunotherapy does guard the brain against melanoma going to the brain, but I haven't had the best results with it. This new immunotherapy looks promising—but also *not*, because of my history. There isn't one right answer, so we are going with BRAF meds for now.

Thank you for praying. Please pray for my family, as these things are hard to walk through.

Also—the other day, when I was feeling sad, I turned my mind to wandering around all my favorite spots in my home, backyard, neighborhood, and church. I imagined all the seemingly insignificant things I do in and around these places (like sitting on my second-floor porch, watching the birds and clouds), all the daily or weekly rituals I have with my people and places (like sitting around the kitchen table with my family, playing games and laughing), the many people connected to me and these places (like the Bauers and their children who sit in front of us at church), and all the holiday traditions I enjoy (like hanging Christmas tree ornaments and white lights). So many good things. I felt so glad for each thing—but I also felt this bittersweet ache, wondering how close I was to saying goodbye to this lovely little life I have been gifted with and thinking about how I wasn't ready to say goodbye. But then I started just being so thankful, in a deeper way, that this is what I have had for so long. Even if I have many, many more months left, I want to savor it all deeply so I can honor it all while still letting go. There is a treasure in hoping for life in God's New Creation and eternity with Christ. And there is a treasure in seeing all the goodness He has given to me these past 55 years as a foreshadowing to all the beauty and goodness He has in store for eternity.

May you, during this Lenten season, find those things that are true treasures in your life—and may they be a foretaste to what is ahead in eternity with our Resurrected Lord and Savior Jesus Christ.

Love,

Leslie

· · ·

March 4, 2023

Dear friends,

Just a quick note to say that my surgery has been moved to March 20th. My radiation is still this Tuesday. Although I'm eager to have the other tumor in my brain removed through surgery (and to find out if it *is* a tumor or if it is trauma to that area), I am glad for a little reprieve, time-wise. The past months have just been one overwhelming wave after another. I want these next two weeks to be really low key and quiet around my home (working on my puzzle, baking, reading, decorating pages in my collage/commonplace book, being outside—whether I actually do these things, I don't know, but I like the hope of them).

Thank you for praying boldly for me and for my family.

Much love and gratefulness for you!

Leslie

MARCH 19, 2023

Ned here.

Leslie had wanted to write a post today to ask you all to pray for her brain surgery happening tomorrow morning at 7:30 a.m. But this morning at 10 a.m. Leslie had a severe seizure. Fortunately, the girls were all here and called 911 (I was at a church meeting).

The ER folks were great and took really good care of Leslie. They took a CAT scan that found increased swelling but nothing more. So they gave her some extra drugs, and the surgery is going to go on as planned tomorrow morning.

The girls and I spent the afternoon with Leslie in her hospital room, reading books while she napped.

We didn't have either volume of *Every Moment Holy* with us because we were rushing out to the ER, so if you have it, please pray the "Liturgy for the Morning of a Medical Procedure" with us tomorrow.

And in the meantime, reflect on these wonderful words of comfort from Psalm 46:1–7:

God is our refuge and strength, a very present help in trouble. Therefore we will not fear though the earth gives way, though the mountains be moved into the heart of the sea, though its waters roar and foam, though the mountains tremble at its swelling. There is a river whose streams make glad the city of God, the holy habitation of the Most High. God is in the midst of her; she shall not be moved; God will help her when morning dawns. The nations rage, the kingdoms totter; he utters his voice, the earth melts. The Lord of hosts is with us; the God of Jacob is our fortress.

Psalm 46
Ned Bustard

. . .

MARCH 20, 2023

Ned here again.

Leslie is a bit too wiped out from the brain surgery to post.

Dr. Hernandez (her neurosurgeon) said he was aggressive and he thinks he got it all. He sent part of the mass to pathology, and they all agree that they think it was both the melanoma and scar tissue from the last surgery. They're probably going to do an MRI tomorrow to double check what they got. But he said the surgery itself was a success. He thinks they'll probably keep her for at least the next two days.

The girls and I have been taking shifts sitting with Leslie through the afternoon (only two guests are allowed in at a time). I hear from them that the sushi here in the cafeteria is good. I'm a bit peeved they don't sell Cherry Coke or sweet tea. Leslie has thrown up a few times (and I'm glad to report I did NOT throw up) and has a lot of pain in her head. The nurse has been very responsive to her needs and takes a lot of time to carefully explain to me that she is giving Leslie 12 cc's of zxyloprquertyzime and a pill of yourejustmakingitup, and that she is placing a request with the doctor for some somethingperzol to help with the pain.

I have carved 75% of a new linoleum block for my next book and did a preliminary sketch for a new *Every Moment Holy* print. Elspeth finished reading a book today and Maggie and Carey almost finished their books.

Please pray for her to be able to rest tonight and (obviously) that the pain in her head will go away.

Thank you for your prayers, love, and support!

. . .

MARCH 21, 2023

Leslie had a rough night in the TNU but around 3 a.m. things started to turn around. When we arrived she was looking good. They say if she behaves herself, she may even go home tomorrow. But I think it will more likely be Thursday.

She spent time today sitting up and time sleeping. Of course, her main complaint is that her head hurts.

Her nurse was grand. She took great care of Leslie and was a whole lot of fun to talk to.

We did nothing all day at the hospital but are all exhausted!

. . .

MARCH 22, 2023

We just talked to Leslie's neurosurgeon. A new MRI shows that there is some remaining tumor to remove. He wants to go back in because she can't go on immunotherapy with it in there. So she's probably having surgery again on Friday.

Please pray for her spirits (she is very discouraged), for peace when she gets her next MRI (she's feeling really anxious and overwhelmed by it), a successful surgery, a smooth recovery, comfort for my girls, the ability for me to work, and (of course) a miraculous healing from the cancer.

. . .

MARCH 23, 2023

Last night we came home to a very special surprise—an original oil painting of Leslie by our friend Bruce Herman. He wanted to add Leslie to his "Ordinary Saints" series. Bruce wrote to me, "Leslie seems (in the painting) to be the calm, still point in a turbulent space. I pray that in the days ahead she, and you, and your daughters find that still point of the turning world that is Christ in you, the hope of glory." We are all overwhelmed by its beauty and the generosity it represents. I'd like to express what this means to me and the girls . . . but words fail.

Today's update: It was mostly a quiet day today for Leslie. The brain doc came back in to visit her to make sure SHE wanted him to operate tomorrow (and that she wasn't just being bullied by her family). She confirmed it was her wish as well, so we are on the docket for brain surgery tomorrow. As I type this update she is getting an MRI.

So pray for Leslie tomorrow (in the afternoon, I think, but I'm not sure). Pray for protection from danger (it is *brain surgery* after all) and pray that all of the big tumor will finally be removed.

And, of course, pray for healing. The data is all against Leslie beating this cancer, but if you're praying, then you believe in a God who is bigger than the data.

. . .

MARCH 24, 2023

Dr. Hernandez just came out—he said that the surgery went well. He wasn't sure if what was removed was tumor or radiation leftovers, but he said that the bits of brain around it looked like healthy brain—which is what he wanted to see. The operation took a really long time, so that was nerve-racking. We are all coming down now from that unpleasant adrenaline rush. A few hours to go in recovery, then we will be allowed up to see her.

...

MARCH 27, 2023

Leslie got her golden ticket! The hospital released her this afternoon.

Leslie made me show the nurse the new painting by Bruce Herman to prove that her hair doesn't always look as crazy as it does right now.

We talked with Dr. Hernandez again and he said the MRI showed that he got all the big tumor. That's the good news. The bad news is it looks like there might be other small tumors that have popped up. More for y'all to pray about, right? Also pray for her overall recovery—two major surgeries in one week have taken their toll, and it will be a few weeks until she is likely to feel like herself again.

...

MARCH 28, 2023

Back in the ER.

Last night Leslie found she couldn't move her left leg. It seems like there's a little bit of bleeding in the brain, near one of the tiny tumors they saw before (not on the side where the surgery was). Dr. Hernandez is in surgery but apparently was able to look at the scans and weigh in. They think that the swelling is coming from the bleeding on the right and the surgery on the left. We're waiting for the neurologist to come down. They say that most likely they won't be going back in the brain, but we'll see. She's definitely getting admitted today so they can monitor all the things.

...

Today has been very difficult and full of tears. But the caregivers at Lanc General have been exceptional.

Leslie is back in TNU and they are working hard to reduce swelling and get excess blood out of her brain—in hopes that this will help her left leg work again (the left motor controls are where the blood/tumor are).

One very happy surprise today was receiving a gift from a very eclectic group of people. A bunch of friends from around the country secretly recorded *The Goodness of the Lord in the Land of the Living*. Leslie was overwhelmed by their generosity and was pleasantly surprised that she still liked her poems![208]

. . .

Okay, three posts in one day is quite excessive, but it has been QUITE a day.

Honestly, the way the doctors were talking this morning, I fully expected to be writing to you all now explaining about how Leslie died today.

BUT we got great care in the ER, the TNU team is grand, and they got good drugs in her.

This afternoon they did a CT scan and said she is "stable." The nurse then explained to us that "stable" means *good*—that they never say "good," only "stable" or "worse."

The oncologist came by later and explained that right now they are going to take good care of her in the hospital and wait to see the blood get reabsorbed into her body. That should help her regain the use of her leg. He also said that he was going to talk to the cyberknife doctor and see if we can knock out these little tumors that have been popping up in her brain.

Where does that leave us? In need of more prayer of course. Prayers for healing, and prayers for our family to be able to keep running this marathon. Elspeth is off work for a few weeks, Maggie is working remotely, and Carey is on spring break (and a very *restful* break it has been, huh?), but still, this experience has been taking its toll on my girls.

. . .

march 29, 2023

After yesterday's emotionally grueling roller coaster, I had hoped for a bit of quiet and boring. But Day Ten of this part of the cancer saga was filled with lots of doctors visiting and lots of changes.

When I arrived at the hospital this morning, Leslie was talking to a brain doctor about what was happening and what she could expect moving forward. Dr. Cross was warm and caring and very clear in her communication. Also, she had a bright yellow handbag that Leslie adored. We were also visited by Dr. Hernandez (he just stopped in to say "hi" between surgeries. Leslie gave him her poetry book and kids lit book as thank you presents). We were also visited by a radiation doctor and an oncologist from our cancer center.

Here is where we are at:

There is a bunch of blood pushing down on her brain, and it's keeping her leg (and her arm a bit) from working. That blood will drain over the next week or so. Hopefully she will get some use back in her limbs when the blood is absorbed back into her body. There is also a fine web of small tumors in Leslie's brain that can't be treated with the cyberknife. These will be treated with radiation over ten sessions (beginning next week), in the hopes of wiping them out. Sadly, they will take Leslie's hair and could impact her short-term memory. We will also begin a new form of immunotherapy as soon as possible. Neither of these treatments are guaranteed, but there is *some* hope that good can come from them—the oncologist told us they wouldn't suggest them if they didn't have a chance of working.

What to pray for:

- Feeling to return to Leslie's left side
- Rest in her new room (it is a rather unpleasant place compared to where she was staying in the TNU)
- A transfer to good rehab facility (there is one across the street from the cancer center—that would be ideal)
- Successful radiation and immunotherapy (wouldn't it be nice if Leslie was healed?)
- Peace and restoration for our daughters—this has been physically, mentally, and spiritually grueling for them
- Billable hours for me—in theory I should be working, and I *do* have several projects I need to get done, but I haven't had the time or energy to do them
- A deep hope and confidence in the sovereignty and goodness of God for all five of us, regardless of if Leslie is healed or if things speed up and go badly

Around dinnertime, Leslie was moved out of the TNU and into a regular room. There were *so* many people who lamented her leaving. Seriously. I even had one nurse come up and hug me. Over and over I heard the caregivers comment that Leslie is such a delight, and that while other patients are often draining and unappreciative, Leslie made giving care a joy. And let me tell you, not only is she a nice person, Leslie is a bold evangelist. She doesn't force Christ into conversations weirdly, but as she rests in her bed in this liminal space between the Now and the Not Yet, Leslie unashamedly declares her hope in Jesus. Many times I thought of the apostle Paul who, it says at the end of Acts, "welcomed all who came to him, proclaiming the kingdom of God and teaching about the Lord Jesus Christ with all boldness and without hindrance" (28:30–31).

I know my posts don't have the beauty and poetry (literally) of Leslie's posts, so to help correct that, I will end this one with a new poem that just came our way today. It is a poem-prayer that Elizabeth Wickland (one of The Black Barn members who came to our Square Halo conference) wrote for Leslie and has been using to pray for her. I think it is gorgeous, and the weaving motif is so appropriate as we begin attacking the web of tumors in Leslie's brain.

LESLIE'S ODYSSEY
Elizabeth Wickland

Like Penelope, unweave
the shroud that makes its progress
on the loom of Leslie's life.
Untie the strangling knots;
You are making all sad things
untrue; You are making
all things new; for Leslie,
Lord, please do. Reweave
hope and wholeness
in the secret, darkened places
as in the dark, in the secret
you once wove her whole
with hope for how she
would shine bright as yellow;
we are not ready

to lose that hope,
nor to wear the shroud
that weaves itself in her.
A day will come when her beauty
will be shrouded by death;
Today is not that day, we pray.
Today, evict the shadows
that wear her beauty
like a disguise, masquerading
as what is real in the land
of the living. Like Penelope,
weave light from this tangle
of darkness; turn mourning
to joy, the goodness of the Lord
in the land of the living.

...

MARCH 30, 2023

An actual post from Leslie today:

I wanted to share with you how lovely today was, with some ordinary beauty. It was such a lovely day. Breakfast was delicious (I just had to add a little bit of extra salt and pepper—but it was a cheesy omelette and home fries, and that was fun). Then later today one of the chaplains came by and we had a lovely time talking about Jesus and C.S. Lewis and hope. My family was with me throughout the day. We were together at different times today. Maggie read out loud to me from a book that she loves called *Malibu Rising* and later Ned read to me from the Chronicles of Narnia, and it all was just lovely. I spent two hours this afternoon just listening to my favorite music—the innocence mission. I just let the beauty of their words wash over me. There were other fun things, too, like Easter candy, Caesar salad, and brownies. A big highlight of the day was when my pastor came and ministered to my family, praying over me and serving us all the Lord's Supper. It was so wonderful. I'm looking forward to listening to the innocence mission again tonight and to just being quiet. As we look around the corner to rehab, I ask for prayers of endurance and hope lifted up on my behalf. Please pray I can place my expectations in God's care and work.

. . .

MARCH 31, 2023

We might not have mentioned it, but in light of Leslie being in the hospital, the memorial service for her mom was postponed. So no one should head down to Wilmington—we won't be there.

Today started out really bad—with the difficult news that radiation would begin *before* rehab, and therefore Leslie would need to stay in the hospital for another month. But by the end of the day we heard that rehab will come and evaluate Leslie on Monday (and will likely place her in the rehab facility across the street from her cancer center). We also learned that radiation won't happen until after the rehab. So please pray for Leslie to have great success in rehab, because I literally can't take care of her in our little row home with a zillion stairs if she can't be somewhat mobile.

Speaking of prayer, we are so blessed that our friend Maile has organized a 6 a.m.–6 p.m. prayer and fasting day for Leslie tomorrow. AND our friend Deb told a bunch of folks in Ocean City about our woes and encouraged them to be praying for Leslie. It is so humbling to be on the receiving end of all this love and prayer! And let's be honest, the future looks grim for Leslie—it will only be through God's miraculous intervention that Leslie will experience healing from this horrific illness.

On a lighter note, the whole Bustard clan was rejoicing and screaming out the SOJO chant tonight because the House of Sojourner Truth WON the Interregnum competition at The King's College! Both Carey and Maggie were presidents of "Sojo," and the leadership team for the house were Maggie's freshmen when she was president. We are so proud of them.

. . .

APRIL 2, 2023

I brought in a palm-cross for Leslie from church, and sang her some songs from the service as well as tried to summarize the sermon for her.

She had a rough night last night and was sort of groggy when I visited. I learned from the doctor that she has a mild fever that they are treating with antibiotics. Tomorrow we meet with Dr. Brennan and with the doctor from the rehab center. Please pray that those conversations go well.

And speaking of prayer, thanks ever so much to all those folks who fasted and prayed for Leslie yesterday. Following is the prayer they shared when they gathered to end the fasting:

Abba,

Can we be so bold as to call you that? I think you wonder that we would call you anything else. Abba, we give this day to you.

These words of prayer, these hours of fasting—of saying "no" in hopes that you might say "yes"—we give this to you. We come boldly with our requests.

We ask for miraculous healing for Leslie. You know every cell of her body. Her disease and its severity is not a surprise to you. And yet here we stand on the brink of Easter, proclaiming its truth of love and resurrection, and we know there's another power at work here, too. Resurrect Leslie's physical health, we pray. Let her story be one that baffles and inspires those who hear it.

And yet, you are already doing that. In Leslie, we see your Spirit of love and creativity blooming in her life. From her poetry to her words of constant encouragement to her soul warming hugs, you are at work in her, and we are grateful.

We ask for your grace, strength, and wisdom to cover Ned, Carey, Maggie, and Elspeth during this time. Each of them in their unique composition needs something different, and we are trusting that you will meet them where they are, that you will be generous in providing all that they lack.

Lastly, we pray for the medical professionals who are caring for Leslie. Inspire their minds. Guide their hands. Open their hearts to the beautiful story that is unfolding before them in the lives of Leslie, Ned, and their girls.

And now, Abba, we wait for you. We won't presume to know what's best in this situation—only you see all sides, know all things. But we pray from what we believe to be best—healing and wholeness—and yet we submit these requests into your loving care, confident that, no matter what the outcome, you are always a good father.

Thank you for your love. Amen.

. . .

A poem from Malcolm Guite arrived today and I got to share it with Leslie this afternoon as I sat by her bed. In fact, I think I read it to her almost a dozen times.

In the email (to which the poem was attached) Malcom wrote:

> I've finished the sonnet I've been writing in response to Bruce's wonderful portrait of Leslie, both so that I can send it to you and also so that it can become part of this growing multimedia work that is *Ordinary Saints*.[209] So here is the poem, written in response to the portrait but also, I hope, informed by my own knowledge of Leslie, of her poetry, and her whole way of being in the world. I hope you like it.

Of course Leslie and I *loved* it.[210]

· · ·

APRIL 3, 2023

Leslie woke up very disoriented today. They called me in to try and calm her down. Sadly, her delirium has been getting worse throughout the day.

To compound things, we talked this morning with Dr. Brennan and he said that the cancer in her brain has rapidly spread, creating a thin web across her whole brain. He told us there is nothing curative that can be done, and we should focus now on her comfort. He says that she is down to her final days or weeks.

The doctor said not to have any visitors while she is struggling with delirium—I know many who would like to visit, but she just is not able to deal with lots of faces. She doesn't even want me in the room most of the time.

And please, no flowers. We have bunches, and she won't see them. If you really feel compelled to give something:

- I'd like to do a new book for Leslie of her complete writings. If you are interested in supporting her legacy that way, please send money to Square Halo.
- Leslie loves trees and would like to have folks donate nice yellow ones to our church to be planted during the upcoming expansion. If you are interested in supporting that, please send money to Wheatland.
- To help my girls you could donate to the deacon fund at Wheatland so they can assist my daughters with their needs.

Thank you for loving Leslie and praying for her. And don't forget the hope of Easter: *THIS IS NOT THE END.*

· · ·

APRIL 4, 2023

Carey and I went to the hospital this morning. Leslie's delirium has gotten really bad. Currently she is heavily sedated.

Our dear Dr. Brennan said the cancer and bleeding is all over her brain and is causing the delirium—which means that the delirium isn't reversible. The plan now is to stop all treatments that are merely keeping her alive (and possibly adding to her pain) and to only continue treatments that will keep her comfortable.

"Anchoring the Heart in Eternal Hope"
Ned Bustard

In light of her current condition, we are asking that people *do not visit her in the hospital*—even the girls and I have stopped going in because it was causing her a great deal of distress yesterday when I was there. It breaks my heart not to sit with her at the end, but I want what is best for her.

The prayer for Leslie now is that she can rest (in a dreamless sleep, like that given to the weary on Ramandu's Island), waking up soon in the arms of Jesus. And, of course, please pray for me and the girls and all the tears we are (and will be) shedding. Then join us in this slightly modified prayer from *Every Moment Holy,* written by our friend Doug:

> Once again we entrust all things to you, Jesus.
> For you are the Captain of Leslie's passage through this storm.
> You are the King who leads her home from lonely exile.
> You are the Lover who embraces her in the midst of this grief.
> You are the Redeemer of all lost and broken things
>   now yearning to be made new.
> Your mercies are everlasting and your promises are true.
> . . . shepherd her passing—command her resurrection. Amen.[211]

. . .

APRIL 5, 2023

Leslie stabilized last night and was much more in her right mind today. Carey and I got to the hospital and Dr. Brennan met us and we went in and together and told Leslie that she only had a few days (or weeks) left here in the Shadowlands. Then Dr. Brennan asked if I was a hugger. I don't know if I am or not, but I hugged him and asked if he was handing off the baton. He said yes, but that he loved Leslie and I should call or text at any time if he could be of help. It turned out that hospice had an open room today and he was going to release us to their care.

Leslie's brother and his family arrived (we had been planning on doing lunch together today) and they were so happy and surprised to actually get to *see* Leslie, thinking she would've already died last night. We had a sweet time until the ambulance folks arrived and Leslie and I had to go to the new facility. Even in her weakened and agitated state, Leslie had made a big impression on her nurse in the cancer wing and the nurse was crying as Leslie was being rolled out. I gave her a copy of Leslie's poetry book as we left.

The hospice facility and the people working there seem really great. They got us in and set immediately to work making Leslie comfortable. I left her this evening snoring softly. I am so thankful.

. . .

APRIL 7, 2023

After coming home from our first day at hospice, a bunch of men from one of our church's care groups came over to pray for me and my family. It was just one more example of how the Body of Christ has been carrying us through all of these hard times. And then as a bonus, they fixed the gate in our backyard so that Milly-Molly-Mandy can't escape anymore—that would've made Leslie very happy. Then, yesterday, the pastors visited us in hospice and prayed over Leslie and anointed her with oil. Several women from the church also came throughout the day to pray with us—they even brought us some yummy smoothies.

As we were driving home last night, Carey reminded us of a family-favorite song, "Beautiful Scandalous Night." We all keep reflecting on how poetic and painful it is that we are all going though this with Leslie during Holy Week. And last night, after the girls and I left to go to the Maundy Thursday service, one of Leslie's best friends here in Lancaster kept vigil with her through the whole night.

One of Leslie's favorite traditions for Maundy Thursday was to read a story from *Stories from the Christian Year* by Walter Wangerin, Jr. (I bet you can order it from Byron Borger over at Hearts & Minds Bookstore—Leslie would have). So the girls and I rummaged through the house and, as we were pulling together a late-night dinner, read that story together, as Leslie would've liked. It is a funny, deep, and heart-warming story in which a young boy searches all over the church building trying to find Jesus. Apologies for a bit of a spoiler, but toward the end it says, "She told me where Jesus was at! Not far away from me at all. Closer to me than I ever thought possible. In my mama! He never had been hiding. I'd been looking wrong. My mighty mother was his holy temple all along."[212]

I have always loved that story, but this time it hit me in a new way, because I was reminded through Wangerin's words that my mighty wife has been God's holy temple for me all along . . .

. . .

We had a nice day at hospice. Leslie is sleeping well and they have a sharp tartan blanket on her bed that she would love—if she opened her eyes.

The doctor talked to us today about how she is doing, what kind of care they are giving her, and what to expect about how long she has to live (from a few days up to a week). I prayed this prayer from *Every Moment Holy* over her this afternoon:

O God My Father,
O Christ My Brother,
O Spirit My Comforter,
Leslie is ready.

Now meet her at this mortal threshold
and deliver her to that eternal city;
to your radiant splendor;
to the table and the feast and
the festival of friends;
to the wonder and the welcome
of her heart's true home.

She waits for your word.
Bid her rise and follow,
and she will follow you gladly
into that deeper glory,
O Spirit her True Guide,
O Christ her True King,
O God her True and Loving Father,
    receive Leslie now.[213]

APRIL 9, 2023

Christ is Risen! He is risen indeed.

Last night friends treated us to dinner at Luca, and this morning we went to church. The service was beautiful and they prayed for Leslie. Then friends brought over Easter dinner for us and *Easter baskets!* A bunch of Wheatland folks had all chipped in to bless the girls, and it was so encouraging. And just before we went to visit Leslie some friends from The King's College stopped by for a quick visit.

When we arrived at hospice we found Leslie sleeping peacefully. I was too excited to let her sleep and immediately read to her a wonderful email we got last night from Dana Gioia—one of Leslie's literary heroes. He had just received her book and wrote, *"The Goodness of the Lord in the Land of the Living* is a radiant collection." The whole letter was beautiful and I was so excited to get to read it to her.

We spent the rest of the afternoon listening to NeedtoBreathe with her and singing along for her (on the way home we blasted Charlie Peacock tunes).

Before praying over her and leaving Leslie for the evening, Carey read John Updike's "Seven Stanzas at Easter" to her.

. . .

APRIL 11, 2023

I've given up the pointless chore of wiping the tears away from my cheeks. Can the groom rejoice as long as the bride lays dying? The days may come when the tears stop flowing . . . or maybe not. Perhaps my new calling is only to weep.

That being said, today had much good in it. As we sat by Leslie's bed we told her about three joyful things that happened today, and we read poetry to her. Of course, we read her one of her favorite poems, the one that always made her laugh—"Litany," by Billy Collins.

. . .

APRIL 14, 2023

My beloved Leslie awakened on Mercy's shores just before sunrise today. Our friend Doug penned these lovely words about her:

> Leslie's greatest gift was in her generous service, in the way she enabled others around her to more vibrantly love God and their neighbors—and to more creatively express that love in all facets of their lives. Leslie embodied so naturally the glad, eternal vision that animated her service. She was not afraid to live life at a walking pace, noting the small beauties and savoring the small delights of the hours, the people, and the creation around her. Her eyes so often seemed to sparkle with the light of a better kingdom, with a wordless beckoning, an invitation, as if she knew some wonderful secret and was forever waiting for the rest of us to catch on. Leslie was a mysterious mixture of open arms, warm smiles, listening ears, and enfolding heart. She was a poet, but she was also a poem. To those blessed to know her, Leslie was both a giver, and a gift.

Thank you—one and all—for your prayers, words of encouragement, and support. This is a time of great sadness for my girls and me, but we mourn with hope, knowing that very soon we will meet her in Heaven.

ABOUT THE COVER

I began painting Leslie a short time before she entered the final phase of a terminal illness. Though she had not yet entered hospice care, I had an intuition that I needed to start the painting right away. In my fifty years of painting, it is rare that a painting effortlessly unfolds—but this is indeed what happened with *See You Soon, Leslie.*

The image seemed to paint itself. The background, which Malcolm Guite mentions in his moving sonnet, began as an experiment: layering a heavy impasto of Naples yellow—a particularly warm and beautiful color—over a preexisting abstract image dominated by resonant blues and greens. This delicious yellow was thickly applied, like frosting on a cake, over the cooler underlayers associated with lush foliage—a garden—something Leslie often turns to in her poetry. Somehow the blazing warmth of the upper layers seems fitting, knowing that beneath that glory is the earthy green of her garden. I speak in the present tense here because to read her poetry is to hear her speaking in our now.

We never actually met in person, but Leslie and I exchanged letters during the COVID-19 pandemic, as she shared her poems and I sent her a drawing— a little study of the contemplative Magdalen. Through Ned and his daughters, and through other mutual friends who were close to Leslie, I've come to know her as the saint she is—an "ordinary" saint of extraordinary warmth and generosity of spirit.

May her memory be eternal.

—*Bruce Herman*

. . .

A PORTRAIT OF LESLIE

Malcolm Guite

Out of the turbulence, out of the wild
Haphazardness of background strokes, the brush
Still finds its form and forms her face:
So full of life and, lovely, like a child
Still making her own mischief, with a rush
Of energy. And yet we also trace
A woman's wisdom in her concentration
On the still point, the whole point of it all,
Which was and is and always will be love:
Creative love and love in all creation.
This painting finds the poet in her, all
The heighth and depth she bodies forth as form,
To find her balance on the point of love,
When lovers know there's nothing left to prove.

ENDNOTES

PART I

1 *Editor:* As of the printing of this book, the full text of her CaringBridge journal is still available at https://www.caringbridge.org/visit/lesliebustard..

2 There has been a Margaret Ellen in our line of the Bustard family for at least four generations.

3 Elspeth is the Scottish form of Elizabeth. It means "chosen by God." Iona is the island where Saint Columba and his companions established a monastery after leaving Ireland in 563. The Book of Kells was likely made on Iona.

4 In part, riffing off Bilbo's "Bag End," but also because many books end up here.

5 In Noldorin (an Elvish dialect predating Sindarin) this is translated as "Tower of Magic."

6 Yes, this is a blatant rip-off of *The Avengers,* but keep in mind, he was just a little kid.

7 It is no surprise to any young student of the Bible that names and naming is important. In addition to the names of God (Creator, I am who I am, Yahweh, the Lord, Jehovah Jirah) Moses named his first son Gershom, saying, "I have been a stranger in a strange land" (Ex. 2:22) and then named his second son Eliezer. Eliezer is *Eli,* meaning God, and *ezer,* meaning "helper" (Ex. 18:4). By naming his son Eliezer, Moses bore witness to God as his strong helper during the hard times leading the Hebrews out of Egypt. Naomi, Ruth's mother-in-law, renamed herself "Mara," to reflect the bitter turn her life had taken (Ruth 1:20),and Jesus renamed Simon to Peter and said of him, "Upon this rock I will build my church" (Matt. 16:18).

8 Steven Roach, *Naming the Animals* (Baltimore, MD: Square Halo Books, 2020), p. 37.

9 Symons was originally Symonds, but the "d" was dropped when my father's parents moved to America from England in the early 1900s. I have heard it mispronounced Simmons. Bustard may have come from the word bastard; however, Ned likes to highlight the bustard bird—the largest, heaviest flying bird in the world. My mother-in-law prefers to pronounce Bustard with a French flair, "Boos-stahrd." I, on the other hand, gamely say (especially when introducing myself to a classroom full of middle-schoolers), "It's Bustard, like mustard, but with a B."

10 I highly recommend that everyone read Curt Thompson's *The Soul of Desire: Discovering the Neuroscience of Longing, Beauty, and Community* (Downers Grove, IL: InterVarsity Press, 2021).

11 Annie Dillard, *The Writing Life* (New York: Harper Perennial, 2013, orig. publ. 1989), p. 32.

12 Frederick Buechner, *Wishful Thinking: A Seeker's ABC* (New York: HarperOne, 1973), p. 119.

13   Billy Collins, "Introduction to Poetry,"
     Poetry Foundation, https://www.
     poetryfoundation.org/poems/46712/
     introduction-to-poetry.

14   Andi Ashworth, *Real Love for Real Life:
     The Art and Work of Caring* (Colorado
     Springs, CO: Waterbrook Press, 2002),
     p. 22.

15   Edith Schaeffer, *The Hidden Art of
     Homemaking: Creative Ideas for
     Enriching Everyday Life* (Wheaton, IL:
     Tyndale, 1971), p. 33.

16   Schaeffer, *Hidden Art,* p. 32.

17   Charlie Peacock, "Making Art Like a
     True Artist," from *It Was Good: Making
     Art to the Glory of God,* ed. Ned
     Bustard (Baltimore, MD: Square Halo
     Books, 2007), p. 243.

18   Denis Haack, "A Stick Becomes a Staff
     of God: Reflections on Faithfulness in
     the Ordinary & the Routine," Ransom
     Fellowship, May 29, 2007, https://
     ransomfellowship.org/article/a-stick-
     becomes-the-staff-of-god-reflections-
     on-faithfulness-in-the-ordinary-the-
     routine/.

19   Peacock, "Making Art," p. 248.

20   Jennifer Allen Craft, *Placemaking and
     the Arts: Cultivating the Christian Life*
     (Downers Grove, IL: IVP Academic,
     2018), p. 71.

21   Sara Groves, "Add to the Beauty,"
     track 5 on *Add to the Beauty,* INO
     Records, 2005.

22   Craft, *Placemaking and the Arts,* p. 17.

23   C.S. Lewis, *An Experiment in Criticism*
     (Cambridge, UK: Cambridge Universi-
     ty, Press, 1967), p. 19.

24   Francis Schaeffer, *Art and the Bible*
     (Downers Grove, IL: InterVarsity
     Press, 1973), p. 26.

25   Alan Jacobs, "Prophet of the Hu-
     man-Built World: An Introduction to

     John Ruskin," *Comment,* March 1, 2019,
     https://comment.org/prophet-of-the-
     human-built-world-an-introduction-
     to-john-ruskin/.

26   Mary McCleary, "Artist's Statement,"
     accessed October 4, 2023, https://
     www.marymccleary.com/statement.

27   Malcolm Guite, "The Church's Ban-
     quet," in *After Prayer* (Norwich, UK:
     Canterbury Press, 2019), p. 4.

28   *Editor:* You can hear Leslie read this
     poem aloud on "Leslie Bustard in
     the Land of the Living," interview by
     Jonathan Rogers, *The Habit* podcast,
     February 16, 2023, https://thehabit.
     co/leslie-bustard-in-the-land-of-the-
     living/?utm_source=rss&utm_medi-
     um=rss&utm_campaign=leslie-bus-
     tard-in-the-land-of-the-living.

29   *Editor:* A version of this essay (one
     of Leslie's first published pieces) first
     appeared on *Risen Motherhood.* Leslie
     frequently wrote and taught on the
     subject of women serving as ezers, or
     "strong allies." More of her writings
     on this topic will be appear in the
     forthcoming book *Strong Allies: Cre-
     ating, Cultivating, and Restoring,* from
     Square Halo Books (2025).

30   Henry Francis Lyte, "Praise, My Soul,
     the King of Heaven," 1834.

31   John McKinley, "Necessary Allies—
     God as Ezer, Woman as Ezer," a paper
     presented at the 67th Annual Meeting
     of the Evangelical Theological Society,
     November 17–19, 2015, https://www.
     wordmp3.com/details.aspx?id=20759.

32   Charles Donelan, "Georges Rouault's
     Miserere et Guerre: This Anguished
     World of Shadows," *Santa Barbara In-
     dependent,* September 6, 2007, https://
     www.independent.com/2007/09/06/
     georges-rouaults-miserere-et-guerre-
     this-anguished-world-shadows/.

33   Donelan, "Georges Rouault's Miserere et Guerre."

34   Steven Roach, *Naming the Animals: An Invitation to Creativity* (Baltimore, MD: Square Halo Books, 2021), p. 69

35   Roach, *Naming the Animals,* p. 70.

36   Thomas S. Hibbs, *Rouault–Fujimura: Soliloquies* (Baltimore, MD: Square Halo Books, 2009), p. 29.

37   Hibbs, *Rouault–Fujimura,* p. 23.

38   Hibbs, p. 58.

39   Hibbs, p. 49.

40   Hibbs, p. 52.

41   In private conversation with author.

42   Brad Littlejohn, "Virtue in the Twilight of a Pandemic," *Breaking Ground,* May 11, 2021, https://breakingground.us/walking-by-the-light-of-virtue-in-the-twilight-of-a-pandemic/.

43   Sandra Bowden, used with permission.

44   Ibid.

45   Hibbs, p. 43.

46   Hibbs, p. 55.

47   Curt Thompson, MD, *The Soul of Desire: Discovering the Neuroscience of Longing, Beauty, and Community* (Downers Grove, IL: InterVarsity Press, 2021), p. 172.

48   Andi Ashworth, *Real Love for Real Life: The Art and Work of Caring,* 2nd ed. (Nashville, TN: Rabbit Room Press, 2012, orig. publ. 2002), p. 56.

49   Ashworth, *Real Love for Real Life,* pp. 63–64.

50   Douglas McKelvey, "A Liturgy for Feasting with Friends," from *Every Moment Holy, Vol. 1* (Nashville, TN: Rabbit Room Press, 2017), p. 113.

51   Written for the birth of a child to friends in our church care group.

52   *Editor:* This essay was originally published as the introduction to *Wild Things and Castles in the Sky: A Guide to Choosing the Best Books for Children,* an anthology of essays Leslie curated and co-edited..

53   Marilyn Chandler McEntyre, *Caring for Words in a Culture of Lies* (Grand Rapids, MI: William B. Eerdmans, 2009), p. 2.

54   James K.A. Smith, "Healing the Imagination: Art Lessons from James Baldwin," *Image Journal,* accessed October 25, 2021, https://imagejournal.org/article/healing-the-imagination-art-lessons-from-james-baldwin/.

55   Ibid.

56   C.S. Lewis, "On Stories," in *On Stories: And Other Essays on Literature* (New York: HarperOne, 1982, orig. publ. 1966), p. 20.

57   C.S. Lewis, *The Voyage of the Dawn Treader* (New York: HarperTrophy, 1952), p. 1.

58   McEntyre, *Caring for Words,* p. 124.

59   Eugene Peterson says, in *Eat this Book: A Conversation in the Art of Spiritual Reading,* "The Holy Scriptures are story-shaped. Reality is story-shaped. The world is story-shaped. Our lives are story-shaped . . . We enter this story, following the story-making, storytelling Jesus, and spend the rest of our lives exploring the amazing and exquisite details, the words and sentences that go into the making of the story of our creation, salvation, and life of blessing" (Grand Rapids, MI: Wm. B. Eerdmans, 2006, p. 62).

60   Helen L. Taylor, *Little Pilgrim's Progress* (Illustrated Edition), envisioned and illustrated by Joe Sutphin (Chicago: Moody Publishers, 2021), p. 301. Used by permission.

61 McEntyre, *Caring for Words*, p. 115.

62 James Romaine, "What the Halo Symbolized: Vincent van Gogh's Sower with Setting Sun," from *Art as Spiritual Perception: Essays in Honor of E. John Walford* (Wheaton, IL: Crossway, 2012), p. 212.

63 "To Theo van Gogh, Saint-Rémy-de-Provence, on or about Friday, 20 September 1889 (Letter #805)," The Van Gogh Museum, accessed October 25, 2023, https://www.vangoghmuseum.nl/en/highlights/letters/805.

64 "Theo van Gogh to Vincent van Gogh. Paris, Saturday, 3 May 1890," Van Gogh Letters, accessed October 25, 2023, https://vangoghletters.org/vg/letters/let867/letter.html.

65 Martin Bailey, "The Artist Whom Van Gogh Most Admired—And Whose Work Fetched Record Prices," *The Art Newspaper*, October 4, 2019, https://www.theartnewspaper.com/2019/10/04/the-artist-whom-van-gogh-most-admiredand-whose-work-fetched-record-prices.

66 See Malcolm Guite, "Good Ground: A Sonnet on the Parable of the Sower," October 10, 2015, accessed September 15, 2023, https://malcolmguite.wordpress.com/2015/10/10/good-ground-a-sonnet-on-the-parable-of-the-sower/.

67 For an example, see page 84 in *Beauty Given By Grace: The Biblical Prints of Sadao Watanabe* (Square Halo Books).

68 My two favorite books on homemaking are *Home: A Short History of an Idea* by Witold Rybcznski, which helped me understand the evolution of the home from the Middle Ages to the Modern age, and *The Not So Big House: A Blueprint for the Way We Really Live*, by Sarah Susanka, which challenges the McMansion way of living and encourages "rightsizing" the American home with quality materials and personalized details.

69 Eugene Peterson, *Eat This Book: A Conversation in the Art of Spiritual Reading* (Grand Rapids, MI: Wm. B. Eerdmans, 2006), p. 18.

70 Peterson, *Eat This Book*, p. 18.

71 Joanna Gaines, "Magnolia Table with Joanna Gaines: Episode 1," *Magnolia*, January 1, 2021, https://magnolia.com/blog/article/428731/magnolia-table-with-joanna-gaines-episode-one/.

72 This title is inspired by the movie *That Thing You Do*, a Bustard favorite and a fun summer movie.

73 C.S. Lewis, "The Weight of Glory" from *The Weight of Glory and Other Addresses* (New York: HarperCollins, 1949), p. 42.

74 *Editor:* These are Leslie's own words, from a poem begun but not completed.

75 Marc Chagall, *"L'Ange,"* WikiArt, https://www.wikiart.org/en/marc-chagall/an-angel-1956.

76 For recipe, see p. 149 of this book.

77 This soup recipe is from my friend Mary Kucks, but it was passed on to her from another friend, Elise Battle. The recipe has since been shared among many other friends, and my daughters often make it for their friends.

78 Original recipe by Michael L. Ervin, found in *Fresh from Central Market: Favorite Recipes from the Standholders of the Nation's Oldest Farmer's Market*, ed. by Phyllis Pellman Good (New York: Good Books, 2009).

79 C.S. Lewis, *Prince Caspian: Return to Narnia* (New York: Houghton Mifflin Harcourt, 1951), p. 150.

80 The Greek words Jesus says are *"ego eimi"* which is translated "I am." Instead of saying to the disciples, "It's Jesus," He declares He is God.

81 Keith Winder, "When Storms Strike," sermon, Wheatland Presbyterian Church, February 3, 2019.

82 J.R.R. Tolkien, *The Fellowship of the Ring* (New York: Houghton Mifflin Harcourt, 1954), p. 123.

83 Tolkien, *Fellowship of the Ring*, pp. 54–55.

84 Tolkien, p. 359.

85 Marva J. Dawn, *Keeping the Sabbath Wholly: Ceasing, Resting, Embracing, Feasting* (Grand Rapids, MI: Wm. B Eerdmans, 1989).

86 J.R.R. Tolkien, *The Hobbit* (New York: Houghton Mifflin Harcourt, 1937), p. 263.

87 I discovered this recipe in *Victoria Magazine* and have been using the filling recipe every fall since, especially for my Thanksgiving Day pie. This recipe can be found online at "Deep-Dish Apple Pie," *Victoria Magazine*, October 1, 2017, https://www.victoriamag.com/deep-dish-apple-pie-recipe/.

88 See Lisa Ludwinski, "Sister Pie All-Butter Dough," *Food & Wine*, October 15, 2021, https://www.foodandwine.com/recipes/sister-pie-all-butter-pie-dough.

89 *Editor:* Leslie originally gave this talk at Wheatland Presbyterian Church, then published a version of it on her blog, *Poetic Underpinnings*, on November 29, 2021. To see a video of Leslie reading this testimony before her church congregation, please visit https://www.wheatlandpca.org/media/717146-2976309-14378517/leslie-bustard.

90 T.S. Eliot, "East Coker," in *Four Quartets* (New York: Harcourt, Brace and World, 1943), p. 28.

91 Seamus Heaney, "Miracle," *100 Poems* (New York: Farrar, Straus and Giroux, 2018), p. 160.

92 The Wyeth dynasty of painters starts with Andrew's father, N.C. Wyeth, and includes Andrew, his sisters Carolyn and Henriette, and his son Jamie.

93 Pittsburgh-born Henry Ossawa Tanner was not only an important American painter, he is also America's first notable African American artist. His career, although started in Philadelphia under the tutelage of realist Thomas Eakins, flourished into a successful European and American career after he moved to Paris, France. He was supported by patrons, won various awards, and inspired many African American painters.

94 Many of my observations here on Tanner's *The Annunciation* and *The Holy Family* are quotes or ideas I have gleaned from *Seeing Art History*, a video series by art historian James Romaine. You can access his video on *The Annunciation* at https://www.youtube.com/watch?v=zs44P8zgfm0.

95 James Romaine, "A History of African American Art: Henry Ossawa Tanner—The Holy Family," *Seeing Art History* on YouTube, https://www.youtube.com/watch?v=xW0OP8kFcwk.

96 *Editor:* This found poem (a poem made by refashioning and reordering longer, non-poetic texts) is based on a speech by Queen Elizabeth II. It was one of the last poems Leslie worked on before she entered hospice care.

97 You can listen to BookEnd Christmas on Apple Music (https://tinyurl.com/2dm3n9tx) or on Spotify (https://tinyurl.com/3tet2d4b).

98 Calvin Seerveld, "Helping Your Neighbor See Surprises: Advice to Recent Graduates," in *Contemporary Art and the Church: A Conversation between Two Worlds*, ed. W. David O. Taylor and Taylor Worley (Westmont, IL: IVP Academic, 2017), p. 211.

99 Rainer Maria Rilke, *Letters on Cézanne*, trans. Joel Agee (New York: North Point Press, 1985), p. 77.

100 *Ferris Bueller's Day Off*, directed by John Hughes (Paramount Pictures, 1986).

101 *Editor:* Leslie originally gave this lecture during a special event for All Saints Presbyterian Church (https://allsaints-church.com).

102 Dana Gioia, "Poetry as Enchantment," *The Dark Horse*, Summer 2015, accessed September 20, 2023, https://www.thedarkhorsemagazine.com/Featured/Poetry-As-Enchantment.

103 Ibid.

104 Ibid.

105 A haiku by Issa from *Cherry Blossoms: Japanese Haiku Series III* (Mount Vernon, NY: Peter Pauper Press, 1970).

106 Marilyn Chandler McEntyre, *Caring for Words in a Culture of Lies* (Grand Rapids, MI: William B. Eerdmans, 2009), pp. 150–151.

107 Luci Shaw's other poems "Mary's Song" and "Royalty," also helped start me on this journey with poetry. Both poems are included in Luci Shaw, *Accompanied by Angels: Poems of the Incarnation* (Grand Rapids, MI: Wm. B. Eerdman's, 2006).

108 John Ortberg, "Dallas Willard, a Man From Another 'Time Zone,'" *Christianity Today*, May 8, 2013, https://www.christianitytoday.com/ct/2013/may-web-only/man-from-another-time-zone.html.

109 Makoto Fujimura, *Culture Care: Reconnecting with Beauty for our Common Life* (Downers Grove, IL: InterVarsity Press, 2017), p. 50.

110 Fujimura, *Culture Care*, p. 26.

111 "Roberto Ghezzi," *EContemporary*, accessed October 17, 2023, https://www.elenacantori.com/artists/roberto-ghezzi/.

112 Roberto Ghezzi, "Project and Solo Show in Trieste—Naturographie 2020," August 31, 2020, https://www.robertoghezzi.it/project-and-solo-show-in-trieste-naturografie-2020/.

113 Christians in Visual Arts (CIVA), *SEEN Journal*, Winter 2021.

114 Fujimura, p. 50.

115 This poem was written as a response to a photograph in *Again + Again*, a CIVA (Christians in the Visual Arts) book and traveling art exhibition.

116 *Editor:* In the spring of 2022, a woman connected with Leslie online and, at some point during their conversations, asked Leslie to write a prayer for her to use when homeschooling her kids. Leslie sent her this.

117 Christopher P. Jones, "How to Read Paintings: *The Penitent Magdalen* by Georges de La Tour," *Thinksheet*, June 22, 2020, https://medium.com/thinksheet/how-to-read-paintings-the-penitentmagdalen-by-georges-de-la-tour-de97a696e0e.

118 C.S. Lewis, *Prince Caspian* (New York: Houghton Mifflin Harcourt, 1951), p. 70.

119 Unlike most of the poems in this book, this one was written in the late 1980s.—Editor

120 Walter Wangerin, Jr., Letters from the Land of Cancer (Grand Rapids, MI: Zondervan, 2010), p. 49.

121 Wangerin, Land of Cancer,

122 Timothy Keller, "Growing My Faith in the Face of Death," The Atlantic, March 7, 2021, https://www.theatlantic.com/ideas/archive/2021/03/tim-keller-growing-my-faith-face-death/618219/. Keller would end up dying a little over a month after Leslie.—Editor

123 NeedtoBreathe, "Mercy's Shore," track 1 Out of Body, Electra Records, 2020.

124 Brad Littlejohn, "Walkng by the Light of Virtue in the Twilight of a Pandemic," Breaking Ground, May 11, 2021, https://breakingground.us/walking-by-the-light-of-virtue-in-the-twilight-of-a-pandemic/.

125 Wendell Berry, Hannah Coulter (Berkeley, CA: Counterpoint Press, 2004), p. 148.

126 Douglas Kaine McKelvey, "A Liturgy of Praise for This Day of Life," in Every Moment Holy, Vol. II: Death, Grief, and Hope (Nashville, TN: 2021), p. 43.

127 Editor: Though this essay is one of Leslie's earliest published pieces, it fits best here near the end of this section, as her mom, Anne Symons, passed over into Glory shortly before Leslie did. She too faced cancer, and Leslie tells her story in more detail in Part II of this book.

128 Adapted from Ree Drummond, "Cinnamon Rolls," The Pioneer Woman Cooks (New York: William Morrow, 2009), p. 36.

129 Adapted from Monique, "The Best Cinnamon Rolls You'll Ever Eat," Ambitious Kitchen, December 1, 2022, https://www.ambitiouskitchen.com/best-cinnamon-rolls/.

130 Adapted from Pillsbury Kitchens, "Basic Powdered Sugar Glaze," Pillsbury, August 28, 2018, https://www.pillsbury.com/recipes/basic-powdered-sugar-glaze/cc5416a0-ebee-4168-8df7-fd586cff90e8.

131 Leslie served on the parents' council for The King's College during the years Carey and Maggie attended there. The college asked Leslie to pray at both of their graduations. This is the prayer she offered up during the 2021 service.—Editor

132 Josef Pieper, Happiness & Contemplation, trans. Richard and Clara Winston (South Bend, IN: St. Augustine's Press, 1998), p. 26.

133 Why We Create: Reflections on the Creator, the Creation, and Creating, ed. Jane Clark Scarf and Brian Brown (Baltimore, MD: Square Halo Books, 2023), p. xviii.

134 William Edgar, Created and Creating: A Biblical Theology of Culture (Downers Grove, IL: InterVarsity Press, 2017), p. 189.

135 Pieper, Happiness & Contemplation, pp. 84, 85.

136 Flannery O'Connor, A Prayer Journal (New York: Farrar, Straus· and Giroux, 2013), p. 3.

137 Pieper, p. 26.

138 Martin Schleske, The Sound of Life's Unspeakable Beauty, trans. Janet Gesme (Grand Rapids, MI: Eerdmans, 2020), p. 181.

139 William Shakespeare, "Sonnet 29: When, in disgrace with fortune and men's eyes," accessed October 10, 2023, https://www.poetryfoundation.org/poems/45090/sonnet-29-when-in-disgrace-with-fortune-and-mens-eyes.

140 Theodore Prescott, in private communication with the author, May 15, 2022.

141 Schleske, Unspeakable Beauty, p. 181.

142 Luke LeDuc, "Best Use of the Time," sermon, Wheatland Presbyterian Church, May 8, 2022, Lancaster, PA.

143 *Editor:* "Raðljóst" is an Icelandic word meaning "enough light to find your way by." This is the final poem Leslie wrote.

144 *Editor:* Leslie composed this liturgy for *Every Moment Holy, Vol. III: The Work of the People* (Nashville, TN: Rabbit Room Press, 2023).

PART II

145 *Editor:* Leslie wrote this prayer in her journal during 2020, her first year of cancer treatment.

146 Walter Wangerin, Jr., *Reliving the Passion: Meditations on the Suffering, Death, and Resurrection of Jesus as Recorded in Mark* (Grand Rapids, MI: Zondervan, 1992), p. 28.

147 Wangerin, *Reliving the Passion,* p. 29.

148 John Newton, *Letters of the Rev. John Newton,* ed. Josiah Bull (London: Religious Tract Society, 1869), p. 278.

149 Keith and Kristyn Getty, "O Church Arise," track 10 on *In Christ Alone,* Getty Music Label, 2006.

150 James K.A. Smith, *On the Road with Saint Augustine: A Real-World Spirituality for Restless Hearts* (Grand Rapids, MI: Brazos Press, 2019), pp. 14–15.

151 For recipe, see p. 49 of this book.

152 See Dru Johnson, "Human Rites: The Power of Rituals, Sacraments, and Habits," The Row House, March 13, 2020, https://www.therowhouse.org/rites.

153 Eric Peters, "Update from Eric," *CaringBridge,* March 25, 2020, https://www.caringbridge.org/visit/ericand-daniellepeters-tornadorecovery/journal/view/id/5e7b610154caaf517d-5c23f6.

154 Leslie Bustard, "Why We Should Travel to Narnia When We Can't Leave Our Homes," *Veritas Academy,* April 2, 2020, https://www.veritasacademy.com/headmasters-blog/why-travel-to-narnia-when-we-cant-leave-our-homes.

155 Matthew Monticchio, "Perseverance of the Saints—Matt Monticchio (feat. Hiram Ring and Pageant Music)," YouTube, accessed September 26, 2023, https://www.youtube.com/watch?v=GiHA71UWHpQ.

156 To read the Spring 2020 edition of *Cultivating,* please visit https://cultivatingoakspress.com/category/index/seasons/spring/spring-2020/.

157 *Editor:* To read more about Leslie's experience recording the podcast and to find out where to listen to it, see Leslie Bustard, "Introducing the Square Halo Podcast," The Rabbit Room, May 13, 2020, https://rabbitroom.com/2020/05/introducing-the-square-halo-podcast/.

158 Walter Wangerin, Jr., *Letters from the Land of Cancer* (Grand Rapids, MI: Zondervan, 2010), p. 49.

159 Madeleine L'Engle, *Two-Part Invention: The Story of a Marriage* (New York: HarperCollins, 1988), p. 123.

160 Martin Schleske, *The Sound of Life's Unspeakable Beauty* (Grand Rapids, MI: Wm. B. Eerdman's, 2020), front cover.

161 Schleske, *Unspeakable Beauty,* p. 124, emphasis added.

162 Keith and Kristyn Getty, "By Faith," track 5 on *Awaken the Dawn*, Getty Music Label, 2009.

163 Switchfoot, "Joy Invincible," track 6 on *Native Tongue*, Fantasy Records, 2019.

164 To read the Summer 2020 issue of *Cultivating*, please visit https://cultivatingoakspress.com/category/index/seasons/summer/summer-2020/.

165 See Gerard Manley Hopkins, "As Kingfishers Catch Fire," Poetry Foundation, https://www.poetryfoundation.org/poems/44389/as-kingfishers-catch-fire.

166 Douglas Kaine McKelvey, "A Liturgy for the Morning of a Medical Procedure," from *Every Moment Holy, Vol. II: Death, Grief, and Hope* (Nashville, TN: Rabbit Room Press, 2021), p. 12.

167 Wallace Stegner, *Crossing to Safety* (New York: Penguin, 1987), p. 339, emphasis added.

168 Douglas Kaine McKelvey, "A Liturgy for the Morning of a Medical Procedure," in *Every Moment Holy, Vol. II: Death, Grief, and Hope* (Nashville, TN: Rabbit Room Press, 2021), pp. 10–11.

169 NeedtoBreathe, "Mercy's Shore," track 1 on *Out of Body*, Elektra Records, 2020.

170 Schleske, *Unspeakable Beauty*.

171 J.R.R. Tolkien, *The Fellowship of the Ring* (New York: Houghton Mifflin Harcourt, 1954), p. 71.

172 NeedtoBreathe, "Child Again," track 5 on *Out of Body*, Elektra Records, 2020.

173 Timothy Keller, "Splendor in the Furnace; 1 Peter, Part I," sermon series, September 12, 1993–December 12, 1993, https://gospelinlife.com/downloads/splendor-in-the-furnace-1-peter-part-1/.

174 Eric Peters, "Found," track 2 on *Birds of Relocation*, self-released, 2012.

175 Josh Garrels, "Sweet River Roll," track 7 on *Over Oceans*, self-released, 2006.

176 To browse the Christmas 2020 issue of *Cultivating*, please visit https://cultivatingoakspress.com/category/index/seasons/holiday-seasons/christmas-2020/; for the Winter 2021 issue, see https://cultivatingoakspress.com/category/index/seasons/winter/winter-2021/.

177 Black Barn Collective, "Art of the Anunciation with Leslie Bustard," YouTube, accessed October 30, 2023, https://www.youtube.com/watch?v=-JnXyQhzHXYI.

178 These recipes are available in Margie Haack's *Place* trilogy (Square Halo Books).

179 See Andrew Roycroft, "Bethlehem Year Zero," featured in Jonathan Rogers, "A Poem for Christmas," The Habit, December 22, 2020, https://thehabit.co/a-poem-for-christmas-2/.

180 *Editor:* Leslie interviewed Ned for her blog and shared the story behind this book's beginnings. To read more, please visit Leslie Bustard, "The Giftgiver," *Poetic Underpinnings*, October 14, 2021, https://www.poeticunderpinnings.com/commonplace/the-backstory-to-the-giftgiver.

181 "Leslie Bustard on Rediscovering Poetry in the Midst of Cancer," interview by Shawn and Maile Smucker, *The Stories Between Us* podcast, February 23, 2021,

182 the innocence mission, "Now in This Hush," track 6 on *Umbrella*, A&M Records, 1991.

183 Malcolm Guite, "Psalm 3: III *Domine, quid multiplicati?*," from *David's Crown: Sounding the Psalms* (London: Canterbury Press, 2021), p. 3.

184 Maurice Manning, "Lent," *Image Journal,* Issue 88, https://imagejournal.org/article/lent-manning/

185 NeedtoBreathe, "Sunshine," track 3 on *Into the Mystery,* Elektra, 2021.

186 Editor: Leslie's website, *Poetic Underpinnings* (https://www.poeticunderpinnings.com/), features many more of her writings than could fit in this book, so please do visit and explore her work!

187 *Editor:* To view samples of the art from this show, see Leslie Bustard, "Poems & Pictures," *Poetic Underpinnings,* September 4, 2021, https://www.poeticunderpinnings.com/commonplace/images-and-words.

188 *Editor:* To read more about the process of putting this book together, see Leslie Bustard, "Wild Things," *Poetic Underpinnings,* November 1, 2021, https://www.poeticunderpinnings.com/commonplace/wild-things-and-castles-in-the-sky.

189 Katy Bowser Hutson, *Now I Lay Me Down to Fight: A Poet Writes Her Way Through Cancer* (Downers Grove, IL: IVP, 2023).

190 *Editor:* To read Leslie's full blog post on this trip to Ireland (and to see more pictures), please visit Leslie Bustard, "Ireland," *Poetic Underpinnings,* October 4, 2021, https://www.poeticunderpinnings.com/commonplace/ireland.

191 Editor: To read more about Leslie's vision for this conference, please see Leslie Bustard, "Creativity, Collaboration & Community: An Invitation to 2022's Inklings Conference," *The Rabbit Room,* December 10, 2021, https://rabbitroom.com/2021/12/creativity-collaboration-community-2022-inklings-conference/.

192 Douglas Kaine McKelvey, "A Liturgy for Dying Well," in *Every Moment Holy, Vol. II: Death, Grief, and Hope* (Nashville, TN: Rabbit Room Press, 2021), p. 37.

193 *Editor:* Leslie later revised and retitled this poem "Unhistoric Acts."

194 The Porter's Gate, "Nothing to Fear (feat. Audrey Assad)," track 2 on *Neighbor Songs,* Integrity Music, 2019.

195 Douglas Kaine McKelvey, "A Liturgy for the Morning of a Medical Procedure," from *Every Moment Holy, Vol. II: Death, Grief, and Hope* (Nashville, TN: Rabbit Room Press, 2021), p. 12.

196 Eliza King ,"I Shall Not Want," track 1 on *I Shall Not Want,* Numa Records, 2020.

197 The 77s, "Nowhere Else," track 2 on *Sticks and Stones,* Lo-Fidelity Records, 1990.

198 *The City for God: Essays Honoring the Work of Timothy Keller* (Baltimore, MD: Square Halo Books, 2022). Editor: Tim Keller would end up dying a month after Leslie.

199 "Making the Most of Our Time (with Leslie Bustard)," *Imagination Redeemed* podcast, July 13, 2022, https://www.anselmsociety.org/blog/ri-2hhxf.

200 See Leslie Bustard, "Kids Books: Summer Reading," Square Halo Books, July 31, 2022, https://www.squarehalobooks.com/squarehalobooks/2022/8/1/summer-reading.

201 See Leslie Bustard, "Poetry for the Lazy Hazy Days of Summer, Part 1," Story Warren, July 20, 2022, https://storywarren.com/poetry-for-the-lazy-hazy-days-of-summerpt-1/; Leslie Bustard, "Poetry for the Lazy Hazy Days of Summer, Part 2," *Story Warren,* July 27, 2022, https://storywarren.com/poetry-for-the-lazy-hazy-days-of-summer-pt-2/.

202 *Editor:* Although this book quickly sold out and is now out of print, most of the poems featured in it are included in Part I of this book.

203 Taylor Leonhardt, "Poetry," track 10 from *Hold Still,* self-released, 2021.

204 Andrew Roycroft, *33: Reflections on the Gospel of Saint John* (Baltimore, MD: Square Halo Books, 2022).

205 Timothy Keller, *Prayer: Experiencing Awe and Intimacy with God* (New York: Penguin Group, 2014), p. 18.

206 *Editor:* To read more about this conference (and the history of Square Halo Books), please see Leslie Bustard, "Culture Care and Conferences," *The Rabbit Room,* January 23, 2023, https://rabbitroom.com/2023/01/square-halo-books-culture-care-and-conferences/.

207 *Editor:* Good news—you're reading this book right now! Thanks to all those who supported her work.

208 *Editor:* You can listen to/watch this wonderful recording here: "The Goodness of the Lord in the Land of the Living," YouTube, March 27, 2023, https://www.youtube.com/watch?v=aipS-lcw61o.

209 *Editor:* To view this series please visit https://ordinary-saints.com

210 To read poem, see p. 365 of this book.

211 Douglas Kaine McKelvey, "A Liturgy for Dying Well," *Every Moment Holy, Vol. II: Death, Grief, and Hope* (Nashville, TN: Rabbit Room Press, 2021), pp. 32–37.

212 Walter Wangerin, Jr., "Maundy Thursday," from *Stories for the Christian Year: The Chrysostom Society,* ed. Eugene H. Peterson (New York: Macmillan, 1992), p. 119.

213 Douglas Kaine McKelvey, "A Liturgy for the Final Hours," from *Every Moment Holy, Vol. 2: Death, Grief, and Hope* (Nashville, TN: Rabbit Room Press, 2021), p. 119.

Acknowledgements

Love for those around her and gratitude toward those who shaped her—whether through their work, love, or example—was a resounding theme for Leslie, so I know there are many, many more people than I can list here who loved Leslie well and are deserving of thanks. If I missed your name on this list, please forgive me: you know and she knows and I'm sure she will thank you herself one day (profusely and with that luminous smile!). For now, I would like to thank the following people on Leslie's behalf:

- The publications and communities that supported and encouraged Leslie in her writing and gave her opportunities to write *more*— in particular, Lancia Smith and the writers of the Cultivating Project, , the Black Barn Collective, The Rabbit Room, Story Warren, Calla Press, and the Anselm Society.
- The friends who read and loved her work and who challenged her to write *better*—Christine Perrin, Amy Maslkeit, Amy Baik Lee, Katy Hutson, Amy Knorr, and Jessica Whipple.
- The writers and poets who enlarged Leslie's imagination and expanded her desire for truth, beauty, and goodness—especially Luci Shaw, Anne Bradstreet, Margie Haack, Karen Peris, Andi Ashworth, Malcolm Guite, Seamus Heaney, Billy Collins, and Dana Gioia.
- All those who, like the friends of the paralyzed man, carried Leslie before Jesus as she fought cancer—her church family at Wheatland, the doctors and nurses who ministered to her, those who faithfully read her CaringBridge journal, and everyone who remembered her in prayer. Her gratitude toward you is evident in her writings and is woven throughout the pages of this book.

I'd also like to thank Luci Shaw, Malcolm Guite, Aaron Belz, Elizabeth Wickland, and Katy Hutson for allowing us to include your full poems in this book, as well as all of the artists whose work adorns this book (some pieces were made particularly for this project!)—especially Hannah Claire Weston, who beautifully illustrated twenty-six of Leslie's tanka poems for a 2021 Square Halo Gallery show.

Special thanks to the following, for their gifts which made this book possible:

Square Halo Books
World's End Images
Veritas Press
Ward & Debbie Keever
Allison Luce
Lynette Stone
Calla Press
Dan Deal
Janet Fickeissen
Davis Carman
Cultivating Oaks Press
Charlie & Andrea Ashworth
ASCHA board members
Jim & Cathy Bourgeois
Jeffery & Dona Barrall
Amy & Yongwon Lee

Lillian Alberici
John & Pamela Pogue
Sandra Bowden
Cameron Anderson
Theodore & Catherine Prescott
Richard & Lisa Nyguist
David & Robin Hibshman
Craig & Tashya Dalen
Daryn & Meg Sauder
Robert & Louise Brewer
Erik & Stephanie Rostad
Elizabeth Jones
June Kuz
The Stephen & Laurel Brown Foundation
John & Christina Gregg
John & Lisa Blowers

Michael & Mary Kucks
Rosemary Johnson
John & Jean Iannotti
Ken & Lisa Cutler
Ruth Goring
Sharon Givler
Rebecca Toews
Matt & Charity Wheeler
Wilma Bender
Don & Karen Peris
Bonnie Bosso
The Cheneys
John & Jean Iannotti
Joanna Collins
Stefanie Peters
William & Donna McLaughlin

And extra special thanks, of course, to Ned. You wouldn't have this book in your hands if he hadn't loved Leslie so faithfully throughout the almost-thirty-three years of their marriage. He championed her writing and did so much to support her work—from designing and publishing her books (including this one) to tending to her legacy even now, during these first months without her. His love for her is generous and abundant, and because of it we are allowed to enjoy Leslie's work more fully. Leslie loved as well as she did because she was so well loved.

—*Théa Rosenburg*

permissions

essays

The essays in this book originally appeared, sometimes in different forms or under different titles, in the following publications:

Calla Press: "A Hidden Life"

Ordinary Saints (Square Halo Books, 2023): "Houses of Cedar and the Homes of God"

One Thousand Words (podcast): "He Who Began a Good Work"

Poetic Underpinnings (Leslie's blog): "Van Gogh, After Millet"; "Disciplined by Hope"; "Ash Wednesday"; "Penitent Magdalen"

Risen Motherhood: "A Necessary Ally"

Why We Create (Square Halo Books, 2023): "Gratitude"

Wild Things and Castles in the Sky (Square Halo Books, 2022): "Love Think Speak"

"The Goodness of Poetry in My Life" was given as a special lecture for All Saints Presbyterian Church.

All remaining essays were originally published in *Cultivating* magazine.

poems

The poems "Virus," "I Gave This Day to God," and "Our Prayers Break on God," are used by permission of Luci Shaw.

The poems "The Church's Banquet," "The Good Ground," and "A Portrait of Leslie" are used by permission of Malcolm Guite.

The poem "Critique" is used by permission of Aaron Belz.

"Treatment is a Gauntlet" and "After Mastectomy" are taken from *Now I Lay Me Down to Fight,* by Katy Bowser Hutson, ©2023 by Katherine Jane Hutson (used by permission of InterVarsity Press, P.O. Box 1400, Downers Grove, IL 60515, USA, http://www.ivpress.com).

All of Leslie's poems were previously published in her book *The Goodness of the Lord in the Land of the Living* (Square Halo Books, 2023), with the exception of: "A Wee Drop in Your Hand," "Because You Should Know," "Courage," "February 4th," "For Hugh Richard," "Luke 19:40," "Mercy," "November Afternoon on My Porch," "One Fall Morning," "(Penultimate) Verse," "Radljóst," "Roller Coasters," "Traveling to Laity Lodge," "What Thirty-Two Looks Like," "Writing Practice," and "XI/MM."

index

RECIPES

LESLIE ANNE BUSTARD spent much of her adult years home-schooling her three girls, and teaching literature, poetry, art appreciation, and writing to other children in various homeschooling co-ops. Leslie also taught middle school literature and writing at a local classical school, as well as produced high school and children's theater. For the past two decades, she and her husband lived in a century-old row house in downtown Lancaster, Pennsylvania, where they loved to offer food and friendship to folks and to collect a plethora of artwork, music, and books. Leslie has written for The Cultivating Project, The Black Barn Online, Veritas Press, Story Warren, Anselm Society, Rabbit Room Press, and Calla Press. Her first book was *Wild Things and Castles in the Sky: A Guide to Choosing the Best Books for Children* (Square Halo Books, 2022). You can find more of Leslie's musings at PoeticUnderpinnings.com, and listen to a number of her podcasts at SquareHaloBooks.com.

recommends

If Leslie invited you over for dinner, most likely she would've tried to send you home at the end of the night with one of these books . . .

WILD THINGS AND CASTLES IN THE SKY: A GUIDE TO CHOOSING THE BEST BOOKS FOR CHILDREN

A passion project for Leslie, this book has been described as "a book about imagination." Brian Brown of the Anselm Society observed that it is "an inspiring and immensely practical gift from forty wise and well-read people to those who want to bring up children marked by meaning."

. . .

NAILED IT: 365 READINGS FOR ANGRY OR WORN-OUT PEOPLE

Karen Swallow Prior says that *Nailed It* is "a devotional that is sharpening, witty, and downright real." Leslie loved it so much that she worked to have Square Halo publish a revised and expanded version of it.

. . .

THE EXACT PLACE | NO PLACE | THIS PLACE

These memoirs are beautifully written reflections on real life that are heartbreaking, funny, and truthful. The author (and these books) were a huge influence on Leslie.

. . .

33: REFLECTIONS ON THE GOSPEL OF SAINT JOHN

Kristyn Getty says, "You will find here beautiful words that let the light in." Leslie discovered this Irish poet for Square Halo to publish and loved to share these poems with her friends.

Learn more about these titles at SquareHaloBooks.com—then order them from your favorite local bookseller. Sure, they are available anywhere quality books are sold, but Leslie liked to support independent booksellers.